1990

ABORTION

edited by JANET PODELL

THE REFERENCE SHELF
Volume 62 Number 4

THE H. W. WILSON COMPANY

New York   1990

THE REFERENCE SHELF

The books in this series contain reprints of articles, excerpts from books, and addresses on current issues and social trends in the United States and other countries. There are six separately bound numbers in each volume, all of which are generally published in the same calendar year. One number is a collection of recent speeches; each of the others is devoted to a single subject and gives background information and discussion from various points of view, concluding with a comprehensive bibliography that contains books and pamphlets and abstracts of additional articles on the subject. Books in the series may be purchased individually or on subscription.

Library of Congress Cataloging-in-Publication Data

Main entry under title:

Abortion / edited by Janet Podell.
     p.   cm. — (The Reference shelf ; v. 62, no. 4)
     Includes bibliographical references (p.).
     Summary: Highlights both sides of the controversial abortion debate, with presentation of the ethical, political and legal views espoused by the pro-choice movement and the anti-abortion camp.
     ISBN 0-8242-0793-9
     1. Abortion—United States—Moral and ethical aspects. 2. Pro-choice movement—United States. [1.Abortion—Moral and ethical aspects.]   I. Podell, Janet.   II. Series.
HQ767.5.U5A22   1990
363.4'6—dc20   90-12924
                                                                      CIP
                                                                       AC

Cover: Prolife and prochoice demonstrators holding signs on the steps of the Supreme Court building in 1989 after the Court ruled on the Missouri abortion case. The Court's decision gave states greater power to limit abortion.
Photo: AP/Wide World Photos

Printed in the United States of America

CONTENTS

PREFACE

An abortion is the forcible removal of a developing baby from the womb of his or her mother, using surgical, mechanical, or chemical means. In some countries, it is an illegal act; in others, it is legal with some or no restrictions; in a few—the People's Republic of China, for example—it is mandatory under certain circumstances.

Abortion and the related practice of infanticide (the killing of newborns) have been practiced for centuries in a wide variety of cultures. Both were common in the ancient world. Infanticide was, and in some places still is, used as a way to restrict population growth and to get rid of unwanted children, including "excess" girls, babies with physical defects, and the second in a pair of twins. In the developed nations of the West, where infanticide is outlawed, population control is accomplished through contraception and abortion. Our goals are not the same as those of the ancient Greeks, say, or of contemporary South American tribes. We want to be able to restrict the size of our families and to enable women to avoid bearing and raising children during part or all of their fertile years; our children are legally protected from the moment they are born, and we would prosecute any parent who killed an unwanted twin. Despite these differences, however, the basic need is the same: to place controls, crude or sophisticated, on the natural capacity of women to bear children. To put it plainly, our society, like many others past and present, tries to eliminate the natural consequences of (hetero)sexual activity without having to eliminate sex.

Some 1.5 million abortions are performed in the United States annually, mostly to women under 30. In Washington, D.C., the nation's capital, there are more abortions than live births each year. In studying the status of abortion in the United States, it is important to understand what motivates the women who have it done. A survey published in *Family Planning Perspectives* in July/August 1988 gave the following answers (more than one answer could be given by a respondent). The vast majority of respondents, 76 percent, said that having a baby would change their lives in some unwanted way, such as by limiting their job choices or education. Sixty-eight percent said that they had an abortion because they couldn't afford a child; 51 percent, because they had problems in their relationship with the father, or didn't want to be single mothers; 31 percent, because they didn't want other people to know that they had had sexual relations; 23 percent, because their husband or boyfriend wanted the abortion. Abnormalities in the baby's development accounted for 13 percent; threats to the mother's health, 7 percent; pregnancy as a result of rape or incest, 1 percent.

It is also important to get a good mental picture of the creature whose life ends when a pregnancy is terminated. Once conception occurs, development is rapid; enormous changes take place every day. By the eighth week of pregnancy, when half of all abortions in the United States take place or have already taken place, almost all the new creature's major internal organs have been formed; the rudimentary heart beats about 160 times a minute; and the developing baby begins to make movements. By the twelfth week, when another 40 percent of abortions have taken place, the heart is completely formed, and the developing baby begins to practice breathing and sucking movements. As the author of one text on gestation explains: "By the end of the first trimester, the fetus is a tiny, but fully formed, human being which weighs 1 oz (30 g) and is 3 in (75 mm) long."

The question of whether or not to keep abortion legal has polarized Americans like no issue since the Vietnam War, for abortion, like war, is a matter of life and death. Activists in both camps claim to have the support of a majority of the American public. They vilify their opponents in the bitterest terms, mount huge demonstrations, conduct lobbying and fund-raising activities, and threaten politicians who vote the other way. The crisis began in 1973, when the Supreme Court voted, in the famous *Roe v. Wade* decision, to legalize abortion in all 50 states, ending a century of antiabortion statutes during which abortions were performed "underground," usually in unsafe and frightening conditions and sometimes resulting in the death of the mother. The majority opinion in *Roe v. Wade* gave each mother the power to decide whether or not to abort the developing baby, a power that diminishes somewhat with each trimester of pregnancy. It was based on a right to privacy that the Justices found to be implicit in the Constitution (although some legal scholars dispute their logic).

Over the next 16 years, an antiabortion movement was formed and mounted a series of challenges to legalized abortion.

In the summer of 1989 it won a partial victory in the case of *Webster v. Reproductive Health Services*, in which the Supreme Court ruled 5-4 that state legislatures may impose restrictions on abortions. (Their ruling upheld Missouri laws that define conception as the beginning of life, deny public funding for abortions, and require physicians performing abortions after the 19th week of pregnancy to determine whether the baby could possibly survive on its own.) Additional cases are on the Court's calendar for the coming year, and the Justices appear to be ranged four-to-four on either side; Justice Sandra Day O'Connor is expected to cast the votes that will tip the balance one way or the other.

The issue of abortion is so emotional that a calm debate between opponents has proved to be almost impossible. Perhaps, at this point, dialogues can only take place on paper, rather than in person. The first section of this book presents several articulations of the feminist view that the right to abortion is central to women's attainment of social and legal equality. Arguments from the opposing camp are aired in Section II. In both sections an attempt has been made to include debates *within* each camp as well. The third section explores some aspects of what life was like before 1973 and what might happen if *Roe v. Wade* were overturned. Questions of ethics, including some raised by advances in medical technology, are discussed in Section IV. The final section is devoted to the possibility of reaching a compromise that the general public can live with.

A note on semantics: People on either side of the abortion debate are very careful to choose words and labels that advance their own views and make them more appealing. Groups that work against legalized abortion call themselves by the positive term "prolife." Groups that support legalized abortion call themselves by the attractive term "prochoice." In the editorial sections of this book, the more specific terms "antiabortion" and "proabortion" will be used. Similarly, the term "developing baby" will be used in preference to the medical term "fetus."

The editor wishes to thank the authors and publishers who kindly granted permission to reprint the material in this collection. Special thanks are due to Steven Anzovin and to Diane Podell of the B. Davis Schwartz Memorial Library, C. W. Post Center, Long Island University.

JANET PODELL

September 1990

I. THE RIGHT TO CHOOSE

EDITOR'S INTRODUCTION

Female bodies are designed to bear offspring. Unless it is disrupted in some way—by physical malfunction, or by deliberate intervention—the reproductive system of an adult female of any species will do what it was designed to do. For most animals this is the way of nature, to which there is no alternative. Humans, however, spend enormous energy trying to manage and control female fertility, because it interferes with other goals—social, economic, political, cultural—that they deem to be more important.

Since the 1950s, the American feminist movement has made reproductive rights one of its primary objectives. It has sought to transfer control over women's fertility from individual men (e.g., husbands and lovers) and male-dominated institutions (e.g., churches) to individual women. All other objectives of the movement—equality of women and men in the workplace, in the courts, in family life, and in every other sphere of endeavor—are considered by most feminists to be dependent on the achievement of this one. In the first article in this section, "A Basic Human Right," originally published just before the Supreme Court issued its decision in the *Webster* case, Gloria Steinem, one of the leaders of American feminism, argues that reproductive freedom should not be subject to any government intervention but should be considered a basic right, like freedom of speech.

So fundamental is abortion to feminist concerns that many feminists refuse to accord the developing baby any status or identity other than as an inanimate appendage of the mother. Cleo Kocol, in her article "Let's Take the Guilt Away," defines an abortion as "just one of many medical procedures," like having one's tonsils removed. Even putting abortion entirely in medical hands can have undesirable consequences, however, as Lisa Chasan points out in "Counselling Abortion," the third article in this section: "Integral to the medical model . . . are biases against women in general, and specifically against the exercise of their right to choose abortion." No woman can wield complete power

8

over her own fertility, Chasan says, unless all women are assumed to be competent moral agents whose decisions should not be subject to anyone else's judgment.

The depth of emotion invested in this issue by abortion advocates is evident in the series of letters that make up the bulk of the fourth selection in this section. These letters were written to the editors of the leftist magazine *The Nation* in response to a column by Christopher Hitchens in which he proposed a series of social reforms—free contraception, free prenatal and childhood health care, mandatory sex education, and a national adoption service—in exchange for a ban on abortions.

Another view, one that has certain elements in common with Hitchens's, is taken by Sidney Callahan in her article "Abortion & the Sexual Agenda." Callahan agrees with the ultimate goal of the feminist movement, full social equality with men, but she denies that such equality can be achieved by oppressing a yet more vulnerable population. She envisions instead a world in which female sexuality and fertility would be respected rather than feared, accommodated rather than controlled—a world in which women could be at ease, not at war, with their own bodies.

A BASIC HUMAN RIGHT[1]

The most crucial question of democracy, feminism, and simple self-respect is not: *What* gets decided? That comes second. The first question is: *Who* decides?

It may seem odd that this fundamental of everything from politics to self-esteem could be learned from an experience as unwelcome as abortion, but that was its source for me. Or rather, *understanding* abortion was. My own had taken place in a time of such isolation, illegality, and fear that afterward, I did my best to just forget. Only a decade later when a new wave of feminism was encouraging women to share "secrets"—allowing us to learn, for example, that as many as one in three or four adult American women probably had risked abortion even when it was criminal

[1]Reprint of an article by Gloria Steinem. First appeared in *Ms.*, July/August 1989. Copyright © Gloria Steinem. Reprinted with permission.

and dangerous—did I begin to think about my own experience as a microcosm of what millions of women had gone through. Belatedly, I questioned why the female half of the human race, whose bodies bear all the consequences of reproduction, were allowed so few of its decisions: on the legality of abortion, contraception, or sterilization; on the workplace or medical treatment of pregnancy and childbirth; on even what was considered "normal" in female sexuality.

Gradually, I figured out . . .

. . . that making every person from a less powerful group feel isolated and guilty, no matter what our numbers and needs, was a psychological necessity of any political system in which one group lives under the decisions of another; in this case, a very old system called patriarchy.

. . . that controlling women's bodies as the most basic means of production, the means of reproduction, was the very definition of patriarchy and a necessity for racist systems besides; so no wonder we got such opposition.

. . . that for me, seeking out an abortion had been the first time I stopped passively accepting whatever happened and took responsibility for my own life; that it was an ethical act, just as refusing to be pressured into an abortion might have been at a different time in my life or for another woman.

I go back to these basics of personal experience (and urge each reader to do the same) because right now, we are again in the position of waiting for someone else to decide; this time, the Supreme Court. We were as active as we could be in advance. Thanks to national outrage at the threat to legal abortion plus leadership from the National Organization for Women, we flooded Washington, D.C., in one of the biggest, most representative marches in history. Thanks to a lot of legal work by a wide variety of groups, we filed a staggering 33 amicus curiae briefs to counter all the anti-choice arguments.

About the only thing we didn't do in advance of this judicial decision was convince the pro-choice majority of voters that reproductive freedom was important enough—and in danger enough—to dictate their choice of President and to turn out at the polls in numbers big enough to counter the turnout of antiabortion groups.

And that's what got us into this jam. Because the last three administrations were elected by such low national turnouts that votes from less than a third of the country seemed like a landslide, Republican platform pledges to appoint antiabortion judges got redeemed. That's the major reason why we are now facing the surrealism of Supreme Court justices who may oppose what at least two thirds of Americans, women and men, believe to be justice.

So here we are again: waiting. This return to old and deep patterns of passivity is an even greater danger than any potential action by the Court. No matter *what* those nine Justices do, we must remember that we as citizens hold the ultimate power to change the law and even the Constitution they interpret, to disobey any law we consider unjust if we're willing to bear the consequences; and that, as women, we live and breathe in the bodies they are trying to control.

To take Vietnam as an analogy: if this country found itself bewildered by trying to invade the home territory of a proud and motivated adversary, can you imagine how bewildered our establishment would be if it seriously tried to invade the reproductive territory of millions of proud and motivated women?

That is, it would be—if we really were proud and motivated.

For instance, suppose the rosy, unlikely best: that the Court only took the Missouri case in order to end controversy by reaffirming the status quo—and it does exactly that. We would be saved the Sisyphean task of fighting in 50 state legislatures for influence over the areas ceded to them. We would also be saved the task of passing a Constitutional Amendment to overturn the idea that U.S. citizenry suddenly included fertilized eggs—an extremist premise that the Missouri statute enshrined in its preamble. (Before you dismiss this possibility, remember that the Human Life Amendment also defines protectable human life as beginning at conception, and that President Bush has endorsed the HLA since arriving in the White House.) Nonetheless, we still would be left with the limitations and liabilities of *Roe* v. *Wade*, a decision that has done too little to help poor women, teenage women, and many others. These 16 years of defending it as the best thing around may have obscured the fact, but it was never what we wanted in the first place. On the contrary, there was a reason why *repeal* appeared in most policy statements and organizational names of the pro-choice movement in the 1960s and early 1970s: the goal was to get the government out of reproductive decision-making by repealing special abortion and contraceptive laws. Though *Roe* v. *Wade* was the Supreme Court's response to that movement, its solution was the compromise of *reform*, not *repeal*.

As long as laws try to govern abortion in a way that no other medical or surgical procedure is legislated, there will be some degree of danger. For one thing, any law is too inflexible for such tasks as deciding whether a particular fetus can survive, or for taking into account the realities of what is medically possible in a particular time and place. For another, the very presence of such laws invites constant political tinkering with their terms; with who gets prosecuted and who does not; with who can interpret them and who cannot. Finally, *Roe* v. *Wade* enshrined a limited idea of state interest in a fetus. Though it did so in all goodwill, with the purpose of protecting the health and welfare of both woman and fetus, the result is impractical at best: how can the law directly relate to an entity it can't directly reach? How can it differentially apply to two people who may be legally separate, but who actually inhabit the same body? At worst, this limited version of state interest leaves the door open to a kind of nationalization of women's bodies throughout their childbearing years.

Really, there are two paths.

They start from two different premises. If reproductive freedom—the right to choose whether, when, and with whom to have children—is a basic human right, like freedom of speech, then state interest lies in protecting that freedom. Women are more needful of this right because of our larger role in reproduction, but it would protect men, too. (For instance, from the forced sterilization allowed by eugenics laws of the nineteenth and early twentieth centuries.)

On the other hand, if there is a state interest in promoting birth over other reproductive choices, then women especially can be subordinated to it. Poor women who depend on Medicaid can be deprived of abortion; so can government employees who depend on health insurance; teenage women can remain the childbearing chattel of families or courts; and pregnant women can be held responsible for damage to the fetus, or even be incarcerated by someone who says he or she represents the fetus.

Clearly, we're already on the second path. Every one of those limitations is already happening to some degree. If reproductive freedom were a fundamental human right, like freedom of speech, then trying to legislate the exact conditions under which one can or cannot give birth to a child, use contraception, have an abortion—or any other of the personal choices that are component parts of this basic freedom—would be as problematical as trying to legislate the exact conditions under which we have freedom of speech.

We give freedom of speech, freedom of assembly, and other basic rights to the individual, limiting state power in the long-term interest of democracy; but reproductive freedom has never been taken that seriously. On the contrary, a man's house may be his castle, but a woman's body is rarely her own.

Nonetheless, with a favorable Supreme Court ruling right now, we could get on the first path one legal ruling at a time, one group at a time. Or we could make a quantum leap by adding reproductive freedom to the list of human rights; and by strategizing about repeal, not reform. We could take on other efforts to limit governmental intervention at local levels.

At a minimum, explaining reproductive freedom would put us back on positive ground, honor each other's choices, and offer protection to women who now feel pressured into abortion (and so may wrongly blame the fact that it is legal at all). It is also a vision of the future. After all, politics may be the art of the possible—but the art of movements is to change politics by envisioning new possibilities.

Suppose, on the other hand, we open our newspapers to find a negative Supreme Court decision, thus making the terms of the future seem worse than the present. Suppose we seem too far down the path of state interference to come back in any conventional way: what then?

Then we are even more in need of seizing the initiative; of saying firmly: *As citizens and women, we will decide.* There are electoral strategies we could adopt; from a short-term targeting of state legislatures to preserve "safe" states to a long-term coalition effort with all those groups who want to see the principle of privacy enshrined in a Constitutional Amendment. Should the news be bad, however, we will also have a special need for civil disobedience and unconventional strategies. Their success depends on our belief in one thing: *the Supreme Court was on trial, not us.* If the Supreme Court has created disrespect for the law by placing it too far outside public practice and belief, that's their problem. This is not an unrealistic conviction. If the Justices restrict or outlaw abortion (or allow states to do so), they will be opposing the 71 percent of Americans who believe abortion should not be criminalized again, the many physicians who believe that antiabortion legislation is an infringement on their right to practice responsible medicine, and a world court of opinion in which, in real life, no other industrialized democracy puts reproductive decisions into the hands of government.

From slavery to voting rights, the Supreme Court sometimes gets on the wrong side of history. This could be one of those times. There's a long tradition of civil disobedience to turn to—and we will if there is no other way of achieving legal, safe, available abortion, and putting decisions back into women's hands. Reproductive freedom *is* a fundamental human right. If Patrick Henry, Frederick Douglass, and Thomas Jefferson had ever been pregnant against their will, they would have been right there rebelling—and so will we.

For instance: organizing not-so-underground railways from antiabortion states to less restrictive ones; expanding such semilegal, early abortion alternatives as menstrual extraction and RU 486; supporting the many physicians who say they will disregard any antiabortion law; looking to allies among religious groups who still have experience in illegal abortion counseling from the days before 1973; using all the public tactics learned during the Vietnam and civil rights movements; taking the U.S. denial of women's rights to the United Nations and the World Court. All these would be just a few of our well-justified actions.

No matter what the Court does with the power we have supposedly (in this case, imperfectly) delegated it, we have three strengths we did not have before feminism and before *Roe* v. *Wade* saved many women's lives and health.

First, we can't be returned by this Court to guilt and isolation. We will be sick with anger at the length and unfairness of this battle, but anger is a step forward from self-blame and depression. We have experienced our right to decide.

Second, we are in the mainstream. Pro-choice numbers in public opinion polls and a half million people marching in Washington have politicians very worried. There are some political experts who believe that identification with the antiabortion extremists will prove a long-term problem for Republicans. In any case, now is the time to translate pro-choice energy into votes and voter turnout; to target antiabortion politicians for defeat;

and to establish reproductive freedom as a human right, not a "single issue" to be bargained away. There is a lot of free-floating anger out there, and it should be channeled into political action.

Third, reproductive issues are part of a convergence of concerns, nationally and globally, that may lead to a new and all-encompassing human right called bodily integrity. There are many elements leading to this need: the abuses of organ transplant policy already beginning between rich countries with recipients and poor countries with donors; blood and urine tests that are required without probable cause or individual suspicion; proposals for mass AIDS testing that amounts to a suspicionless search of the human body; mind-altering drugs that are used for purposes of brainwashing or social control; children and old people who are drugged for easier handling by schools and institutions; the efforts to outlaw forced sterilization in Asia, female genital mutilation in Africa, and other reproductive abuses: all these and more are leading toward a shared and growing belief—the power of a government, *any* government, has to stop at our skins. Our bodies cannot be invaded. They are our castles to rule.

When I was in Washington for the march, I read a newspaper report about an incident that seemed both far away and oddly close. A husband and wife from the People's Republic of China were seeking political asylum in the United States. The wife had been forced to have an abortion under China's one-child-per-family policy—and the couple feared this would happen again.

Our government—the same one now trying to criminalize abortion at home—is opposing their request for asylum. A U.S. immigration service spokesman explained that since China's one-child-per-family rule applied to everyone equally, it couldn't be discriminatory. (I wondered: would a blanket policy against freedom of speech be considered equally okay?) Furthermore, the official said, a population policy is clearly social, so an objection to it cannot be political. (I wondered: is what happens to men called "political," while what happens to women is "social"?)

Of course, there are still questions to be answered. A Chinese official said this one-child policy had been *encouraged* by his government, not *forced*.

Nonetheless, that story stuck with me. If it is true, then marching for reproductive freedom means marching for the rights of that couple, too—and we should say so.

If we unite on the question of "who decides," then the abortion struggle will have been the darkness before the dawn of a new human right.

LET'S TAKE THE GUILT AWAY[2]

Roe v. *Wade*, the Supreme Court decision which legalized abortion, is fifteen years old. Yet, the cultural core of thinking—the mystique, if you will—about abortion has changed little since 1973. Before then, abortion was considered a dirty business, and a nation pretended that it didn't happen. Women with money went off to other cities, states, or nations to take care of unwanted pregnancies. Poor women did whatever they could. This often included methods which cost them their lives. Yet, no matter what method is used to terminate a pregnancy, no matter what the level of financial help available, thinking about abortion didn't vary. Abortion was bad, dirty, and unspeakable because it was against the law, often poorly done in unsanitary surroundings, and many women died as a result.

Yet, the stigma of bearing an illegitimate baby, the trauma of bearing an unwanted child, the horror of giving birth to a child conceived through rape or incest drove women to abortionists at a rate of an estimated one million per year.

Legalizing abortion didn't take away the stigma. The appearance of abortion as a nasty business is still with us. In the beginning, proponents felt that it was prudent to say that no one favored abortion but that it was sometimes a necessity. The rationale was that all other avenues had been explored and, in this particular instance, abortion was the final solution. The anti-abortion element recognized the mistake in this type of pronouncement. They wasted no time linking abortion to genocide.

Abortion rights advocates redoubled their efforts to prove that they were really nice folks. Pussyfooting and disclaimers

[2]Reprint of an article by Cleo Kocol, chairperson of the Feminist Caucus of the American Humanist Association. *The Humanist*. 48:33. My/Je '88. Copyright © 1988 by the American Humanist Association. Reprinted by permission.

abounded. All statements were prefaced with sentences like "Nobody wants to have an abortion," "Abortion is not a procedure taken lightly," "Abortion is a last resort." Is it any wonder that as a nation, a culture, and individuals we believe that abortion is still a nasty business?

Today, polls show that most physicians recognize the necessity for abortion. Lately, however, fewer and fewer doctors elect to perform them. Those who do are looked upon with less than favor by their peers. This unwritten but highly contagious attitude is prevalent everywhere. Women who have abortions seldom speak of them. If they do, they must be properly grieved. They must show repentance: "I hated to do it," "I was depressed for months afterwards," "I would never do it again." The social climate dictates that they must act as if they have done something reprehensible, that guilt must follow. Instead, I venture that most women are relieved that they have spared themselves, their families, and society the consequences of an unwanted pregnancy.

From day one of legal abortion, concerted efforts have been made to overturn the ruling. Fundamentalist and charismatic Christians and pope-dominated Roman Catholics lead those who scream "baby-killer." Women are harassed, clinics picketed and bombed, doctors and liberal politicians targeted, and medically unsound movies shown. The hysterical shout, and the rest of the nation gives up logical thinking to fall in line.

It is time to stop playing the game according to our opponents' rules. Abortion is a procedure we do want, as individuals, as a society, as a nation. It is time to protect the living over the not-yet-formed. A potential life is not a life. A potential for life exists every time there is intercourse, yet a majority of people, including Catholics, routinely employ some kind of birth control in an attempt to limit that potential. Only the fanatical fringe would make sexually abused children bear babies. Only hard-core women haters would sacrifice women to the "unborn."

We must stop leaning over backwards in order not to offend militant anti-abortion radicals. We must create a climate in which people are not afraid to say, "Yes, I had an abortion. Yes, I perform abortions. Yes, you need an abortion. Yes, I want an abortion." Abortions must become just one of many medical procedures.

To say that fetuses and embryos are more important than living women and children should be abhorrent to everyone. Until we have 100-percent-safe birth control, until we have men who do not rape, until we have men who never sexually molest their daughters, granddaughters, and nieces, we have need for abortion.

The time for truth-telling is now. At this time and place, abortion is a necessity.

COUNSELLING ABORTION[3]

"I just want to get it over with," she says clutching herself. I look up from her medical chart and see her face starkly contrasted against the white wall of the counselling room. She is talking about the abortion which she will undergo in about two hours, and I begin to gently probe into the reasons that brought her to this choice.

Given the recent activity of the Supreme Court, the tendency of pro-choice advocates has been to focus on the threats to abortion rights from the legal system. It is just as important, however, to be aware of the threats to abortion that are inherent in the medical system. In most societies today, a legal abortion is the property of the medical domain. Integral to the medical model, however, are biases against women in general, and specifically against the exercise of their right to abortion.

When I graduated from college in 1987, I became an abortion counselor. I work in a free-standing abortion clinic which is both staffed and managed by women, with the exception of the physicians who are predominantly male. As is true of most abortion clinics, the counselors speak with the women before their abortion to describe the possible risks and complications of the procedure and, more importantly, to explore the decision-making process behind their choice. This "counselling session" is mandatory for each woman who desires an abortion at our clinic and was created to provide the doctors with the assurance that the women are giving an informed consent to the abortion.

---

[3]Reprint of an article by abortion counselor Lisa Chasan. Reprinted by permission of the author. First printed in Ja '90 in *Sojourner: The Women's Forum*, 1050 Commonwealth Ave., Boston, MA 02215.

In essence, the counselors judge the certainty of a woman's decision and are expected to send her home if she seems ambivalent. To prepare us for this responsible position, we were provided with forty hours of training covering the fundamentals of reproductive health care, contraception, short-term counselling, observation of the senior counselors, and group "consciousness raising."

At first, I felt that my position as an abortion counselor helped women to obtain caring and safe abortions. In many cases, the counselling session was the first opportunity a woman had to share her thoughts without fear of a negative response. I saw how simply talking in a quiet room could enable a woman to focus her thoughts, separate issues, or identify new goals. I savored the allowance and gift of this time, and the establishment that provided it. Here, women were able to speak freely with each other.

After about one year of counselling, during which I counseled about twenty-five women per week, I began to have concerns about the nature of my job. I started to consider that my role in the clinic might actually be working against the very right which I so strongly wanted to be working for. "Does abortion counselling oppress women?," I asked myself. Does abortion "counselling," by its very definition, imply that the decision to have an abortion will be surrounded by guilt and/or sadness? Does it not assume the existence of emotions which are culturally defined and which will furthermore necessitate discussion with a "professional?" Certainly, in my sessions, I had talked to women who had felt such emotions, but I have also talked with others who have felt calm and clear, and even others who did not want to talk at all. As feminists, we may indeed hope that an abortion can be a "turning point" for a woman, or "empower" her, but in essence what the abortion means to her is knowledge that is hers alone to choose to share.

The mandatory nature of the counselling session at our clinic, as at most, opens the private thoughts of women to our scrutiny and justifies this exposure with the belief that it will "help" the woman. And we, as abortion counselors even with the best of intentions, are given the undisputed right not only to delve into these thoughts, but to evaluate them. If what we find in her mind does not fit in with our presumptions on how a woman choosing an abortion should feel, we have the authority through the medical model to deny her her legal right.

I now believe that we have legitimized the exposure of women's private thoughts in the medical setting so that we can reassure ourselves that the moral structure of our world is being upheld. In other words, the true reason for the establishment of abortion counselling is a lack of trust in the capability of women to act as moral agents. The truth is that we live in a world where the morality of a man who has killed hundreds in a war is not only never questioned, but honored.

I suggest that we stop reacting to this broad-based fear of abortion. Instead of perpetuating the stereotypes surrounding abortion, we must acknowledge the full variety of the experience. All this fear (you can feel it; from the anti-choice faction, and unfortunately from society in general) must be recognized for what it is: fear of power in the hands of women.

MINORITY REPORT/RESPONSES[4]

REPORT

Apparently ridiculing the idea that "unborn children have protectable interests" in its mini-exhortation "March!" (April 10), *The Nation*'s editorialists add sarcastically, "That's more than born children have in a country with soaring infant mortality rates." Why do I find this non sequitur encouraging?

It's just my impression, but the idea that a fetus is "only" a growth in, or appendage to, the female body seems to be advanced with less conviction than was once the case. There was a time when our editorialists would have proudly echoed Gloria Steinem on the fetus, saying that its indubitable and necessary existence posed no problem because it was "a mass of dependent protoplasm" with no more distinction or dignity than an inflamed appendix. One still hears that sort of thing said, but to its credit the "pro-choice" school has turned queasy and shifted to the iron-

⁴Reprint of a column by Christopher Hitchens, "Minority Report." *The Nation*, 248:546, Ap 24 '89. Together with reprints of responses in *The Nation* (248:650+ My 15 '89, and 248:870, Je 26 '89). All copyright © 1989 by The Nation Company, Inc.

ic or, as above, the merely sarcastic. Thus it's more often argued
that the so-called right to life movement is, generally speaking,
led by people who support capital punishment, endorse imperial-
ist war, fetishize nuclear weapons and detest women's liberation.
The abortion issue, in this analysis, is an opportunistic conscrip-
tion of the emotions for the purpose of retarding or negating the
gains made by women since the 1960s.

As far as it goes, that line of argument is based on politically
valid observation. The leading element in the "right to life"
movement is indeed composed of hypocrites, who are either indifferent to the suffering of others or in some cases positively en-
thusiastic about it; who are marketers of religious cretinism; and
who have been thoroughly and revealingly unsettled by one of
the century's most positive developments, the sexual autonomy
of women. As has been said before, the "lifers" pretend concern
for humanity before it is born and after it is dead, and contribute
mightily to the preventable bits of misery in between.

I am not recording an opinion on this in order to protect myself from the wrath to come. I have always been convinced that
the term "unborn child" is a genuine description of material reality. Obviously, the fetus is alive, so that disputation about whether
or not it counts as "a life" is casuistry. The same applies, from a
materialist point of view, to the question of whether or not
this "life" is "human." What other kind could it be? As for
"dependent," this has never struck me as a very radical criticism
of any agglomeration of human cells in whatever state. Children
are "dependent" too.

It is because I actually do mind about this that I am appalled
by the exploitation of the subject by religious and political dema-
gogues. Still, most of them have the excuse of ignorance or de-
pravity. The left should not. If you care to spend a few minutes
talking with the people who attend "right to life" events, the active majority of them working-class women, you will encounter
all kinds of what I am still arrogant or confident enough to call
illusions. But you will also encounter a genuine, impressive, un-
forced revulsion at the idea of the disposable fetus. This revulsion
would deserve respect even if it were "only" emotional. But anyone who has ever seen a sonogram or has spent even an hour with
a textbook on embryology knows that the emotions are not the
deciding factor. In order to terminate a pregnancy, you have to
still a heartbeat, switch off a developing brain and, whatever the

method, break some bones and rupture some organs. As to whether this involves pain on the "Silent Scream" scale, I have no idea. The "right to life" leadership, again, has cheapened everything it touches.

But I don't think that this cheapening should set the standard, as it paradoxically appears to do in the propaganda of the "pro-choice" lot. Here, the emphasis is exclusively or allegedly on the defense of the rights of women. Need the two conceptions be permanently at war? What if there were to be a historic compromise?

If society really wanted to protect the unborn child, it would have, in reason and conscience, to make women a serious proposal. "We" regard the occupant of what is undoubtedly *your* womb as a candidate member of the next generation, and "we" thus claim a right and an interest. "We" do not like what "we" hear about gender abortions, where potential girls are flushed out by couples who want boys (surely the great unintended consequence of a feminist campaign). Nor do "we" like what "we" hear about racial implications of this type of population control. For these and many other reasons, "we" want to define this as a social problem. In return:

(1) Contraception will be available free, under a National Health Service that will also guarantee prenatal, nutrition and health care for any child born to any family (as is still the case even in much poorer capitalist democracies like Britain). Sexual and contraceptive education will be part of the national school curriculum, just as prayer will not need to be.

(2) Since not all taking of life is murder, and since it is immoral and unscientific to maintain otherwise, no woman may be compelled to bear a child if she is the victim of rape or incest, or if her mental or physical health is threatened. These abortions will be performed at no cost by the National Health Service, which will relieve at least some of the people who worry understandably about profit-making abortion "clinics."

(3) The National Health Service will supervise a national adoption service. The current disgrace of private and profit-making adoption rackets, many of them run by religious and racial sectarians, will cease.

Most of these socialist reforms should have been implemented by now in any case. *On these conditions* it would be possible to end the dialogue of the deaf between those who shout "murder" and those who dully reply "no problem." It is a pity that instead of taking this course, the majority of feminists and their allies have stuck to the dead ground of "Me Decade" possessive individualism, an ideology that has more in common than it admits with the prehistoric right, which it claims to oppose but has in fact encouraged.

RESPONSES

Majority Report

New York City

Many on *The Nation*'s staff were appalled by Christopher Hitchens's attack on the women's movement and on the freedom of reproductive choice in his "Minority Report" of April 24. We do not all think alike about abortion, but almost all of us agree that the right to decide to bear a child belongs to the woman— not to the state or, as Christopher puts it, to society. And we believe that the defense of that right is not just a personal matter but a proper concern of the left.

Christopher's uneasiness about abortion seems the most genuine sentiment in his piece, and it is the position with which we can most easily sympathize. For many of us, abortion is a moral dilemma. I and some others on the staff see abortion as a hard choice, but one we would definitely make under certain circumstances. For others, the choice is not so hard. A third group says: I would not have an abortion (or encourage my partner to have one), but each woman must make this choice for herself.

Christopher's distaste for abortion and his ignorance about the women's movement is clear. But it is impossible to tell what his relationship is to what he has written. In his closing paragraphs, when he begins to suggest a policy on abortion, he abandons his own voice and begins to describe the "proposal" that society would make to women if society wanted to protect the "unborn" child. He further distances himself from the proposals he is outlining by having "society" (which does not seem to include women, since it is addressing them) speak as "we," in quotation marks.

When he has society say that "'we' do not like what 'we' hear about gender abortions," does he mean that he does not like what he hears or merely that some people do not like what they hear? This device allows him to drag in all sorts of right-wing propaganda (there is *no* evidence of gender abortion in the United States) without having to take responsibility for it. Unlike Christopher's usual clear and elegant prose, this column contains more voices than the Mormon Tabernacle Choir.

The distancing strategy has another benefit. When readers accuse Christopher of advocating the criminalization of abortion, he will deny that he said anything of the kind—and he didn't. He has "society" say that "'we' want to define this as a social problem," and that "in return" women and children will receive the health benefits that most advanced societies routinely provide. This program seems intended to make it possible for women to avoid abortions. Christopher accuses feminists and their allies of not facing the reality that fetuses are human and alive, but he won't face the reality that the alternative to legal abortion is criminalization.

Christopher is also evasive in his discussion of the nature of reproduction. I agree with him that the fetus is a human life, and I understand that he is truly troubled by the moral dilemma of abortion. But throughout the column he minimizes the connection between the fetus and the woman in whose uterus the fetus is, as he puts it, an "occupant." As historian Linda Gordon has written, "Reproduction involves a relationship that is unique, and treating the fetus as an individual entrapped in a uterus does not adequately express this relationship."

Because Christopher accepts the equation Alive + Human = Child, he views the fetus as having rights. Because he minimizes the mother's role in pregnancy, he does not see her rights as paramount. (On the contrary, he sees the defense of women's rights as selfishness.) Instead, he believes that the rights of fetuses and those of women—"the two conceptions" in his interesting choice of words—need not be "permanently at war." Here is another evasion. Once the fetus is viewed as having rights equal to or greater than those of the mother, the state has almost unlimited ability to intervene in pregnancy, and in many cases has begun to exercise it.

Christopher claims to be concerned about the "racial implications" of abortion, although here again he never makes clear what he means. Yet the defense of fetal rights will have its harshest impact on poor and black women, who are most likely to use the public clinics, hospitals and drug programs that will bring them to the attention of the state. Ellen Willis, writing in

The Village Voice ("The Wrongs of Fetal Rights," April 11), cites a *New England Journal of Medicine* survey that found that 81 percent of court-ordered Caesareans were performed on black, Hispanic and Asian women.

Although Christopher disavows the distortions and demagogy of the antiabortion leadership, his column is full of right-wing buzzwords that keep the debate at a high emotional pitch. He claims that women in the antiabortion movement feel "revulsion at the idea of the disposable fetus," a slur on the character and motivation of women who have abortions. "Emotions are not the deciding factor" he says, and then goes on to talk about "still[ing] a heartbeat, switch[ing] off a developing brain . . . break[ing] some bones." Ninety percent of the abortions in this country are performed in the first trimester, when there are no bones to break.

Christopher writes that "'we' do not like what 'we' hear about gender abortions." According to the American College of Obstetricians and Gynecologists, no statistics are kept on the reasons for abortion. But rumors of widespread gender abortion surface and are reported. The perpetrators are usually said to be members of the diplomatic community, particularly Asians, who so prefer boys to girls that the women have abortions in the fifth month, after amniocentesis has revealed the fetal sex. If there are a few instances of this practice—the Guttmacher Institute thinks there may be—it can hardly be viewed, as Christopher has it, as an ironic consequence of the women's movement. Rather, it would be a consequence of the technology of amniocentesis, and of a lack of respect for women.

Christopher puts forward a "historic compromise" that would presumably remove the need for abortion. Point one is free contraception and sex education, as well as free prenatal care and health care for children. That's certainly nice. But contraception, free and easily accessible or not, doesn't always work, so that even its universal practice will not spell the end of unwanted pregnancy. Nor, as the Children's Defense Fund's admirable work with pregnant teen-agers has made clear, will young people necessarily use contraception when it's available.

Of course society should provide prenatal, nutritional and health care for children, as Christopher suggests, but that doesn't begin to touch the expense of raising children. A survey by the Guttmacher Institute found that the most common reason women gave for having an abortion was that they were unable to afford a child. If society really wanted to assure that anyone could afford to have a child, or another child, we'd need guaranteed jobs, generous parental leave, affordable housing, highly subsidized child care and first-rate public education. But even in Sweden, with sex education, contraceptives available and social benefits far more complete than Christopher advocates, the abortion rate is 18 percent of pregnancies among women of reproductive age.

The second point in Christopher's program has "society" offer the option of free abortion to women in cases of rape or incest, or when the mother's "mental or physical health is threatened." This is where I came in; that's the exact wording of the loophole in the statutes that outlawed abortion in the bad old days. Here Christopher is willing to admit that "not all taking of life is murder." This is an interesting place to draw the line. I have always drawn it where the Supreme Court did in *Roe v. Wade*—when a fetus is mature enough that it could survive outside its mother's body there should be no abortion. But Christopher seems to be saying that abortion is O.K. when women have been forced into pregnancy by rape or incest; when the pregnancy results from accident or mistake, abortion is murder. The unspoken argument seems to be: If a woman chooses to have sex and gets pregnant, she has to have the baby.

And so we come to "society's" final proposal, a national adoption service. Dan Quayle might have suggested this if he had the wit. "Adoption, not abortion" is a slogan that assumes either that pregnancy and birth are passing inconveniences or that nine months of an unwanted pregnancy followed by giving up a child is what you get if you want to have sex. And as Katha Pollitt pointed out in these pages on October 17, 1988, the supply of unwanted babies who will be born once abortion is crimin—excuse me, is defined as a social problem, will far outstrip the demand for them. Nor will adoption help the mother of several children who does not have the financial resources or the energy to raise another one.

Christopher claims that he wants to "end the dialogue of the deaf between those who shout 'murder' and those who dully report 'no problem.'" This formulation is dishonest, because "no problem" is not the feminist position. Christopher's notion of feminism is Gloria Steinem circa 1967, but he seems wholly ignorant of the work of pro-choice socialist feminists like the members of the Committee for Abortion Rights and Against Sterilization Abuse, or of the writing of Rosalind Petchesky and others. I cannot believe that Christopher would argue that the black struggle for civil rights, or the unions' defense of their members, stems from a possessive individualism that has encouraged the right wing. That he can make that claim about feminists and their allies shows, I think, that he does not take feminism seriously as a movement that seeks to transform society—and that he has not made an effort to understand it.

Finally, I am curious about the timing of Christopher's column. His opposition to abortion has been known for years. Yet he waited to air his views in *The Nation* until the increasingly conservative Supreme Court was about to hear *Webster v. Reproductive Health Services*, a case that may indeed limit severely, if not revoke, the right to a legal abortion. Christopher takes this moment to magisterially inform the left how to think about abortion—allying himself, whatever his intentions, with the right-to-life movement he so eloquently denounces.

ELSA DIXLER

Fundamental Difference

Washington

Michael Dukakis had one good moment in his otherwise pitiful presidential campaign. That was when he in effect asked George Bush whether he considered women who had abortions to be murderers. Bush hemmed and hawed, but his advisers quickly realized that labeling such women in this way could send one-fifth of the adult female population to prison. In effect, Bush was told to deny that his antiabortion stance implied that killing a fetus was equivalent to murder.

We recount this episode because it suggests a fundamental point that Christopher Hitchens seems to have missed in his antiabortion essay. There already is a moral and legal consensus in this country that eliminating a fetus is fundamentally different from killing a human being.

Hitchens's essay implies that a life-form becomes human after conception because—presumably—that is when the brain and uniquely human attributes begin to develop. In fact, science now allows us to fertilize the egg outside the womb. That is what in vitro fertilization is all about, and why thousands of women who can't conceive in the old-fashioned way have been able to have children. Doctors doing in vitro fertilization routinely take more than one egg from the woman and fertilize all of them. One fertilized egg is implanted in the woman and the rest are discarded. Does Hitchens regard this as the taking of human life? Does he think a fertilized egg about to be implanted by a doctor in a woman's womb deserves the description "unborn child"? Would he join with his antiabortion comrades, chief among them the Catholic Church, in condemning this procedure and in the process condemning thousands of people to childlessness? Is this position likely to be too reactionary even for Hitchens's antiabortion zeal? Nevertheless, this is where positions like Hitchens's ultimately lead us.

It amazes us that while Hitchens allies himself with the reactionaries who would deny women the right to control their own bodies, he can still consider himself progressive. Maybe Hitchens can live with the principles he outlined in his essay, but he shouldn't be allowed to forget that if he and other antiabortion advocates have their way women will be dying because of them.

JOHN WILLOUGHBY
MARY ANN FAY

Boys' Club

New York City

I'm writing for information on how to start my own chapter of the Men Who Know More About Reproduction and the Evils of Abortion Than Most Women Seem to Know Club, started at *The Village Voice* by Nat Hentoff and expanded to your pages by the erstwhile progressive Christopher Hitchens. While criticizing everything else about their politics and intelligence, Hitchens makes the daring insight that the emotions of working-class women who are horrified by abortion are truer than those felt by the selfish, "Me Decade" women who turn a blind eye to the atrocity that they daily commit without a second thought. It's finally become clear that one of the few who can truly claim to stand squarely between the unintelligent emotionalism of the right and the murderous disingenuousness of the left is Hitchens himself. And not only does he understand the issue with a clarity that has escaped the millions of women who have attempted to grapple with it but he has even presented us with a *program* that finally solves the seemingly intractable difficulties that may have led us down the errant path to abortion, but need to no more.

Now that he has dispelled the curmudgeonly assumption so prevalent on the left that the Bush Administration is unwilling to sink enormous new resources into programs benefiting women, children and the poor, he will also be able to show us the road to equality and world peace that we've no doubt been missing all along.

Bravo, Hitchens! Thousands of years of patriarchy can't have been all wrong!

FRANK SHEED

"Same Old Story"

Montague, Mass.

Christopher Hitchens's "Minority Report" on abortion comes at a bad time, given that abortion for all women, whatever their circumstances, is now under threat by Reagan's Supreme Court. But his combination of sexual utopianism with a total banishing of women as *members* of society would be bad news under any regime. What kind of political imagination argues that society ("we") can make a serious proposal to women (obviously "them") whereby women give up abortion in return for sex education, contraception and adoption organized according to the principles of the masculine "we" explaining true values to women in this article? By 1990 women may not have abortion to give up. So what kind of yes or no does Hitchens imagine as their response? The answer: He doesn't imagine women responding or acting in any way. An unborn child is more real to him than a woman who doesn't want to be pregnant and give birth.

Why is a fetus so much more visible as a suffering being than a woman who carries through an involuntary pregnancy? What does Hitchens think adoption consists of: the delivery of a baby carried for nine months and given birth to by no one? Perhaps it's time for a new strategy for defenders of abortion: the representation of state-enforced pregnancy as involuntary servitude. That's what it is, and a form of peculiarly invasive servitude. Black women in this country were used as breeding machines by white masters throughout our centuries of slavery. Now Hitchens wants to extend this privilege to women of all colors.

And he tells us that resisting such exploitation of women's bodies and energies is "'Me Decade' possessive individualism." Come on! Abortion is much older than that. For over a century it's been at the heart of feminist movements that recognized women's reproductive control as even more basic to their freedom than economic opportunity. One result of legalization in the past decade has been the expansion of decent clinics where abortions are performed on embryos, not fetuses. If Hitchens is so up on embryology, he ought to know the difference. And if he's so up on materialist politics, he ought to know that distant dreams—an enlightened, efficient and pro-woman National Health Service in an increasingly reactionary late-capitalist state—are no basis for the kind of bargain he wants to make: women's bodies and labor (in both senses) as counters in men's grand designs. This is not "a historic compromise." It's the same old story.

ANN ROSALIND JONES

Hands Off!

New York City

Gee, Mr. Hitchens, what a great bunch of brand new ideas you had in your "Minority Report." I can't imagine why the rest of us never thought of nationally available free contraception and sexual and contraceptive education in schools. It's a sure bet that these two measures would cause a sharp decline in unwanted pregnancies, and thus a decline in the necessity for abortions. We should really get moving on these ideas; I'm sure we'll be able to implement them before women lose their rights to safe, legal abortion. And if we can't get the country to go social overnight, well, I guess hundreds of thousands of women will die from botched, illegal abortions. But, oh, I'm sorry, you've heard that all before and it's starting to get on your nerves.

You say "no woman may be compelled to bear a child if she is the victim of rape or incest, or if her mental or physical health is threatened." I love that bit, I really do. Thanks so much for telling me when I will and will not be COMPELLED to give birth. And, since you're so smart, you can have the fancy job of deciding when a woman's mental health is threatened by being pregnant. You could sit on a very tall chair and give the thumbs up or thumbs down and I'll be shuffled off to the Abortion Wing or the Prenatal Care Wing.

You seem to think that "possessive individualism" is a fad, that women insisting on control over their own reproductive systems is a fad. I wonder, what do you think happened in the early 1970s? Do you think a bunch of women got together and said, "We feel like having some abortions. Now, what excuse can we use? Oh,

how about, 'I should be able to do whatever I want with my body'?
Yeah, that's a good one. Grab some posters. Let's go."

So, now we should get together again and think up a new slogan, something more eighties-ish? No, Mr. Hitchens, I don't
think so. We really meant it then and we really mean it now.
There is something timeless in my desire for you to keep *your*
hands off *my* body.

MARYAN NEWBURY

For Bread and Roses
Princeton, N.J.

It is troubling to hear Christopher Hitchens, the socialist,
echoing not only the sentiments of the Pope but the opinions of
the most callow male undergraduates I encounter.

Hitchens tries to distance himself from the conservatives he
sees as "cheapening" the "pro-life" issue. But antifeminism also
has its left-wing sources. Against the narcissistic, presumably
bourgeois feminists who support the pro-choice movement,
Hitchens pits the Working-Class Woman, whom he sees as filling
the ranks of right-to-lifeism. This rhetorical figure, with her supposed sense of family values, feminine self-sacrifice, class solidarity and now—in Hitchens's account—of fetal babyhood, has been
a beloved fantasy of conservative socialists and trade unionists
since the nineteenth century. Hitchens never bothers to check his
own fantasies about the women he claims to have met in antiabortion organizations against a more complex reality: If Catholic and
fundamentalist women support "pro-lifeism," hundreds of thousands of other working-class women seek and use the right to
abortion. If he were investigating a massive right-wing movement
for the open shop, heavily financed by the Catholic Church,
would he be so quick to attribute the views of its members to the
working-class masses? Two-thirds of women obtaining abortions
in the United States have family incomes below $24,000. Just who
does Hitchens think they are, if not working-class women?

Historically, working-class women, just like their middle-class
counterparts, have sought abortions in great numbers and, in the
period of illegality, at great peril to themselves. As for the reverence for the "unborn child" that Hitchens implies is a distinct
class tradition, the evidence before the twentieth century, and before the onset of the concerted crusade of the Catholic Church
against abortion and contraception, indicates that working-class

women felt no deep ambivalence about abortion, nor did they support any ethic of babyhood-from-conception. They feared the medical procedure but had no qualms about escaping the unwanted pregnancies. Women in the United States today continue, implicitly, to observe the traditional boundary between what one could call "being" and "babyhood" as the point when they feel the fetus move, or "quicken," at eighteen to twenty weeks. Less than 5 percent of abortions occur after the sixteenth week of pregnancy.

Hitchens, however, seems uninterested in examining hundreds of years of female experience or in analyzing distinctions that might be critical to his views. To him, materialist philosophy—presumably Marxism?—makes it obvious that a mass of tissue, apparently from the moment of conception, is a child, if an unborn one. Yet this "fact" has never been obvious to the people who are, after all, materially closest to the awakening of life, i.e., women. Even for a self-styled materialist, might not a theory of humanity begin with an examination of the grounding of consciousness? Against Hitchens's smug and crude biological reductionism, I'll take Rosalind Petchesky's brilliant exploration (in *Abortion and Woman's Right*) of the dialectic of personhood, the coming-into-being of the fetus through its own growth and movements in utero, its growing responsiveness and its mother's consciousness of it as a distinct being.

Finally, it's big of Hitchens, concerned as he is with *communitas*, to let rape and incest victims off the hook. But illogical. If abortion is murder, why shouldn't they, too, put in their nine months for the National Adoption Service? The difference seems to lie in coerced versus consensual sex. Any female, girl or woman, who enters into sex voluntarily must bear the consequences. Women as victims deserve, in Hitchens's program, sympathy and empathic public policy; women as actors, in search of pleasure, good times, love or intimacy deserve regulation.

Women need abortions and seek them for a multitude of reasons. These days, after fifteen years of inundation by conservative propaganda, they do so with a range of feelings, from sorrow to regret to fear to a simple longing for relief. What they hold in common is, at the least, a wish to be free of biological necessity and, at the most, a vision of a larger life for themselves—the desires that left-wing feminists have long encapsulated in the slogan "bread and roses." It is disgraceful that a socialist—and in the name of socialism, no less—sees fit to caricature these longings rather than to honor them.

CHRISTINE STANSELL

This Won't Hurt a Bit

Olympia, Wash.

Since Christopher Hitchens is so concerned about the issue of abortion, I (meaning society) would like to propose to men this "historic compromise."

"We," contrary to popular opinion, don't *want* to have abortions. It's not "our" idea of a good time. "We" also understand that not only are the most widely used methods of birth control (the pill, diaphragm, condoms, I.U.D.) not 100 percent effective, they are often inconvenient and downright dangerous. "We" don't like what we hear about medical studies linking high blood pressure and certain types of cancer to the pill, nor did we like losing our sisters to the corporate greed of A. H. Robins and Company in the Dalkon Shield episode. Nor are we comfortable with a return to the deadly practice of back-alley and coat-hanger abortions that a reversal of *Roe v. Wade* would precipitate. "We" feel that placing the responsibility for birth control, and consequently the result of failed birth control, on women is patently unfair. "We" want to define this as a social problem. In return:

(1) Vasectomies will be available free under a National Health Service. They will be compulsory for all males at the beginning of puberty. Prior to his vasectomy, any male may make a donation to the National Sperm Bank. Since each ejaculation contains millions of sperm, this will insure that there will be plenty of those squiggly things around to provide "candidate members of the next generation."

(2) At the time of his vasectomy, a male will receive a "V number" and a "V card," without which he won't be able to get a job, collect unemployment, receive medical treatment, etc. If any man is found without his V card, he will be subject to immediate imprisonment. He will be released only after the necessary operation has been performed.

(3) Of course, abortion will remain legal. However, if a woman becomes pregnant against her will and can identify the father, he will be arrested, vasectomized and made to perform extensive community service in the free day care centers for working parents.

(4) Prenatal care, postnatal care, nutrition advice, etc. will be available and free, as with all health care to all people, just as it should be.

On these conditions it would be possible to end the monologue of the sexists who cry, "not *my* problem." It is a pity that instead of taking this course, the majority of Hitchensists and their allies have stuck to the dead ground of "He Millennia" one-sided pseudo-solutions, reflecting an ideology that has more in common with the prehistoric practice of dragging women around by their hair than it does with the reality of women's lives.

CELIA WARD

Selective Memory
New York City

Women did not have to wait for the "me generation" to hear men like Christopher Hitchens calling them selfish for imagining they could control their own reproductive capacities. Nineteenth-century eugenicists portrayed WASP women as shirking the duties of motherhood. Teddy Roosevelt in 1903 accused women of endangering the race by their "desire to be 'independent'—that is, to live one's life purely according to one's own desires" and ignoring the needs of "the race." There is one political view that unites most men—that women should "remember the children!" As if we were the ones who forget them.

TEMMA KAPLAN

ABORTION & THE SEXUAL AGENDA[5]

The abortion debate continues. In the latest and perhaps most crucial development, pro-life feminists are contesting pro-choice feminist claims that abortion rights are prerequisites for women's full development and social equality. The outcome of this debate may be decisive for the culture as a whole. Pro-life feminists, like myself, argue on good feminist principles that

[5]Reprint of an article by Sidney Callahan, associate professor of psychology at Mercy College. *Commonweal*. 113:232–8. Ap 25 '86. Copyright © 1986 by Commonweal Foundation.

women can never achieve the fulfillment of feminist goals in a society permissive toward abortion.

These new arguments over abortion take place within liberal political circles. This round of intense intra-feminist conflict has spiraled beyond earlier right-versus-left abortion debates, which focused on "tragic choices," medical judgments, and legal compromises. Feminist theorists of the pro-choice position now put forth the demand for unrestricted abortion rights as a *moral imperative* and insist upon women's right to complete reproductive freedom. They morally justify the present situation and current abortion practices. Thus it is all the more important that pro-life feminists articulate their different feminist perspective.

These opposing arguments can best be seen when presented in turn. Perhaps the most highly developed feminist arguments for the morality and legality of abortion can be found in Beverly Wildung Harrison's *Our Right to Choose* (Beacon Press, 1983) and Rosalind Pollack Petchesky's *Abortion and Woman's Choice* (Longman, 1984). Obviously it is difficult to do justice to these complex arguments, which draw on diverse strands of philosophy and social theory and are often interwoven in pro-choice feminists' own version of a "seamless garment." Yet the fundamental feminist case for the morality of abortion, encompassing the views of Harrison and Petchesky, can be analyzed in terms of four central moral claims: (1) the moral right to control one's own body; (2) the moral necessity of autonomy and choice in personal responsibility; (3) the moral claim for the contingent value of fetal life; (4) the moral right of women to true social equality.

1. The moral right to control one's own body. Pro-choice feminism argues that a woman choosing an abortion is exercising a basic right of bodily integrity granted in our common law tradition. If she does not choose to be physically involved in the demands of a pregnancy and birth, she should not be compelled to be so against her will. Just because it is *her* body which is involved, a woman should have the right to terminate any pregnancy, which at this point in medical history is tantamount to terminating fetal life. No one can be forced to donate an organ or submit to other invasive physical procedures for however good a cause. Thus no woman should be subjected to "compulsory pregnancy." And it should be noted that in pregnancy much more than a passive biological process is at stake.

From one perspective, the fetus is, as Petchesky says, a "biological parasite" taking resources from the woman's body. During pregnancy, a woman's whole life and energies will be actively involved in the nine-month process. Gestation and childbirth involve physical and psychological risks. After childbirth a woman will either be a mother who must undertake a twenty-year responsibility for childrearing, or face giving up her child for adoption or institutionalization. Since hers is the body, hers the risk, hers the burden, it is only just that she alone should be free to decide on pregnancy or abortion.

This moral claim to abortion, according to the pro-choice feminists, is especially valid in an individualistic society in which women cannot count on medical care or social support in pregnancy, childbirth, or childrearing. A moral abortion decision is never made in a social vacuum, but in the real life society which exists here and now.

2. The moral necessity of autonomy and choice in personal responsibility. Beyond the claim for individual *bodily* integrity, the pro-choice feminists claim that to be a full adult *morally*, a woman must be able to make responsible life commitments. To plan, choose, and exercise personal responsibility, one must have control of reproduction. A woman must be able to make yes or no decisions about a specific pregnancy, according to her present situation, resources, prior commitments, and life plan. Only with such reproductive freedom can a woman have the moral autonomy necessary to make mature commitments, in the area of family, work, or education.

Contraception provides a measure of personal control, but contraceptive failure or other chance events can too easily result in involuntary pregnancy. Only free access to abortion can provide the necessary guarantee. The chance biological process of an involuntary pregnancy should not be allowed to override all the other personal commitments and responsibilities a woman has: to others, to family, to work, to education, to her future development, health, or well-being. Without reproductive freedom, women's personal moral agency and human consciousness are subjected to biology and chance.

3. The moral claim for the contingent value of fetal life. Pro-choice feminist exponents like Harrison and Petchesky claim that the value of fetal life is contingent upon the woman's free consent and subjective acceptance. The fetus must be invested with maternal valuing in order to become human. This process of "humanization" through personal consciousness and "sociality" can only be bestowed by the woman in whose body and psychosocial system a new life must mature. The meaning and value of fetal life are constructed by the woman; without this personal conferral there only exists a biological, physiological process. Thus fetal interests or fetal rights can never outweigh the woman's prior interest and rights. If a woman does not consent to invest her pregnancy with meaning or value, then the merely biological process can be freely terminated. Prior to her own free choice and conscious investment, a woman cannot be described as a "mother" nor can a "child" be said to exist.

Moreover, in cases of voluntary pregnancy, a woman can withdraw consent if fetal genetic defects or some other problem emerges at any time before birth. Late abortion should thus be granted without legal restrictions. Even the minimal qualifications and limitations on women embedded in *Roe v. Wade* are unacceptable—repressive remnants of patriarchal unwillingness to give power to women.

4. The moral right of women to full social equality. Women have a moral right to full social equality. They should not be restricted or subordinated because of their sex. But this morally required equality cannot be realized without abortion's certain control of reproduction. Female social equality depends upon being able to compete and participate as freely as males can in the structures of educational and economic life. If a woman cannot control when and how she will be pregnant or rear children, she is at a distinct disadvantage, especially in our male-dominated world.

Psychological equality and well-being is also at stake. Women must enjoy the basic right of a person to the free exercise of heterosexual intercourse and full sexual expression, separated from procreation. No less than males, women should be able to be sexually active without the constantly inhibiting fear of pregnancy. Abortion is necessary for women's sexual fulfillment and the growth of uninhibited feminine self-confidence and ownership of their sexual powers.

But true sexual and reproductive freedom means freedom to procreate as well as to inhibit fertility. Pro-choice feminists are also worried that women's freedom to reproduce will be curtailed through the abuse of sterilization and needless hysterectomies. Besides the punitive tendencies of a male-dominated healthcare system, especially in response to repeated abortions or welfare pregnancies, there are other economic and social pressures inhibiting reproduction. Genuine reproductive freedom implies that day care, medical care, and financial support would be provided mothers, while fathers would take their full share in the burdens and delights of raising children.

Many pro-choice feminists identify feminist ideals with communitarian, ecologically sensitive approaches to reshaping society. Following theorists like Sara Ruddick and Carol Gilligan, they link abortion rights with the growth of "maternal thinking" in our heretofore patriarchal society. Maternal thinking is loosely defined as a responsible commitment to the loving nurture of specific human beings as they actually exist in socially embedded interpersonal contexts. It is a moral perspective very different from the abstract, competitive, isolated, and principled rigidity so characteristic of patriarchy.

How does a pro-life feminist respond to these arguments? Pro-life feminists grant the good intentions of their pro-choice counterparts but protest that the pro-choice position is flawed, morally inadequate, and inconsistent with feminism's basic demands for justice. Pro-life feminists champion a more encompassing moral ideal. They recognize the claims of fetal life and offer a different perspective on what is good for women. The feminist vision is expanded and refocused.

1. From the moral right to control one's own body to a more inclusive ideal of justice. The moral right to control one's own body does apply to cases of organ transplants, mastectomies, contraception, and sterilization; but it is not a conceptualization adequate for abortion. The abortion dilemma is caused by the fact that 266 days following a conception in one body, another body will emerge. One's own body no longer exists as a single unit but is engendering another organism's life. This dynamic passage from conception to birth is genetically ordered and universally found in the human species. Pregnancy is not like the growth of cancer or infestation by a biological parasite; it is the way every human being enters the world. Strained philosophical analogies fail to apply: having a baby is not like rescuing a drowning person, being hooked up to a famous violinist's artificial life-support system, donating organs for transplant—or anything else.

As embryology and fetology advance, it becomes clear that human development is a continuum. Just as astonomers are studying the first three minutes in the genesis of the universe, so the first moments, days, and weeks at the beginning of human life are the subject of increasing scientific attention. While neonatology pushes the definition of viability ever earlier, ultrasound and fetology expand the concept of the patient in utero. Within such a continuous growth process, it is hard to defend logically any demarcation point after conception as the point at which an immature form of human life is so different from the day before or the day after, that it can be morally or legally discounted as a nonperson. Even the moment of birth can hardly differentiate a nine-month fetus from a newborn. It is not surprising that those who countenance late abortions are logically led to endorse selective infanticide.

The same legal tradition which in our society guarantees the right to control one's own body firmly recognizes the wrongfulness of harming other bodies, however immature, dependent, different looking, or powerless. The handicapped, the retarded, and newborns are legally protected from deliberate harm. Prolife feminists reject the suppositions that would except the unborn from this protection.

After all, debates similar to those about the fetus were once conducted about feminine personhood. Just as women, or blacks, were considered too different, too underdeveloped, too "biological," to have souls or to possess legal rights, so the fetus is now seen as "merely" biological life, subsidiary to a person. A woman was once viewed as incorporated into the "one flesh" of her husband's person; she too was a form of bodily property. In all patriarchal unjust systems, lesser orders of human life are granted rights only when wanted, chosen, or invested with value by the powerful.

Fortunately, in the course of civilization there has been a gradual realization that justice demands the powerless and dependent be protected against the uses of power wielded unilaterally. No human can be treated as a means to an end without consent. The fetus is an immature, dependent form of human life which only needs time and protection to develop. Surely, immaturity and dependence are not crimes.

In an effort to think about the essential requirements of a just society, philosophers like John Rawls recommend imagining yourself in an "original position," in which your position in the society to be created is hidden by a "veil of ignorance." You will have to weigh the possibility that any inequalities inherent in that society's practices may rebound upon you in the worst, as well as in the best, conceivable way. This thought experiment helps ensure justice for all.

Beverly Harrison argues that in such an envisioning of society everyone would institute abortion rights in order to guarantee that if one turned out to be a woman one would have reproductive freedom. But surely in the original position and behind the "veil of ignorance," you would have to contemplate the possibility of being the particular fetus to be aborted. Since everyone has passed through the fetal stage of development, it is false to refuse to imagine oneself in this state when thinking about a potential world in which justice would govern. Would it be just that an embryonic life—in half the cases, of course, a female life—be sacrificed to the right of a woman's control over her own body? A woman may be pregnant without consent and experience a great many penalties, but a fetus killed without consent pays the ultimate penalty.

It does not matter (*The Silent Scream* notwithstanding) whether the fetus being killed is fully conscious or feels pain. We do not sanction killing the innocent if it can be done painlessly or without the victim's awareness. Consciousness becomes important to the abortion debate because it is used as a criterion for the "personhood" so often seen as the prerequisite for legal protection. Yet certain philosophers set the standard of personhood so high that half the human race could not meet the criteria during most of their waking hours (let alone their sleeping ones). Sentience, self-consciousness, rational decision-making, social participation? Surely no infant, or child under two, could qualify. Either our idea of person must be expanded or another criterion, such as human life itself, be employed to protect the weak in a just society. Pro-life feminists who defend the fetus empathetically identify with an immature state of growth passed through by themselves, their children, and everyone now alive.

It also seems a travesty of just procedures that a pregnant woman now, in effect, acts as sole judge of her own case, under the most stressful conditions. Yes, one can acknowledge that the pregnant woman will be subject to the potential burdens arising from a pregnancy, but it has never been thought right to have an interested party, especially the more powerful party, decide his or her own case when there may be a conflict of interest. If one considers the matter as a case of a powerful versus a powerless, silenced claimant, the pro-choice feminist argument can rightly be inverted: since hers is the body, hers the risk, and hers the greater burden, then how in fairness can a woman be the sole judge of the fetal right to life?

Human ambivalence, a bias toward self-interest, and emotional stress have always been recognized as endangering judgment. Freud declared that love and hate are so entwined that if instant thoughts could kill, we would all be dead in the bosom of our families. In the case of a woman's involuntary pregnancy, a complex, long-term solution requiring effort and energy has to compete with the immediate solution offered by a morning's visit to an abortion clinic. On the simple, perceptual plane, with imagination and thinking curtailed, the speed, ease, and privacy of abortion, combined with the small size of the embryo, tend to make early abortions seem less morally serious—even though speed, size, technical ease, and the private nature of an act have no moral standing.

As the most recent immigrants from non-personhood, feminists have traditionally fought for justice for themselves and the world. Women rally to feminism as a new and better way to live. Rejecting male aggression and destruction, feminists seek alternative, peaceful, ecologically sensitive means to resolve conflicts while respecting human potentiality. It is a chilling inconsistency to see pro-choice feminists demanding continued access to assembly-line, technological methods of fetal killing—the vacuum aspirator, prostaglandins, and dilation and evacuation. It is a betrayal of feminism, which has built the struggle for justice on the bedrock of women's empathy. After all, "maternal thinking" receives its name from a mother's unconditional acceptance and nurture of dependent, immature life. It is difficult to develop concern for women, children, the poor and the dispossessed—and to care about peace—and at the same time ignore fetal life.

2. From the necessity of autonomy and choice in personal responsibility to an expanded sense of responsibility. A distorted idea of morality overemphasizes individual autonomy and active choice. Morality has often been viewed too exclusively as a matter of human agency and decisive action. In moral behavior persons must explicitly choose and aggressively exert their wills to intervene in the natural and social environments. The human will dominates the body, overcomes the given, breaks out of the material limits of nature. Thus if one does not choose to be pregnant or cannot rear a child, who must be given up for adoption, then better to abort the pregnancy. Willing, planning, choosing one's moral commitments through the contracting of one's individual resources becomes the premier model of moral responsibility.

But morality also consists of the good and worthy acceptance of the unexpected events that life presents. Responsiveness and response-ability to things unchosen are also instances of the highest human moral capacity. Morality is not confined to contracted agreements of isolated individuals. Yes, one is obligated by explicit contracts freely initiated, but human beings are also obligated by implicit compacts and involuntary relationships in which persons simply find themselves. To be embedded in a family, a neighborhood, a social system, brings moral obligations which were never entered into with informed consent.

Parent-child relationships are one instance of implicit moral obligations arising by virtue of our being part of the interdependent human community. A woman, involuntarily pregnant, has a moral obligation to the now-existing dependent fetus whether she explicitly consented to its existence or not. No pro-life feminist would dispute the forceful observations of pro-choice feminists about the extreme difficulties that bearing an unwanted child in our society can entail. But the stronger force of the fetal claim presses a woman to accept these burdens; the fetus possesses rights arising from its extreme need and the interdependency and unity of humankind. The woman's moral obligation arises both from her status as a human being embedded in the interdependent human community and her unique lifegiving female reproductive power. To follow the pro-choice feminist ideology of insistent individualistic autonomy and control is to betray a fundamental basis of the moral life.

3. From the moral claim of the contingent value of fetal life to the moral claim for the intrinsic value of human life. The feminist pro-choice position which claims that the value of the fetus is contingent upon the pregnant woman's bestowal—or willed, conscious "construction"—of humanhood is seriously flawed. The inadequacies of this position flow from the erroneous premises (1) that human value and rights can be granted by individual will; (2) that the individual woman's consciousness can exist and operate in an *a priori* isolated fashion; and (3) that "mere" biological, genetic human life has little meaning. Pro-life feminism takes a very different stance to life and nature.

Human life from the beginning to the end of development *has* intrinsic value, which does not depend on meeting the selective criteria or tests set up by powerful others. A fundamental humanist assumption is at stake here. Either we are going to value embodied human life and humanity as a good thing, or take some variant of the nihilist position that assumes human life is just one more random occurrence in the universe such that each instance of human life must explicitly be justified to prove itself worthy to continue. When faced with a new life, or an involuntary pregnancy, there is a world of difference in whether one first asks, "Why continue?" or "Why not?" Where is the burden of proof going to rest? The concept of "compulsory pregnancy" is as distorted as labeling life "compulsory aging."

In a sound moral tradition, human rights arise from human needs, and it is the very nature of a right, or valid claim upon another, that it cannot be denied, conditionally delayed, or rescinded by more powerful others at their behest. It seems fallacious to hold that in the case of the fetus it is the pregnant woman alone who gives or removes its right to life and human status solely through her subjective conscious investment or "humanization." Surely no pregnant woman (or any other individual member of the species) has created her own human nature by an individually willed act of consciousness, nor for that matter been able to guarantee her own human rights. An individual woman and the unique individual embryonic life within her can only exist because of their participation in the genetic inheritance of the human species as a whole. Biological life should never be discounted. Membership in the species, or collective human family, is the basis for human solidarity, equality, and natural human rights.

4. The moral right of women to full social equality from a pro-life feminist perspective. Pro-life feminists and pro-choice feminists are totally agreed on the moral right of women to the full social equality so far denied them. The disagreement between them concerns the definition of the desired goal and the best means to get there. Permissive abortion laws do not bring women reproductive freedom, social equality, sexual fulfillment, or full personal development.

Pragmatic failures of a pro-choice feminist position combined with a lack of moral vision are, in fact, causing disaffection among young women. Middle-aged pro-choice feminists blamed the "big chill" on the general conservative backlash. But they should look rather to their own elitist acceptance of male models of sex and to the sad picture they present of women's lives. Pitting women against their own offspring is not only morally offensive, it is psychologically and politically destructive. Women will never climb to equality and social empowerment over mounds of dead fetuses, numbering now in the millions. As long as most women choose to bear children, they stand to gain from the same constellation of attitudes and institutions that will also protect the fetus in the woman's womb—and they stand to lose from the cultural assumptions that support permissive abortion. Despite temporary conflicts of interest, feminine and fetal liberation are ultimately one and the same cause.

Women's rights and liberation are pragmatically linked to fetal rights because to obtain true equality, women need (1) more social support and changes in the structure of society, and (2) increased self-confidence, self-expectations, and self-esteem. Society in general, and men in particular, have to provide women more support in rearing the next generation, or our devastating feminization of poverty will continue. But if a woman claims the right to decide by herself whether the fetus becomes a child or not, what does this do to paternal and communal responsibility? Why should men share responsibility for child support or child-rearing if they cannot share in what is asserted to be the woman's sole decision? Furthermore, if explicit intentions and consciously accepted contracts are necessary for moral obligations, why should men be held responsible for what *they* do not voluntarily choose to happen? By pro-choice reasoning, a man who does not want to have a child, or whose contraceptive fails, can be exempted from the responsibilities of fatherhood and child support. Traditionally, many men have been laggards in assuming parental responsibility and support for their children; ironically, ready abortion, often advocated as a response to male dereliction, legitimizes male irresponsibility and paves the way for even more male detachment and lack of commitment.

For that matter, why should the state provide a system of day-care or child support, or require workplaces to accommodate women's maternity and the needs of childrearing? Permissive abortion, granted in the name of women's privacy and reproductive freedom, ratifies the view that pregnancies and children are a woman's private individual responsibility. More and more frequently, we hear some version of this old rationalization: if she refuses to get rid of it, it's her problem. A child becomes a product of the individual woman's freely chosen investment, a form of private property resulting from her own cost-benefit calculation. The larger community is relieved of moral responsibility.

With legal abortion freely available, a clear cultural message is given: conception and pregnancy are no longer serious moral matters. With abortion as an acceptable alternative, contraception is not as responsibly used; women take risks, often at the urging of male sexual partners. Repeat abortions increase, with all their psychological and medical repercussions. With more abortion there is more abortion. Behavior shapes thought as well as the other way round. One tends to justify morally what one has done; what becomes commonplace and institutionalized seems harmless. Habituation is a powerful psychological force. Psychologically it is also true that whatever is avoided becomes more threatening; in phobias it is the retreat from anxiety-producing events which reinforces future avoidance. Women begin to see themselves as too weak to cope with involuntary pregnancies. Finally, through the potency of social pressure and the force of inertia, it becomes more and more difficult, in fact almost unthinkable, *not* to use abortion to solve problem pregnancies. Abortion becomes no longer a choice but a "necessity."

But "necessity," beyond the organic failure and death of the body, is a dynamic social construction open to interpretation. The thrust of present feminist pro-choice arguments can only increase the justifiable indications for "necessary" abortion; every unwanted fetal handicap becomes more and more unacceptable. Repeatedly assured that in the name of reproductive freedom, women have a right to specify which pregnancies and which chil-

dren they will accept, women justify sex selection, and abort unwanted females. Female infanticide, after all, is probably as old
a custom as the human species possesses. Indeed, all kinds of selection of the fit and the favored for the good of the family and
the tribe have always existed. Selective extinction is no new program.

There are far better goals for feminists to pursue. Pro-life
feminists seek to expand and deepen the more communitarian,
maternal elements of feminism—and move society from its male-
dominated course. First and foremost, women have to insist upon
a different, woman-centered approach to sex and reproduction.
While Margaret Mead stressed the "womb envy" of males in other
societies, it has been more or less repressed in our own. In our
male-dominated world, what men don't do, doesn't count. Pregnancy, childbirth, and nursing have been characterized as passive, debilitating, animal-like. The disease model of pregnancy
and birth has been entrenched. This female disease or impair-
ment, with its attendant "female troubles," naturally handicaps
women in the "real" world of hunting, war, and the corporate fast
track. Many pro-choice feminists, deliberately childless, adopt the
male perspective when they cite the "basic injustice that women
have to bear the babies," instead of seeing the injustice in the fact
that men cannot. Women's biologically unique capacity and privilege has been denied, despised, and suppressed under male domination; unfortunately, many women have fallen for the phallic
fallacy.

Childbirth often appears in pro-choice literature as a painful,
traumatic, life-threatening experience. Yet giving birth is accurately seen as an arduous but normal exercise of lifegiving power,
a violent and ecstatic peak experience, which men can never
know. Ironically, some pro-choice men and women think and talk
of pregnancy and childbirth with the same repugnance that ancient ascetics displayed toward orgasms and sexual intercourse.
The similarity may not be accidental. The obstetrician Niles
Newton, herself a mother, has written of the extended threefold
sexuality of women, who can experience orgasm, birth, and nursing as passionate pleasure-giving experiences. All of these are involuntary processes of the female body. Only orgasm, which
males share, has been glorified as an involuntary function that is
nature's great gift; the involuntary feminine processes of childbirth and nursing have been seen as bondage to biology.

Fully accepting our bodies as ourselves, what should women want? I think women will only flourish when there is a feminization of sexuality, very different from the current cultural trend toward masculinizing female sexuality. Women can never have the self-confidence and self-esteem they need to achieve feminist goals in society until a more holistic, feminine model of sexuality becomes the dominant cultural ethos. To say this affirms the view that men and women differ in the domain of sexual functioning, although they are more alike than different in other personality characteristics and competencies. For those of us committed to achieving sexual equality in the culture, it may be hard to accept the fact that sexual differences make it imperative to talk of distinct male and female models of sexuality. But if one wants to change sexual roles, one has to recognize pre-existing conditions. A great deal of evidence is accumulating which points to biological pressures for different male and female sexual functioning.

Males always and everywhere have been more physically aggressive and more likely to fuse sexuality with aggression and dominance. Females may be more variable in their sexuality, but since Masters and Johnson, we know that women have a greater capacity than men for repeated orgasm and a more tenuous path to arousal and orgasmic release. Most obviously, women also have a far greater sociobiological investment in the act of human reproduction. On the whole, women as compared to men possess a sexuality which is more complex, more intense, more extended in time, involving higher investment, risks, and psychosocial involvement.

Considering the differences in sexual functioning, it is not surprising that men and women in the same culture have often constructed different sexual ideals. In Western culture, since the nineteenth century at least, most women have espoused a version of sexual functioning in which sex acts are embedded within deep emotional bonds and secure long-term commitments. Within these committed "pair bonds" males assume parental obligations. In the idealized Victorian version of the Christian sexual ethic, culturally endorsed and maintained by women, the double standard was not countenanced. Men and women did not need to marry to be whole persons, but if they did engage in sexual functioning, they were to be equally chaste, faithful, responsible, loving, and parentally concerned. Many of the most influential women in the nineteenth-century women's movement preached and lived this sexual ethic, often by the side of exemplary feminist men. While the ideal has never been universally obtained, a culturally dominant demand for monogamy, self-control, and emotionally bonded and committed sex works well for women in every stage of their sexual life cycles. When love, chastity, fidelity, and commitment for better or worse are the ascendant cultural prerequisites for sexual functioning, young girls and women expect protection from rape and seduction, adult women justifiably demand male support in childrearing, and older women are more protected from abandonment as their biological attractions wane.

Of course, these feminine sexual ideals always coexisted in competition with another view. A more male-oriented model of erotic or amative sexuality endorses sexual permissiveness without long-term commitment or reproductive focus. Erotic sexuality emphasizes pleasure, play, passion, individual self-expression, and romantic games of courtship and conquest. It is assumed that a variety of partners and sexual experiences are necessary to stimulate romantic passion. This erotic model of the sexual life has often worked satisfactorily for men, both heterosexual and gay, and for certain cultural elites. But for the average woman, it is quite destructive. Women can only play the erotic game successfully when like the *"Cosmopolitan* woman," they are young, physically attractive, economically powerful, and fulfilled enough in a career to be willing to sacrifice family life. Abortion is also required. As our society increasingly endorses this male-oriented, permissive view of sexuality, it is all too ready to give women abortion on demand. Abortion helps a woman's body be more like a man's. It has been observed that *Roe v. Wade* removed the last defense women possessed against male sexual demands.

Unfortunately, the modern feminist movement made a mistaken move at a critical juncture. Rightly rebelling against patriarchy, unequal education, restricted work opportunities, and women's downtrodden political status, feminists also rejected the nineteenth-century feminine sexual ethic. Amative, erotic, permissive sexuality (along with abortion rights) became symbolically identified with other struggles for social equality in education, work, and politics. This feminist mistake also turned off many potential recruits among women who could not deny the positive dimensions of their own traditional feminine roles, nor their allegiance to the older feminine sexual ethic of love and fidelity.

An ironic situation then arose in which many pro-choice feminists preach their own double standard. In the world of work and career, women are urged to grow up, to display mature self-discipline and self-control; they are told to persevere in long-term commitments, to cope with unexpected obstacles by learning to tough out the inevitable sufferings and setbacks entailed in life and work. But this mature ethic of commitment and self-discipline, recommended as the only way to progress in the world of work and personal achievement, is discounted in the domain of sexuality.

In pro-choice feminism, a permissive, erotic view of sexuality is assumed to be the only option. Sexual intercourse with a variety of partners is seen as "inevitable" from a young age and as a positive growth experience to be managed by access to contraception and abortion. Unfortunately, the pervasive cultural conviction that adolescents, or their elders, cannot exercise sexual self-control, undermines the responsible use of contraception. When a pregnancy occurs, the first abortion is viewed in some pro-choice circles as a *rite de passage*. Responsibly choosing an abortion supposedly ensures that a young woman will take charge of her own life, make her own decisions, and carefully practice contraception. But the social dynamics of a permissive, erotic model of sexuality, coupled with permissive laws, work toward repeat abortions. Instead of being empowered by their abortion choices, young women having abortions are confronting the debilitating reality of *not* bringing a baby into the world; *not* being able to count on a committed male partner; *not* accounting oneself strong enough, or the master of enough resources, to avoid killing the fetus. Young women are hardly going to develop the self-esteem, self-discipline, and self-confidence necessary to confront a male-dominated society through abortion.

The male-oriented sexual orientation has been harmful to women and children. It has helped bring up epidemics of venereal disease, infertility, pornography, sexual abuse, adolescent pregnancy, divorce, displaced older women, and abortion. Will these signals of something amiss stimulate pro-choice feminists to rethink what kind of sex ideal really serves women's best interests? While the erotic model cannot encompass commitment, the committed model can—happily—encompass and encourage romance, passion, and playfulness. In fact, within the security of long-term commitments, women may be more likely to experience sexual pleasure and fulfillment.

The pro-life feminist position is not a return to the old feminine mystique. That epousal of "the eternal feminine" erred by viewing sexuality as so sacred that it cannot be humanly shaped at all. Woman's *whole* nature was supposed to be opposite to man's, necessitating complementary and radically different social roles. Followed to its logical conclusion, such a view presumes that reproductive and sexual experience is necessary for human fulfillment. But as the early feminists insisted, no woman has to marry or engage in sexual intercourse to be fulfilled, nor does a woman have to give birth and raise children to be complete, nor must she stay home and function as an earth mother. But female sexuality does need to be deeply respected as a unique potential and trust. Since most contraceptives and sterilization procedures really do involve only the woman's body rather than destroying new life, they can be an acceptable and responsible moral option.

With sterilization available to accelerate the inevitable natural ending of fertility and childbearing, a woman confronts only a limited number of years in which she exercises her reproductive trust and may have to respond to an unplanned pregnancy. Responsible use of contraception can lower the probabilities even more. Yet abortion is not decreasing. The reason is the current permissive attitude embodied in the law, not the "hard cases" which constitute 3 percent of today's abortions. Since attitudes, the law, and behavior interact, pro-life feminists conclude that unless there is an enforced limitation of abortion, which currently confirms the sexual and social status quo, alternatives will never be developed. For women to get what they need in order to combine childbearing, education, and careers, society has to recognize that female bodies come with wombs. Women and their reproductive power, and the children women have, must be supported in new ways. Another and different round of feminist consciousness-raising is needed in which all of women's potential is accorded respect. This time, instead of humbly buying entrée by conforming to male lifestyles, women will demand that society accommodate to them.

New feminist efforts to rethink the meaning of sexuality, femininity, and reproduction are all the more vital as new techniques for artificial reproduction, surrogate motherhood, and the like present a whole new set of dilemmas. In the long run, the very long run, the abortion debate may be merely the opening round in a series of far-reaching struggles over the role of human sexuality and the ethics of reproduction. Significant changes in the culture, both positive and negative in outcome, may begin as local storms of controversy. We may be at one of those vaguely realized thresholds when we had best come to full attention. What kind of people are we going to be? Pro-life feminists pursue a vision for their sisters, daughters, and granddaughters. Will their great-granddaughters be grateful?

II. THE RIGHT TO LIVE

EDITOR'S INTRODUCTION

In a debate so charged with emotion, it is not surprising that the participants should view their efforts in quasi-mythic terms, as the renewal of historic crusades. Proabortion activists see themselves as a liberation movement to secure the civil rights of an oppressed group. Antiabortion activists compare themselves to the abolitionists of the 19th century, struggling to convince the public that it is wrong to classify any fellow human beings as sub-human and therefore liable to be killed or enslaved at someone else's pleasure. As the rightist author Lewis E. Lehrman has written, "I suggest not merely that the issues of slavery and abolition are historically analogous. Rather I say that they are, in a crucial sense, the same issue. Both are but particular cases of recurring challenge to the first principles of the American Revolution, which forbid the violation of the God-given rights of any person, no matter how convenient such a violation might be for some powerful individual or faction, or even the majority." In pursuit of this goal, antiabortionists have engaged in a variety of tactics that include political lobbying, civil disobedience, and occasionally terrorism (the firebombing of abortion clinics).

Like the abolitionist movement, the antiabortion movement has a strong connection to organized religion. In "The Abortion Wars," the first selection in this section, Tim Stafford describes a previous campaign by Christians to outlaw abortion in the Roman Empire, where the fight was also against infanticide. Stafford also traces the evolution of the position taken by evangelical Protestants on the issue. By the end of the 1980s, all the evangelical churches in America were opposed to abortion, and a number of mainstream Protestant churches were beginning to reconsider their more liberal stances. The second selection, "Prolife: What Does It Really Mean?," is a debate between three prominent evangelicals over the movement's priorities. They agree on the existence of a biblical mandate to protect developing babies in the womb, but disagree on whether antiabortion activism should be part of a larger effort to fight nuclear war, hunger, homelessness, drug and alcohol addiction, racism, and environmental deterioration.

Theological disagreements have made evangelical Protestants generally unfriendly to Catholics, but their common interest in outlawing abortion has brought the two groups together in recent years. In the third selection, Cardinal Joseph Bernardin of the Archdiocese of Chicago calls for a "comprehensive defense of human life from conception to natural death," encompassing issues of warfare and euthanasia as well as abortion; he also calls on Catholics to extend help and support to pregnant women and poor families and to listen to them with compassion.

The final article, "After Roe" by Richard John Neuhaus, analyzes which of a variety of legal arrangements will be politically feasible once *Roe v. Wade* is overturned, as he anticipates it will be.

THE ABORTION WARS[1]

Ours is not the first abortion war. Two previous periods saw protracted contests over whether abortion would be accepted or proscribed.

The first was in the early centuries of Christianity, when faith spread within a Greco-Roman culture that considered abortion (and infanticide) routine. The second was in America during the mid-nineteenth century when abortions became widespread, freely advertised in virtually every newspaper.

The third abortion war is now approximately 25 years old and shows no sign of peace. Living in a battle zone, we can easily focus on the tactics of the moment and forget the wider context. The danger in forgetting is that when the situation suddenly shifts, as it did in 1973 with *Roe* v. *Wade* and again this year with *Webster*, we get thrown off. Suddenly the tactics we had honed become irrelevant, and the goals we had set are outdated.

[1]Reprint of an article by staff writer Tim Stafford. *Christianity Today*. 33:16-20. O 6 '89. Copyright © 1989 by *Christianity Today*. Reprinted by permission.

The First War

People commonly suppose that abortion is an invention of modern, technological medicine. In fact, it was well known in Greco-Roman society. Plato's *Republic* made abortion or infanticide obligatory if the mother was over 40. In Aristotle's ideal society, abortion would be compulsory for families that exceeded a certain size.

Aristotle also made a distinction that would develop a life of its own: the "formed" versus the "unformed" fetus. Aristotle believed that human life was present in the fetus when distinct organs were formed, 40 days after conception for males and 90 for females. This was a metaphysical, not a moral, distinction; Aristotle would abort both "formed" and "unformed" fetuses. But some Christians—Augustine of Hippo and Thomas Aquinas in particular—would later adopt his distinction. It survived in various forms right down to the arbitrary trimesters of *Roe* v. *Wade*.

Both Plato and Aristotle believed that a child had life long before birth; it was just that the welfare of society and family were more important to them than the rights of a child. The Roman empire made the same assessment while adopting the Stoic belief that life begins only at birth. Abortion was common. As Michael Gorman puts it in *Abortion and the Early Church*, the Roman empire was paradoxically "pro-family but not fundamentally antiabortion. . . . That the fetus is not a person was fundamental to Roman law. Even when born, the child was valued primarily not for itself but for its usefulness to the father, the family and especially the state."

Many Romans opposed abortion, but Gorman says, "Pagan antiabortion statements are consistently mindful of the welfare and rights of the state, the father, the family and even occasionally the woman, but never those of the fetus. . . . Christians discarded all pagan definitions of the fetus as merely part of the mother's body. To Christians, the fetus was an independent living being."

From the first, Christians were outspokenly opposed to abortion on the basis of the child's right to life. The *Didachē*, an early second-century document summarizing Christian belief and practice, declares, "Thou shalt not murder a child by abortion/destruction." Clement of Alexandria, Tertullian, Jerome, Basil the Great, Ambrose—all pronounced against abortion. Tertullian wrote eloquently in his *Apology*, aimed at non-Christians: "To hinder a birth is merely a speedier man-killing; nor does it matter whether you take away a life that is born, or destroy one that is coming to the birth. That is a man which is going to be one; you have the fruit already in the seed."

That is how Western society came to be antiabortion. Although the church's antiabortion arguments were consistent and insightful, the change in society was due more to the fact that Christians won the empire to their faith. Not long after Constantine legalized Christianity, it was made illegal for a father to kill his children. Roman abortion laws were never changed, but as the institutional church's role grew more important, ecclesiastical penalties for abortion—their severity was between those for manslaughter and murder—became meaningful legislation for the entire society.

No one can say to what extent behavior changed. What is sure is that a stable antiabortion consensus, based on Christian values, had been formed. It endured intact throughout the medieval period and into modern times.

Through Augustine, Aquinas, Luther, Calvin, and on to Barth and Bonhoeffer, Christian theologians have condemned abortion in the clearest terms. Aristotle's distinction between the formed and unformed fetus was carried on by some, for whom abortion was only murder 40 days after conception. (Yet even before then, it was a violation of developing humanity, and thus still wrong.) Therapeutic abortion, in which the life of the unborn can be sacrificed to save the life of a mother, was sometimes allowed. But the values of Greco-Roman society, in which the life of a child had meaning only as state or family granted it meaning, would not resurface for 1,500 years.

The Second War

There were no written laws against the practice of abortion in colonial America; courts operated on the basis of English common law, by which abortion was illegal after "quickening," the time when a mother could feel the movement of her unborn child in the womb. The "quickening" distinction seems to have been a survival from the Aristotelian idea of a "formed" fetus, as it filtered through centuries of theological discussion.

"Quickening" might not have survived on the strength of its history alone, though; it had practical significance as well. There were no reliable pregnancy tests, and so until quickening, no one could be certain whether a woman was actually pregnant or merely experiencing some kind of menstrual "blockage." Doctors treated a "blockage" by doing just what they would do to carry out an early abortion. Before quickening, it was impossible to say whether an abortion was intended. There was no point in outlawing behavior that could not be ascertained.

In fact, since "quickening" was generally only known to the woman involved, it was legally difficult to try any kind of abortion case. American courts steered a lenient course with the few cases that came before them. In 1803 Britain passed a strong and clear antiabortion law, but it was not until 1821 that Connecticut passed the first American antiabortion statute. By 1840 most states still had no such law, and those that did rarely enforced them.

A dramatic change began in the decades after 1840: the number of abortions shot up. American conception dropped precipitately: the average American woman bore seven children in 1800, three and a half by 1900. Estimates of abortions ranged between one-fifth and one-third of all pregnancies. Before, abortion had been the refuge of desperate, unmarried women; now most abortions were by married women, using it as birth control. Abortion operations were not regarded as particularly dangerous, and the belief in quickening made them seem innocent as well. This was a period of rapid industrialization, with growing cities and easy transportation by railroad. Along with many aspects of American life, abortion became commercialized.

In 1838 Charles and Anna Lohman, adopting the names of Dr. Mauriceau and Madame Restell, began to advertise extensively in the *New York Herald*. They were the first to seize an opportunity offered by a new kind of newspaper that sold cheaply, circulated widely, and depended on advertising revenues to make a profit. Madame Restell's business flourished; she soon opened branch offices in Boston and Philadelphia, and moved into a lavish mansion on Fifth Avenue.

Others imitated her. Soon newspaper ads offered a whole portfolio of potential abortionists. They had the political and economic influence to protect themselves; historian James Mohr notes, in one example, that "between 1849 and 1857 there were only thirty-two trials in Massachusetts [under a new, toughened law] for performing abortions and not a single conviction." Newspapers avoided the subject. Only one, the sensational *National Police Gazette*, reported on and crusaded against abortion. (Not coincidentally, it did not take abortion advertising.)

The increase in abortion, however, led to a counterreaction. The most visible group opposing abortion were "regular" doctors. The American Medical Association (AMA), formed in 1847, took up antiabortion as its cause. Though the AMA was a group with insignificant power, and the medical profession was at an all-time low in prestige, "regular" doctors did raise the issue before the legislature.

The religious establishment did not. Protestant clergy had considerable prestige and were important in other reform movements of the time—notably temperance—but to the dismay of doctors, most churches ignored the issue. No one really knows why; perhaps the topic was too delicate. Catholics, mainly immigrants, were not having abortions like Protestants, and Catholic leaders were at that time in no position to exert political influence.

The rising feminist movement was against abortion. Not even the most radical considered abortion to be an instrument of freedom for women; on the contrary, abortion was understood to be an aspect of male domination, whereby (outside marriage) men tried to conceal the results of their seduction, or (inside marriage) women behaved tragically because of the terrible conditions of a home governed by a tyrannical husband.

In 1870, under a new editor, the *New York Times* began to campaign actively against abortion. Their investigative reports were too sensational for other newspapers to let pass; soon widespread press attention forced prosecutors to act. The more they acted, the more sensational news was available to report (the bodies of young women found dismembered in trunks; numbers of babies found buried in basements). Marvin Olasky notes in *The Press and Abortion* that Madame Restell became "an object of general hatred in New York City. Occasionally, her carriage would be chased down Fifth Avenue by a volley of rocks, and by shouts of 'Madame Killer.'" In 1878 she was arrested and could not buy her freedom as she had in previous cases. The night before she was to be tried she committed suicide. The *Times* headlined the news: "End of a Criminal Life."

Gradually, through the century, laws were toughened. The quickening distinction was dropped. Under the Comstock Act of 1873, abortion advertising became illegal nationally. By the end of the century, abortion was illegal everywhere; and while veiled advertising continued (the Comstock Act was seldom enforced), observers reported that abortions greatly decreased.

The antiabortion crusade was successful despite the fact that only regular physicians publicly worked for it. They were not a particularly influential group, but they did have confident scientific knowledge on their side. Doctors had known since early in the century that the "quickening" distinction was without merit—that the development of the unborn child was gradual from the time of conception.

Some recent histories have commented on the quickening distinction as though it had preserved a right to abortion for women, but that is a classic case of imposing modern thinking on a historical situation. The law and common belief had always held that it was wrong to abort a child once it had life, after quickening. The doctors could presume that society's moral commitments would lead to the banning of abortion once enough people understood that life was at stake from the beginning.

The Third War

Yet the success of the nineteenth-century crusade was short-lived. The life of an unborn child is easy to ignore—invisible and voiceless. The *New York Times*, which had led the press crusade to stop abortions in the 1870s, suddenly stopped reporting on it at all in 1896, when Adolph Ochs assumed ownership and introduced two new slogans: "All the News That's Fit to Print" and "It Does Not Soil the Breakfast Cloth." Abortion news was apparently not fit to print, for it did soil the breakfast cloth.

The *National Police Gazette* no longer crusaded against abortion either; it now took abortion ads. Other newspapers reported occasionally on lurid abortion cases, but journalism professor Olasky notes a change. In the late nineteenth century, press coverage often referred to abortion as the killing of unborn children. Stories in the twentieth century rarely mentioned the unborn; the focus was exclusively on the dangers of abortion to women.

Doctors also lost interest. By early in the twentieth century the AMA had regulated the irregulars (whose nineteenth-century abortion practices had threatened to take away patients and income from regular doctors) out of business, and had no more need to appeal to the legislature for the control of medical business. Doctors could regulate themselves—but showed little interest in interfering with the practices of their fellow regulars.

There was, therefore, no one to show an interest in the lives of the unborn. The American clergy never had. Sexual behavior grew more promiscuous in the Roaring Twenties, and perhaps the failure of Prohibition made America less interested in moral reform. The Soviet Union legalized and promoted abortion, to the acclaim of some. Population-control groups such as Planned Parenthood began cautiously and privately to favor abortion. So did some doctors, mainly on the basis of their claim to know what was best for the welfare of their patients without governmental interference.

Contrary to popular assertions, the number of women who died from "back-alley abortionists" was small; according to the Kinsey Report, 85 percent of abortions were done by doctors, and the number of annual deaths declined steadily, to an estimated 300 by 1967. The deaths were tragic whatever the number, but far more significant in putting abortion back on the public agenda was doctors' discomfort with the rigidity of the antiabortion laws.

Perhaps the most important thing to remember about the beginning of the third abortion war was that it seemed to be about a relatively small change in the law—"abortion reform," as it was called. The "right to abortion" was not an issue, at least for women; if anyone's rights were at stake, they were the doctor's. In 1959 the prestigious American Law Institute (ALI) published a new "model code" for state legislatures. It would allow a doctor to perform abortions in cases of rape, incest, serious deformity, and whenever the doctor believed there was risk to the mental or physical health to the mother. The word *believed* was significant, because it meant a doctor was virtually immune from prosecution so long as he would claim, whatever the medical facts, that he had believed them threatening. Few imagined that such terminology could become an open door to abortion on demand.

Protestants, and even many Catholics, had historically recognized the validity of what is called therapeutic abortion. Abortion reform purported to expand the categories of those tragic decisions. Suppose that the birth of a child conceived by rape threatened to destroy the mother's mental stability; could not an abortion be considered life saving?

Such "hard cases" were real, and proabortionists could expand on them at length. They were received sympathetically in the press, and seemed, in the light of publicity, to be far more numerous than they really were. One well-publicized event brought the abortion issue into public view.

In 1962 an Arizona "Romper Room" TV hostess named Sherri Finkbine learned that a drug she had been taking during pregnancy, thalidomide, had caused numerous birth defects in Europe. She applied for a therapeutic abortion and was granted one by a committee of three doctors. But Finkbine talked to reporters before the scheduled abortion, to warn others about the dangers of thalidomide.

The hospital, wary of public scrutiny, refused to allow the abortion until an advance court judgment was made that the abortion was legal. A judge said that he could make no ruling unless someone had filed a complaint. No one was complaining, but cautious hospital officials were not willing to go ahead without official assurances. The legally complex case was presented in the press as a woman persecuted by an inhumane, hypocritical legal system. Ultimately, Finkbine traveled to Sweden to have an abortion. Her story had a strong emotional hook, enabling many Americans to identify with the plight of a woman who believed she was bearing a deformed child.

In 1967 the AMA voted in favor of legal reform. In the same year the National Organization for Women came out in favor of abortion, and feminists joined the cause. A number of states passed reforming legislation, along the ALI recommended lines, which would give physicians greater latitude in performing therapeutic abortions.

Another issue arose, adding to the apparent urgency: the "population explosion." In a few short years, experts said, the world would starve to death unless population growth could be stopped. This was one of those crises that rises in a media-saturated society, riveting attention until it mysteriously disintegrates. It made abortion into a strangely conservative cause, and raised a very different set of issues: not abortion as tragic choice, but abortion as crusade to save the world. The campaign for abortion-law reform began to turn into a campaign for abortion-law repeal. In 1969, the National Association for the Repeal of

Abortion Laws (NARAL) was formed. Many denominations—
Lutherans, Methodists, Presbyterians—supported their cause.

But the movement was beginning to outdistance its popular
support. The American public was sympathetic to therapeutic
abortion, but solidly against abortion on demand. In 1970 New
York, Alaska, Hawaii, and Washington repealed their abortion
laws; by then, 13 other states had passed some form of reform legislation. But after 1970 resistance arose, and only one more state,
Florida, passed a reform bill. In several other states, reform or
repeal were rebuffed. In New York, the legislature tried to reim-
pose abortion controls, but these were vetoed by Gov. Nelson
Rockefeller.

Thus the proabortion movement shifted its energy toward
the courts, a tactical shift that was to prove fateful.

Who Was Against?

Press accounts of the late sixties and early seventies gave a
clear picture of who stood against abortion: the Roman Catholic
Church. This stereotype of antiabortionists was actively encouraged by proabortionists, who believed it would paint the opposition as narrow and sectarian. Actually, in the general public,
Protestants were as likely to be against abortion as Catholics. Yet
there was some truth to the caricature: Catholics brought determination and national organization to the cause. The bishops
could and did draw up a national plan for opposing abortion,
while Protestant antiabortionists remained splintered and disor-
ganized.

It is startling to review the change in evangelical feeling as re-
flected in the pages of this magazine. The November 8, 1968, issue of *Christianity Today* carried several articles on contraception
and abortion. One leading biblical scholar wrote, "Clearly, then,
in contrast to the mother, the fetus is not reckoned as a soul." A
theologian mentioned the ALI reform proposals favorably. The
articles concluded with "A Protestant Affirmation," the consensus of 25 evangelical scholars. On abortion, it read, "Whether or
not the performance of an induced abortion is sinful we are not
agreed, but about the necessity of it and permissibility for it under certain circumstances we are in accord." The statement spoke
of "a tragic moral choice" and endorsed the American College of
Obstetricians and Gynecologists' statement favoring therapeutic

abortions for the life and health of the mother, in cases of rape, incest, or deformities.

By the next year, though, red flags had begun to fly. An editorial noted that under a new Maryland law numerous abortions were being approved on the basis of mental health. "No doubt most state abortion laws need revision," the editorial stated.

Evangelist Francis Schaeffer, who had only recently become well known, was making an impact among evangelicals with his strong warnings against abortion. Harold O. J. Brown, who would soon write strong *Christianity Today* editorials against abortion, felt Schaeffer's influence. So did a Bible college student named Randall Terry, who would become the leading spokesperson for Operation Rescue.

By 1971 there was no more talk in *Christianity Today* about therapeutic abortion. The direction reform was leading was clear. "Let it be no great surprise when America is subjected to severe judgment," an editorial read. In the same year, however, the Southern Baptist Convention "urged Baptists to work for legislation permitting abortion under certain conditions. These include: rape, incest, deformity, emotional health."

Roe v. *Wade*

Few anticipated the complete victory that *Roe* v. *Wade* gave to proabortionists in 1973. Though the Supreme Court claimed to offer no opinion about when human life began, it implicitly set the time at birth; and though the new law divided pregnancy into equal trimesters, allowing that the fetus might receive some protection in the last three months before birth, in practical terms—because it stipulated that abortion could be done at any time if the mother's mental health was believed to be in danger—the Court assured that an abortion could be done up until the very moment of birth.

Christianity Today greeted *Roe* v. *Wade* with a firestorm of criticism. "Christians should accustom themselves to the thought that the American state no longer supports, in any meaningful sense, the laws of God." That was a revolutionary thought to most evangelicals.

But *CT* was ahead of many evangelicals. In its news report on *Roe* v. *Wade*, it quoted prominent Southern Baptist pastor W. A. Criswell: "I have always felt that it was only after a child was born and had life separate from its mother that it became an individual person, and it has always, therefore, seemed to me that what is best for the mother and for the future should be allowed." (He has since repudiated this position.) It would be years before such a statement from an evangelical leader would be unthinkable. According to Brown, evangelicals simply could not imagine themselves lining up with Roman Catholics, nor could they imagine that the Supreme Court of their beloved nation (which they thought of as Protestant) would support a cause directly opposed to Christian values.

Few in the press seemed to understand how radical the justices' decision had been. *Time* gave it two pages in the back of the magazine; *Newsweek* gave it one. An editorial in the *Christian Century* proclaimed that "this is a beautifully accurate balancing of individual vs. social rights. . . . It is a decision both proabortionists and antiabortionists can live with."

Roe v. *Wade* demonstrates that fundamental moral conflicts should not be decided by fiat. The absolute polarization we currently experience is directly traceable to the Supreme Court's decision to take abortion out of politics and declare it a settled question. Those who opposed abortion had suddenly no recourse except radical action. The discussion had been about where to draw the line among tragic choices; the justices erased the line completely and said there was no room for further discussion.

Antiabortionists may someday have reason to remember this lesson, if they gain the power to stop abortion by fiat. As we have seen, restricting abortion works best when it is based on a wider consensus about the value of life. The first centuries of the church gained this consensus through centuries of witness. They spoke passionately against abortion as a part of their faith; they also suffered for their faith. Ultimately, their faith triumphed, and legal changes followed.

By contrast, the nineteenth century, though it passed antiabortion laws, seems not to have built a strong, public consciousness of the humanity of a fetus.

Ethicist Stanley Hauerwas touches on this issue when he notes the frustration of antiabortionists who fail to convince their opponents that a fetus is a human being. He says that more than logic is needed. "Christian arguments about abortion . . . have not merely failed to convince: they have failed to suggest the kind of 'reorientation' necessary if we are to be the kind of people and society that make abortion unthinkable. . . . Even if [we succeed politically], our success may still be a form of failure if we 'win' without changing the presuppositions of the debate."

This is what Christians in the first three centuries managed to do. They changed the world, not just the law.

PROLIFE: WHAT DOES IT REALLY MEAN?[2]

ABORTION IS NOT THE ONLY ISSUE
Ronald J. Sider

Everyone supports life, but inconsistencies pop up on the way to its practical protection.

For example, why do so many liberal and radical activists champion nuclear disarmament to protect the sanctity of human life and then defend the destruction of one-and-one-half-million unborn American babies each year? Are "sexual freedom" and affluent lifestyles finally more important than helpless, inconvenient babies?

Why does Sen. Jesse Helms, one of the most visible opponents of abortion, support government subsidies for tobacco? Is the political clout of North Carolina's influential tobacco growers more important to this prolife advocate than the fact that smoking kills 350,000 Americans a year?

Why do Marxists destroy millions of lives and impose totalitarian governments on millions more in order to create an "ideal life for all"? Is economic justice (such as it is—the effective income differentials between Communist party members and ordinary citizens is often greater than differentials in capitalist societies) more important than religious and political freedom?

Why do prominent American televangelists lend support to South Africa's racist government? Is not racism that tortures and murders a prolife issue?

[2]Reprint of a composite article by Ronald J. Sider, professor of theology and culture at Eastern Baptist Theological Seminary and executive director of JustLife and Evangelicals for Social Action; Charles E. White, associate professor of Christian thought and history at Spring Arbor College; and senior editor Kenneth S. Kantzer, professor of biblical and systematic theology at Trinity Evangelical Divinity School. *Christianity Today.* 33:28–38. Jl 14 '89. Copyright © 1989 by *Christianity Today*, Charles E. White, and Ronald J. Sider.

Why do many Westerners join the crusade for nuclear disarmament and neglect poverty and starvation among the poor? Is the growing danger that a nuclear holocaust may destroy us more important to affluent Westerners than the present annual murder by malnutrition of millions of persons?

What does it really mean to be prolife? Is there a consistent prolife stance?

The answer, of course, depends on one's basic values. If one endorses Marx's philosophical materialism, then sacrificing millions of people on the way to a secular utopia is not inconsistent. If one knows that the fetus is merely a physical appendage of the mother and not an independent human life, then favoring abortion and opposing nuclear war are not inconsistent. If freedom is a higher value than justice, then majoring on religious and political liberty even at the expense of a decent life or even life itself for the poor is not inconsistent. If Peter Singer is correct and people and animals have essentially the same value, then speciesism joins racism and sexism as dreadful evils. It all depends on what one means by life.

Defining Life

Whether consciously or unconsciously, one's definition of what it means to be "prolife" emerges from one's deepest beliefs. My understanding of what it means to be prolife is grounded in what the Bible says about life.

Every part of God's creation is very good and very special because it results from the loving design of Almighty God. But it is in no sense divine, as some of the New Age religions suggest. It is finite, limited, and dependent. You and I are not divine, even though we have a special status above all other earthly created things that the Bible ascribes to persons.

As persons created in the divine image, however, we are very special. The dignity and worth of every human being flows from divine decree, not human decision. Our essential dignity does not come from government fiat, social usefulness, or self-actualization. It comes from the Creator of the galaxies who selected human beings alone out of the almost infinite multitudes of the created order to bear the divine image. No matter how poor and defenseless, old and weak, crippled and deformed, young and helpless, human beings enjoy a God-given worth and dignity that sets them apart from the rest of creation.

Today, however, this special status is under attack from another direction. Some secular thinkers denounce as speciesism any claim that persons have a higher status than monkeys or moles. The Bible, on the other hand, elevates persons to a unique status only slightly lower than the angels (Psalm 8). We have been given dominion over every other living creature (Gen. 1:26–28). But dominion is not devastation. We insult the Creator of the garden if we rape and destroy it.

The opening chapters of Genesis sketch a glorious picture of the fullness of life intended for humanity by the Creator. A harmony of right relationships prevailed everywhere—with God, with each other, and with the earth. Although it is not used here, the Hebrew word *shalom* (peace) is perhaps the best word to signify this fullness of life enjoyed as Adam and Eve walked in obedient relationship to God and responsible stewardship over God's garden.

Sin, however, shattered this *shalom* and disrupted relationships with God, neighbor, and earth. But God refused to abandon us. Beginning with Abraham, God called out a special people to be his instrument of revelation and salvation for all. Through Moses and the prophets, the judges, and the writers of wisdom, God patiently showed his chosen people how to live the abundant life.

As in the garden, God said that *shalom* starts with a right relationship with himself. But it also includes right relationships with the neighbor: economic fairness; respect for all persons, including a special concern for the poor and weak; faithful family life; fair courts; and, of course, an end to war.

Moses starkly clarified the options at the end of Deuteronomy. Life in every sense would follow if Israel obeyed God's commands; if they disobeyed, death and evil would follow. "I call heaven and earth to witness against you this day that I have set before you life and death . . . ; therefore choose life that you and your descendants may live" (Deut. 30:19).

They chose death. Worshiping idols and oppressing the poor, they defied the Author of Life. Still, God would not give up. God's prophets looked ahead to a time when the Messiah would come to restore life and *shalom*. In Christ, we receive abundant life. "I am come that they might have life and that they might have it more abundantly" (John 10:10).

Why Human Efforts Fail

Increasingly since the eighteenth-century Enlightenment, however, secular thinkers have promoted purely human paths to wholeness of life. If only we will offer quality education to all; if only we will modify our social environment; if only we will change the economic system; if only we will undertake this or that bit of human engineering—secular thinkers promise a new person and a new social order freed from the stupidity and selfishness of the past. The Marxist promise that utopia will follow the abolition of private property is merely one of the more naive versions of the Enlightenment's secular humanism.

Christians know this is dangerous nonsense. Certainly we can and should effect significant changes by improving social structures. But no amount of social engineering will create unselfish persons. Tragically, the human problem lies far deeper than mere (even very unjust) social systems. It lies in the proud, rebellious self-centered heart of every person. A transforming relationship with the living God is the only way to heal the brokenness at the core of our being.

That is why Jesus told Nicodemus that he must be born again (John 3:1ff.). It is only as we believe that God has sent his only Son to live and die for us that we experience genuine life—indeed, eternal life (John 3:16). As the Gospel of John says so beautifully and powerfully, eternal life begins now as we believe in Christ because "this is eternal life, that they know thee the only true God, and Jesus whom thou has sent" (17:3). As the Spirit begins to transform believers, we enjoy the first fruits of eternal life even now. Thus, already in this life, we enjoy an abundant life as we live in Christ, and our personalities are now being reshaped according to the pattern of his perfection.

But even the *shalom* of abundant Christian living pales by comparison with the glorious life of the age to come. "For to me to live is Christ and to die is gain" was Paul's confident cry (Phil. 1:21; cf. Acts 20:24).

Physical human life is not the highest value. There are many things worth dying for. To say that Christians seek to reverse the nuclear-arms race because human life is exceedingly precious is not to say that life here on earth is the ultimate good. "Thy lovingkindness is better than life," the psalmist exclaimed (63:3). Jesus taught that we should sacrifice eyes, limbs, possessions—

indeed, even life itself—for the sake of the kingdom of God and the harmony of right relationships that make up the righteousness of that kingdom (Matt. 6:25–34; 18:7–9; Luke 12:13–31).

Because Christians know that Jesus is the resurrection and life (John 11:25), they will sacrifice their own physical life for freedom, justice, peace, and evangelism. Jesus has conquered death in all its terror. Therefore, we know that death is only a temporary transition to life even more abundant.

The Coming Kingdom

The biblical vision of the fullness and perfection of eternal life in the coming kingdom is finally the only adequate answer to the question: What is life really all about? What, after all, is genuine living? True life is eternal life in the presence of the risen Lord in a kingdom of *shalom* from which all the devastation of sin has been cast out.

But this biblical teaching about eternal life does not refer to some ethereal, spiritual fairyland totally unrelated to human history and the created order. Paul clearly teaches that this groaning creation will be freed of its bondage and decay and will experience the glorious liberty of the children of God (Rom. 8:18–25). In Colossians, he describes God's cosmic plan of redemption. God intends to restore all things (that is not a universalist claim that all persons will be saved), whether in heaven or on earth (i.e., everything in the created order), to their original wholeness (Col. 1:15–20).

How God will do that we do not know. The coming kingdom is certainly not a purely human construction that we weld together with slow incremental improvements. There will be fundamental disjuncture between fallen history as we know it and the *shalom* of heaven. Revelation 21:1ff. describes the coming kingdom as a new heaven, a new earth, and a new Jerusalem. But notice, on the other hand, that it is a city and it is called earth. And God dwells with us, wiping away tears, banishing pain and death. Poverty, warfare, broken families, and abortion will give way to an unspeakable fullness of life in the presence of the Lord of life.

If there is a fundamental break between life now and the coming kingdom, there is also significant continuity. The Book of Revelation says that the kings of the earth will bring their glory into the holy city (21:24–26). The crystalline river of life waters the tree of life, whose leaves are given for the healing of the nations (22:2). Apparently God intends to transform all that is good in human culture, purify it of all sinful distortion, and make it a part of the abundant life of the eternal kingdom.

Until Christ's return, all attempts to realize that fullness of life in American or any other society will have only very imperfect results. On the other hand, history demonstrates that it is possible to combat racism, end slavery, and foster democracy.

To be consistently prolife, then, is to allow the full biblical picture of life abundant that God gave at creation and will finally restore at the eschaton to shape our thought and action. Such a view demands that we say no to abortion and the nuclear-arms race, no to murder by environmental pollution, economic oppression, and euthanasia.

Obviously, in each case, one would have to construct a careful ethical argument showing that abortion or nuclear war or whatever was incompatible with the biblical teaching on life and *shalom*. Here I do not have time to do more than sketch arguments that I have developed elsewhere.

Ultimate Abortion?

Abortion is wrong. Both the Bible and biology point away from the modern notion that the fetus is merely a physical appendage of the mother rather than an independent human being. We must act on the belief that from the moment of conception, we are dealing with a human being created in the image of God. We must stop aborting millions of unborn babies each year.

But if annually aborting millions is wrong, then walking down a path that increases the likelihood of the ultimate abortion, where a nuclear exchange obliterates hundreds of millions of people, is also wrong.

Most evangelical Christians stand within the just-war tradition. Under certain circumstances, the just-war tradition permits killing to promote justice and peace. But the just-war tradition teaches that aiming at civilians is murder. Nuclear weapons are clearly targeted at civilians as well as military and industrial targets located in the middle of population centers. Precisely because using nuclear weapons targeted at noncombatants would be murder, prolife people must redouble their efforts to reverse the nuclear arms race. Adm. Hyman Rickover, the man who built

America's nuclear navy, declared when he retired that we will destroy ourselves if we do not abolish nuclear weapons. Even President Ronald Reagan, who clearly does not espouse pacifism, endorsed the goal of a nuclear-free world. Prolife people should work hard for bilateral and multilateral, verifiable steps to move toward that goal.

Similarly, if human life is precious, then it is a terrible sin to stand idly by in suffocating affluence when we could prevent the death by malnutrition and starvation of 12 million children each year. And yet some Christians urge us to focus all or most of our attention on combating abortion, apparently placing concern for the poor in a category that is less urgent.

Nor does the list of consistently prolife issues end with abortion, the nuclear-arms race, and poverty. In the United States alone, 350,000 persons die prematurely each year because of cigarette smoking. William Pollin, director of the U.S. National Institute on Drug Abuse, pointed out recently that these 350,000 deaths from smoking are "more than all other drug and alcohol abuse deaths combined, seven times more than all automobile fatalities per year, . . . and more than all American military fatalities in World War I, World War II, and Vietnam put together." The global death toll from cigarette smoking already runs in the tens of millions.

Alcoholism enslaves 10 million Americans. Their personal tragedies entangle another 30 million family members, close friends, and coworkers in a hell of crippling car accidents, fires, lost productivity, and damaged health that cost the nation $120 billion annually.

Racism in India, South Africa, and South Philadelphia maims and kills. More than 200,000 black children in affluent South Africa die every year of starvation.

The rape of our environment, finally, is also a prolife issue. The United States loses three million acres of agricultural land each year. Annually, erosion carries away 6.4 billion tons of topsoil—enough to cover all cropland in Maine, New Hampshire, Vermont, Massachusetts, Connecticut, Rhode Island, New York, New Jersey, Pennsylvania, Delaware, Maryland, Alabama, California, and Florida with one inch of soil. Since farming began in North America, one-third of all our topsoil has been lost forever. Every day, erosion and development remove enough productive land to feed 260,000 for a year. In a world of hunger and starvation, that is a prolife issue.

A hasty survey of the current religious scene in the United States might lead one to despair of any realistic possibility of promoting this consistent prolife agenda. But that would be a superficial judgment. Increasingly today, especially in the churches, there is a growing movement of Christians who care about justice and freedom, the sanctity of unborn life and the lives of the poor, the family and the environment, an end to murder on the highways, and concern over the nuclear-arms race.

In short, if biblical norms set the Christian's agenda, then we will reject one-issue approaches in favor of a commitment to all that for which God has a concern.

Target for Left and Right

What does it mean to be prolife? It means letting the Author of Life set our agenda. It means saying no to right-wing ideological agendas that make freedom, family, and the crusade against abortion more important than justice and nuclear disarmament. It means saying no to left-wing ideological agendas that do the reverse. It means letting the balance of biblical concerns set the priorities for our political engagement.

A biblically consistent prolife stance will say no to abortion and nuclear weapons, no to the deadly pollution of our lungs and our environment, no to racism and sexual promiscuity. A biblical prolife stance will say yes to the unborn and the underemployed, yes to justice and freedom, yes to the family and nuclear disarmament.

Championing that whole agenda will produce harsh attacks from Left and Right. One side will attack us for our stance on the poor and the arms race. The other side will attack for our defense of the unborn and the family. Being willing to be the target for both left-wing and right-wing ideological attack is the price Christians must pay for biblical faithfulness today.

The acid test of the integrity of the Christian prolife movement in this generation will be whether we have the courage to let God, rather than competing secular ideologies, shape our agenda.

[CHARLES WHITE RESPONDS: JustLife is right that God cares about the ends of achieving economic justice and peace as much as he cares about ending abortion, but it is arrogant to think that it has a God-given mandate for the human means it has chosen to achieve those ends. Looking at the ten House and Senate votes it picked to evaluate during the 1988 national elections, one can see that for JustLife "economic justice" simply means spending more on social programs and less on the military. While spending millions of dollars to set up job-training programs, increase federal subsidies for school lunch programs, and to supplement college budgets may actually help the poor, there is a large body of evidence to suggest that such spending not only wastes money, but actually hurts the poor by rewarding exactly the kind of behavior they need to eliminate. Further, to call such income redistribution "economic justice" borders on dishonesty. Where is the justice in taking money from those who have earned it and giving it to those who have not? One group's economic justice is another group's socialism.

JustLife's humanly chosen means for promoting God's end of peace are similarly suspect. Here again the positions JustLife has chosen to support show their agenda. For example, they are against the testing or deployment of any new weapons system. This unilateral restraint may encourage similar behavior in the Soviets, but it may also tempt them the way Allied weakness encouraged the Nazis in the 1930s. Why support a position that could even remotely encourage the possibility of a nuclear war?

JustLife wants to prevent nuclear war at all costs. They rightly know the destruction of humanity is contrary to God's will. But if we believe what the Bible says about God's control of the affairs of the nations, we should realize that obeying God's will is the key to national safety. Israel could not buy security when she armed herself to the teeth through alliance with Egypt, nor could she quiet her enemies when she bought them off with economic assistance. The only way she could be safe was to obey the law of God.

Likewise, if we can learn anything from Israel's experience, we should realize that the best way to avoid the judgment of God is to rid our nation of the sin of abortion. At least on this question we clearly know God's will: Stop the killing. If I prevent one death by blocking the entrance to an abortion clinic, or if I help to stop millions by campaigning for a reversal of *Roe* v. *Wade*, I am obeying God. I do not have that certainty when it comes to preventing nuclear war or eliminating poverty.

Since obedience to God is more important than anyone's political agenda, Christians ought to unite in the campaign to outlaw

abortions. Allowing abortions as a national policy is more likely
to bring the Soviet missiles down upon us than is some mistake
in military strategy.]

WHY ABORTION MATTERS MOST
Charles E. White

Ever since Constantine's conversion in 312, Christians have
tried to use their political power to make their societies more
pleasing to God. Hosius, bishop of Cordoba, tried to persuade
Constantine to become a Christian as they marched east together
toward Rome. After the emperor saw the cross in the sky, the
good bishop continued to suggest policies God would favor. In
529 a later emperor, Justinian, replaced all the laws of the Roman
empire with a single code that he hoped would bring all of society
into conformity with God's will. At the turn of the twelfth century, Pope Innocent III proclaimed himself a latter-day Melchize-
dek who had combined both church and state into a unified
Christian community, with himself at its head.

After the Protestant Reformation, Christians no loger
claimed to have enacted God's will as law throughout the whole
world, but they still tried to set up a perfect government on the
smaller sections of earth they controlled. Under Calvin's guidance, the citizens of Geneva attempted to set the pay scale for the
local printshops and to regulate what people would eat, drink,
and even wear. King James I of England went so far as to publish
a *Book of Sports* suggesting Sabbath recreations for his subjects,
and some Puritans moved to New England rather than endure its
levity.

In Catholic countries, the Roman church has tried to enact
its policies through the Christian-Democrat political party. More
recently the Moral Majority informed Americans that it was immoral to sign over control of the Panama Canal.

And now, many Christians are attempting to shape public policy, challenging the church to be more consistent in its advocacy
of life. Led by Joseph Cardinal Bernardin on the Catholic side
and Evangelicals for Social Action executive director Ron Sider
on the Protestant, these Christians want believers to broaden
their concern as they use the political process to advance the kingdom of God. Directing their appeal especially to Christians who
are working to stop abortion, these "consistent Christians" urge
prolifers to champion a whole range of other issues just as pas-

sionately as they fight abortion. The Catholics say the "consistent ethic of life" involves opposing nuclear war, stopping capital punishment, and changing current policy on Central America as well as ending abortion. My colleague on these pages, Ron Sider, and the organization he represents, JustLife, says that to be "consistently prolife" Christians must add promotion of "economic justice" and opposition to nuclear war to their antagonism to abortion.

Unquestionably, the motives of the "consistent Christians" are commendable. Like each of the leaders and groups since Hosius, they are right to urge that God's will be done on earth as it is in heaven. Unfortunately, when it actually comes to implementing what they believe to be God's will, they have not succeeded.

Confusing Principles with Policies

One reason why the results are usually mixed when groups with good motives try to promote God's cause in society is the complexity of moral issues. Unfortunately, few political issues present us with simple moral choices. Most political choices consist of two elements: the ends and the means. The ends suggest where we want to go and the means propose how we should get there. Just as travelers must decide both what their destination is and what is the best route to get there, so politicians must first decide what they want to accomplish and then determine how to do it. To accomplish anything political, people must agree on both the ends and the means. In the same way, to be consistently Christian in one's political position, both the ends and the means have to be correct.

Those who call for the church to be "consistent Christians" are undoubtedly correct when they say that our political ends, the goals of our political action, must be morally correct. They rightly urge us to be certain that the goals we are pursuing, the ends we want to accomplish, are truly Christian. Where they are incorrect is that they sometimes forget the complexity of politics. This mistake leads them to confuse principles with policies, ends with means.

Because of this error they tend to think that if they are right about the ends, then they must also be right about the means. They think that anyone who disagrees with them must be ignorant of the scriptural ends God wants us to attain, so they pile on a few more Bible verses to persuade the ignorant to be consistent. They forget the complexity of political issues, not realizing that many Christians who disagree with them share their God-given ends but differ about the human means to reach those ends.

Does God *really* have a position on the location of the capital of the Roman empire, the closing of the Academy in Athens, the legitimacy of Prince John as king of England, the wages of printers in Geneva, the use of Maypoles in Morris dances, the composition of Italy's forty-seventh postwar government, the Panama Canal Treaty, and the funding of "star wars"? Apparently so, if we listen to all who claim to speak in his name. Unfortunately, however, the Almighty has not chosen to make his political position obvious to all his followers.

If God does indeed have a position on these and other political issues, he does not reveal it clearly through the only authoritative source we have, the Bible. Christian legislators will search the Scriptures in vain for unmistakable direction on how to vote on federal day-care funding or any other specific legislative item. The Bible is not an oracle to be consulted for mystical guidance in every decision. It is, rather, the history of a nation that God established, gave a perfect law, and then judged when it departed from his standards. From the specifics of Israel's laws, history, and experience with God we may infer the general principles of his dealings with all nations. For instance, God told Amos that one reason he was punishing Israel was that "they sell the needy for a pair of sandals" (Amos 2:6). So low was the price of labor that poor people were cheaply sold into slavery. From this one case we see the general principle that God sets himself against any society that exploits the poor.

Hearing God's words through the prophets to Israel, measuring the nation's performance against the standard of his law, and reading his commandments to the church in the New Testament teach us that God cares intensely about justice, integrity, faithfulness, and compassion. It does not, however, give us much guidance about how we should structure our governments or economies to achieve those goals. The Bible is silent when we ask it whether God favors monarchy over democracy, or whether he prefers socialism to feudalism. Apparently God considers it more important to give us general guidelines for society than to give us specific direction on every political decision. In his Word he tells us much more about the kind of society he wants than about what we should do to establish it. Instead of revealing the forms our governments and economies should take, God gives us the standards to use in judging our nations. In his Word he gives us the criteria for deciding the ends toward which our societies should move, but relatively little about the means we should use to achieve those ends.

In American political life most issues involve only means. When the majority of Democrats and Republicans argue about the economy, they agree that the end they are trying to reach is increased prosperity for all Americans. But they disagree about the means that will bring us that end result. Republicans generally think prosperity will come if we get the government off the peoples' backs. Democrats usually think giving the government more money and power will help people. Both sides agree on where they want to go—the end; they disagree on how we should get there—the means.

A few political issues, however, involve ends. Before the Civil War, Americans disagreed about slavery. This was a dispute about ends, not means. The question was not what was best for blacks, but what kind of national government we should have. Some said slavery was wrong, and should not be tolerated by a government designed to protect human freedom. Others felt that slavery was right, and the main role of the government was to protect property rights. Since slaves were property, the government needed to defend the institution of slavery. This disagreement between those who were for and against slavery was a fundamental conflict over the goals of American society. It was a debate about the ends for which our government was established. Was the government's primary role to promote human freedom or to protect private property? This was not a conflict about the means of making life better for black people. It was about ends: Should blacks be free or slaves?

Three Lively Issues

Those who espouse the consistent life ethic think they know the mind of the Lord on several political issues. Because the Protestant organization JustLife has taken a stand on specific political issues and even published ratings for individual politicians, it can serve as an example of this view.

JustLife has picked three issues about which it thinks it knows God's will: abortion, economic justice, and the nuclear arms race. JustLife is right to say that God's will is plain in its opposition to abortion, economic injustice, and war. The elimination of these three wrongs is clearly God's goal for our society. Saving lives by ending abortion, poverty, and the threat of nuclear war is certainly an end that God wants us to reach.

The problem with JustLife is that it forgets that having the right end is only part of the answer. The issue is more complex. In the real world of politics, we have to have the correct means to achieve our good ends. Good intentions are not enough. Most Americans have good intentions about peace and the economy. Almost every American politician professes to agree with God's goals for our national life in these two areas. They all say they want to help the poor and to promote peace. Their ends are godly, but the means are uncertain.

For example, is economic justice best served when the government redistributes the people's money or when it lets market forces determine who gets what? Some people point to the thinking of economist John Maynard Keynes and the experiences of the Great Depression and New Deal to argue that government intervention is necessary for a fair economy. Others cite Charles Murray's book, *Losing Ground*, which shows that poverty decreased in the fifties when the government ignored it, and increased when the poverty programs of the sixties were created. These thinkers say the government only hurts the poor when it redistributes income.

Similarly, people do not agree whether nuclear war is more likely to be prevented if we unilaterally disarm, arm ourselves to the teeth, or take some moderate way in between. Some think that the turn-of-the-century European arms race made World War I inevitable, and others feel that recent progress in arms reduction came only because the United States rearmed itself after the weakness of the Carter years.

Unfortunately, there is one obvious area where not every American political figure shares God's goal for our society: abortion. God's Word makes it clear that he wants society to protect weak, innocent, and defenseless people. Scriptures such as Psalm 139:13-16, Jeremiah 1:5, Luke 1:15, and Exodus 21:22-25 make it clear that God considers the unborn child a person, someone whom he can know and fill with the Holy Spirit, and an individual

whose death must be avenged. Proverbs 24:11-12 calls upon us
to prevent the killing of innocent people. Some Americans want
the government to fulfill God's mandate by outlawing abortion,
while others ignore his law and want government to protect so-
called freedoms that end all too often in abortion. Here there is
a clear division that involves ends, not means. This is not a conflict about the means of making life better for unborn children.
It is about ends: Should some unborn children be alive or dead?

In the areas where our society says it shares God's goals, we
need to apply our minds to figuring out the best way to achieve
them. We need to use our God-given reason to investigate the
laws God built into nature and human society so that we can structure our government and economy to reach the ends God
planned for it. In the areas where our nation does not agree with
God's standards, we face a different task. When people do not accept God's ends we need to call them to repent—to turn around
and start going in his direction.

Like the prophets of old we must announce God's will for society. When speaking about ends, we have a special authority. On
the authority of God's Word we promise blessing for obedience
and judgment for sin. We say, "Thus saith the Lord." To do less
is to be unfaithful.

But we must not say, "Thus saith the Lord," when God has not
spoken. He calls us to proclaim his standards, but he has not au-
thorized us to tell people the ways and means to attain those standards. Evidently the Lord feels general revelation is sufficient for
this task, because nothing in his special revelation specifically directs us to employ certain means. To pretend that it does simply
confuses the investigation in the same way the theologians mud-
died the waters when they used the Bible to find the answers to
Galileo's questions about the heavens. What is worse, it makes us
false prophets, putting words in God's mouth.

Specifically, we cannot pass laws against poverty, nor can we
legislate away the possibility of nuclear war. The means of eliminating poverty and the potential for nuclear war can be legiti-
mately challenged. We can, however, work toward making
abortion illegal. The means are clear: overturn the Supreme
Court ruling that made abortions legal (*Roe* v. *Wade*), and enact
a human-life amendment to the Constitution.

With each of these issues—nuclear weapons, poverty, the environment, and abortion—all Christians can and should use a

variety of techniques to call attention to (and help solve) the problem. Pacifists may promote a ban on weapons development, and antiabortionists may try to close clinics. We may disagree on the extent to which these techniques will affect public policy, but we cannot say with certainty that God favors one technique over the other. We can, however, agree on the means to eliminate or severely reduce the number of abortions performed: make abortion illegal.

Thus, JustLife is biblically faithful in its stand against abortion. This issue is one where clear biblical principles apply. It is also an issue where the conflict is over ends. JustLife is also being faithful to God when it calls for economic justice and for peace. These, too, are obviously revealed in the Bible as goals God has for society. But in our society, few people are against the ends of eliminating poverty and preventing war. The conflict in these two areas is over the best means to use to achieve these ends. JustLife is not being biblically faithful when it identifies one particular political position as the God-ordained means to achieve these godly ends. Here it is going beyond the Word of God into areas where God has not authoritatively spoken. It is making conclusions it has reached on its own and passing them off as God's inerrant revelation.

God's Will vs. Man's Ways

JustLife's inability to distinguish between the ends God has ordained and the means people favor also leads it into counterproductive political judgments. Consider their rating of candidates in the last national election. Colorado Sen. William Armstrong is one of the most outspoken evangelicals on Capitol Hill. He shares JustLife's commitment to the ends of ending poverty and preventing war. Yet he disagrees with JustLife about the best means to achieve those ends. Because he hopes that the Strategic Defense Initiative (SDI, or "star wars") will slow the arms race, and thinks that less government is the way to prosperity, his JustLife approval rating was only 36 percent. On the other hand, Ohio's Howard Metzenbaum, a long-time champion of the ACLU's seemingly anti-Christian agenda, received a much higher rating. He consistently votes to promote abortion, but because he shares JustLife's commitment to income redistribution and arms reduction, he earned a 67 percent favorable rating. Can

JustLife seriously contend that Metzenbaum's votes are almost twice as pleasing to God as are Armstrong's?

JustLife should stop its talk about a "consistent ethic of life" and make it clear that there is only one issue facing our government where Americans openly disagree about the ends we are trying to reach: abortion. God's will is clear on the ends and means, and rejecting God's will in this matter is such a moral monstrosity that it dwarfs all other squabbling about means. Christians should not be as concerned with questions of means like educational funding and the testing of antisatellite weapons in space as they are with the deaths of infants. The people in JustLife shoud stop trying to divert the concern, energy, and money of committed Christians away from the God-given ends of the prolife movement and into side issues relating to human means. They should give priority to the one issue where there is a clearly defined method of fulfilling God's will, and then, with other Christians, seek his mind about how to do his will in other areas. JustLife ought to support those who share its commitment to God's ends, and work with them where there is disagreement to discover God's means for achieving them.

Support for abortion is not a minor flaw, it is a sin. Those who support abortion have blood on their hands. JustLife should not join hands with such people, but they should make the antiabortion cause their priority.

[RON SIDER RESPONDS: I agree with Charles White that divine revelation (whether general or special) does not provide direct guidance on specific political choices. Since there is a big gap between biblical principles (or ends) and prudential judgments, it is wrong to equate one's political choices with God's will. Unfortunately, White overstates this point and applies it inaccurately to JustLife.

For example, White correctly argues that the Bible is silent about whether God prefers democracy. But the biblical affirmation that each person has unique value and the warning that sinful people will use absolute power for selfish ends lead toward the conclusion that decentralized political power—as in a democracy—is the direction in which biblical principles point.

The fact that JustLife wants to apply biblical principles in this careful way in no way justifies the charge that we identify one particular political position as "the God-ordained means." We do, however, claim that divine revelation demands a biblically balanced agenda that is concerned not only for life but also for peace and justice.

I will concede one small point. JustLife's 1988 election study guide used percentages in our ratings that led some persons to reach conclusions that we in no way intended. Therefore, we will not use percentages again in that way.

From the beginning, however, JustLife has consistently supported only political candidates who oppose abortion and the nuclear-arms race and seek justice for the poor. Our words and actions have been public and consistent for three years. In mid-1988, I wrote: "JustLife denounces as fraud any attempt by pro-abortion politicans to hide behind other votes in order to claim they are substantially pro-life!" JustLife has never supported a Ted Kennedy or Howard Metzenbaum or any other prochoice politician.

Nor is White correct that on the issue of abortion we have "absolute certainty" about the means. Should we join Operation Rescue's campaign of civil disobedience or work with National Right to Life through the normal political channels? Or should we focus, not on the political process, but on a private volunteer approach as White seems to prefer in the case of the poor? Believing, as White and I do, that God opposes abortion does not solve the question of means in this case any more than in the case of peace and justice.

Finally, White charges that JustLife diverts Christians from the issue of abortion. In fact, JustLife makes an antiabortion stance more attractive to many people who have long identified the prolife movement with what they consider reactionary politics unconcerned with minorities, the poor, and the dignity of women. Precisely when they see antiabortion people who are vigorously seeking equality for women and justice for blacks and the poor, then they are able to rethink and abandon their prochoice stand. JustLife attracts allies to the crusade against abortion.]

IF BOTH SIDES WOULD LISTEN . . .
Kenneth S. Kantzer

What are the real differences between White and Sider and between other evangelicals for whom they speak? To begin with, antiabortionists are convinced that antinuclear-war pacifists are usurping their "prolife" battle cry. They feel including the nuclear question under the prolife umbrella makes the term confusing because it tacks on to it a variety of controversial issues (pacifism, for example).

On the other hand, antinuclear "prolifers" consider antiabortionists to be extraordinarily inconsistent when they restrict their opposition to the evil of abortion. They are doubly faulted, so the argument goes, for limiting the issue to what may prove to be the lesser of the moral questions facing our generation. If 50 million Americans are destroyed—or, possibly, most of the human race—the issue of one million abortions per year will become insignificant.

These two approaches to affirming life also differ regarding the means by which we can best obtain the agreed-on good ends. Sider is certainly right when he stresses that a true biblical concern about human life should drive us to oppose nuclear warfare and that we should be at least as much opposed to nuclear warfare as to free abortion. But White is also right when he points out there are many ways to battle against nuclear warfare. One can be irrevocably opposed to nuclear war (after all, who could possibly *favor* it?), yet be thoroughly convinced that unilateral disarmament or mutual disarmament without guarantees and inspection would create a greater chance of war.

Fight Evil, Not Each Other

What shall we say, then, to the millions of evangelicals who stand on one side or the other of these divisive issues?

To those who feel "prolife" refers to abortion, the nuclear question, economic issues—the "consistent life ethic" camp—we say:

1. Stop wasting your time and ours arguing that the God of the Bible is opposed to nuclear war, poverty, and to injustice. We already know that. As evangelicals, we believe that human beings are created in the image of God and that all of human life is sacred. We are all committed to the lordship of Christ, and his message is prolife across the board. Evangelicals are also committed to the authority of the Bible, and its teaching is clear: abortion, nuclear slaughter, war, poverty, injustice—all are wrong.

2. Recognize that God may call individuals to a particular task. Evangelicals are opposed to all of these wrongs, but God may well call some of us to special areas of his kingdom. A Christian physician is committed to evangelism, but he has been spe-

cially called to heal the body through medical science. Similarly, it is legitimate and fully consistent with scriptural instruction about the Christian life for an individual to be opposed to all forms of evil, but to devote his talent and energies against one specific evil in the world.

3. Make appropriate distinctions. For example, all evangelicals must be opposed to nuclear war. But it is one thing to oppose nuclear war and quite another thing to advocate unilateral nuclear disarmament as do John Stott and the Catholic bishops (though Evangelicals for Social Action does not). Similarly, one must recognize that it is possible to oppose nuclear war, yet not espouse pacifism.

4. Finally, direct your arguments to the issues that really divide us. For example, we all agree that Christians are to help the poor. The disagreement comes in determining the best way to help the most people. Are massive government handouts the best approach, or will that only enslave the poor to perpetual poverty *and* bankrupt our government? How can we best get help to those who are really needy without destroying the initiative and motivation to work on the part of many? We do not expect a perfect solution to the problem of poverty and economic injustice, but we are sincerely troubled as to what is best for all citizens in a world of limited resources.

These are the problems that trouble the soul of evangelicals. It is on these issues that we desperately need light. We welcome gladly all the data you can provide that will help us answer these awesomely important, and also terribly difficult, issues that we must face as Bible-believing Christians. Share with us all the God-given wisdom you possess to help us on to the right answers. We need your wisdom, and we are grateful for all you can give us—not for exhortations to believe what we already know, but for Spirit-guided wisdom to find better paths to our commonly shared goals.

Prolife or Antiabortion?

And to those who view abortion as the one issue all Christians should fight with equal vigor:

1. Signal loud and clear to all men and women that you stand unequivocally for the sanctity of human life. Show us that although you have chosen to fight abortion, you are equally con-

cerned about the potential destruction of human life through nuclear war, and that you consider slow death through poverty and hunger to be a prolife issue. These causes are infinitely important to us, and we must do all we can, with God's help, to rid our nation and the world from these evils. It would help now and then if you would take time out from your war against abortion to lend support to those who campaign for the millions dying of hunger in sub-Sahara Africa and for the tens of thousands who are undergoing continual racial indignity in South Africa. Show us that you, too, oppose a nuclear holocaust that could destroy 50 million people if either of the superpowers launches its missiles.

2. Make distinctions to show you have thought through the implications of laws against abortion. Should an exception be made for the life of the mother? We think so. Should we pass laws to force a woman who has been raped to carry the child to birth? Ordinarily we do not force a person to risk his life to save the life of another—even though morally we think such a person ought to be willing to take the risk. Not all morally wrong acts should be specifically prevented by law and punished as crimes.

3. Give us assurance that you are prepared for the consequences of a strict law against abortion. Tens of thousands now aborted would be brought to term, many to families who do not want them. Will the church lead the way in providing support to those troubled families? Some of those babies will be deformed. Are we prepared to share in the care of these handicapped children? Will we dig into our pockets to provide for their nurture or adopt them into our homes when that is best? Are we willing to make the sacrifices, emotional as well as financial, that will be required to welcome them into the human family and provide for their needs? If we cannot respond with an unblinking "yes" to these questions, we have no right on moral grounds to oppose their abortions.

4. Do not forget that we live in a democracy where we are the rulers. Some evangelicals have turned from political persuasion to taking things into their own hands. They have moved to the streets, and in some cases have openly endorsed violence as a means to drive abortion clinics out of existence. While I defend the right of any Christian to demonstrate peacefully against a perceived evil, and acknowledge that in extreme cases force is justified in fighting moral evil, I do not believe this battle should be fought in the streets. It is not the wisest strategy in a day of gener-

al disrespect for law and quick appeal to violence. This seems an unusually bad time to revert to violence in order to achieve good laws.

5. Be willing to work together with others to secure the best laws for protecting life. Theodore Hesburgh, retired president of Notre Dame University, writes: "If given a choice between the present law of abortion on demand, up to and including viability, or a more restrictive law, such as a limitation of abortion to cases of rape, incest, and serious threat to the mother's life, the majority of Americans polled consistently have supported the more limited option." He acknowledges that "there is not a consensus in America for the absolute prohibition of abortion," but "there is and was a moral consensus . . . for a stricter abortion law. A remarkably well-kept secret is that a minority is currently imposing its belief on a demonstrable majority."

Americans now clearly have it in their power to pass legislation outlawing the vast majority of abortions. Surely the path of moral and political wisdom would dictate support for a second-best law that would eliminate the deaths of nearly a million unborn children every year.

And now a final word to both camps: The real solution to the moral dilemma of our nation is not a law against abortions, nuclear buildup, or poverty—desirable as each of these may be. And that is why we must commit ourselves ever anew to the task of highest priority—that of winning all men to the gospel of Jesus Christ, who alone can save men and women from their sins.

Christians *ought* to be the first to speak out boldly in behalf of human life. We *confess* as a cardinal doctrine of our faith that human beings are made in the image of God and have infinite value in God's sight. If that religious belief does not shape the whole of our life, including our thinking about abortion, infanticide, euthanasia, nuclear war, poverty, and much more, we have not really begun to fathom the power and depth of the gospel.

ABORTION: CATHOLICS MUST CHANGE HEARTS
AS WELL AS LAWS[3]

A day or two after the U.S. Supreme Court announced its most recent abortion decision—in the *Webster* case—last July, a local television news program carried a story about several busloads of prochoice advocates who had gone to Springfield, Illinois to lobby the state legislature. A reporter interviewed one of them: a middle-aged woman, well-dressed and very articulate. With a calm, gentle voice she explained that she had never been involved in such a political effort before.

When asked what prompted her involvement now, she replied with rising anger and bitterness that the Supreme Court's decision was quite unacceptable. The interview ended with her reciting, "How dare they! How dare they!"—referring to the Supreme Court justices. The glint in her eye and the sharp edge in her voice at the end of the interview revealed the depth of her emotional reaction to the court's decision in *Webster*, an intensity of feeling shared by many other women and men.

Nevertheless, despite extensive coverage of the *Webster* decision and its aftermath, many people remain confused about the specific issues in the abortion controversy. To some extent this is understandable because much of the media attention has focused on the emotional and political dimensions of the story.

Some think that in 1973 the U.S. Supreme Court decided that a woman has an absolute constitutional right to an abortion, that she has an unlimited right to do with her body whatever she pleases, that she can terminate her pregnancy at whatever time and in whatever way and for whatever reason she chooses. But this is not true. In its landmark case, *Roe v. Wade*, the court explicitly rejected these notions.

A careful reading of its decision in that case reveals that the court tried to balance the rights of the woman with the state's interest in protecting "the potentiality of human life." Conflicts of rights are often difficult to resolve. In a pregnancy, the matter

[3]Reprint of an article by Cardinal Joseph Bernardin. *U.S. Catholic*, 54:31–3. D '89. Reprinted with permission from *U.S. Catholic*, published by Claretian Publications, 205 West Monroe, Chicago, IL 60606. Copyright © 1989 by Cardinal Joseph Bernardin.

is even more complex. Within our society there are diverse opinions and beliefs about when human life truly begins. The court attempted to resolve the issue by turning to the three trimesters of pregnancy.

It said that during the first three months of pregnancy, approximately, the abortion decision is solely a matter between a woman and her doctor. At about the beginning of the second three months, the state may "regulate the abortion procedure in ways reasonably related" to the health of the mother. Only at the beginning of the third trimester, however, does the state's interest in protecting "the potentiality of human life" become "compelling" because the unborn child would usually be "viable" at that time—that is, capable of living outside the mother's womb, although with artificial help. This meant that a state could regulate or even forbid abortion only from the beginning of the third trimester onward.

In effect, this controversial decision and another one issued on the same day by the court struck down the abortion laws of most states. When state legislatures and municipalities drafted and passed new abortion laws in light of the court's rulings, these were often contested; some of them were eventually considered by the Supreme Court. During the last sixteen years, a majority of the Supreme Court struck down many of these new statutes and, in effect, went well beyond *Roe v. Wade*. They emphasized the woman's right to an abortion to the extent that it severely diminished the state's ability to protect its interest in the life of the unborn child.

Legal scholars and others, including some of the current justices themselves, have criticized the initial *Roe v. Wade* decision because of the flimsy grounds on which it was based and the rigid framework of the trimester approach. Moreover, medical technology and practice have made it possible for unborn children to become viable before the third trimester. Further, it is quite arbitrary to hold that human life can be protected only from the point of its viability outside the mother's womb.

In the *Webster* case, the justices were quite divided. Justice Antonin Scalia declared that the court should reverse itself on *Roe v. Wade*. The rest of the majority were unwilling to do so but, instead, gave considerable power to regulate abortions back to the state legislatures where decisions about such a sensitive and disputed topic should rightfully be made in a democracy. This sets the stage for the next step in the public debate, which will presumably take place in every state legislature.

The U.S. Catholic bishops and many others have been vocal in their opposition to abortion and will continue to participate in the public debate. The basis of the Catholic Church's opposition to abortion is centrally located in its moral and social teaching.

The basic moral principle is that direct killing of the innocent is always wrong. This means that Catholics must defend innocent life in the multiple cases of abortion, warfare, and care of the handicapped and terminally ill. During the past five years, I have often spoken of the need for a consistent ethic of life that provides a sound basis for the development of a comprehensive defense of human life from conception to natural death.

This moral principle about the immorality of the direct killing of the innocent, however, does not stand alone. It is related to other dimensions of Catholic social teaching. The opposition to abortion in the civic sphere is rooted in the conviction that civil law and social policy must always be subject to continual moral analysis. Simply because a civil law is in place does not mean that it should be blindly supported. In *Roe v. Wade* the court said that the abortion decision before the viability of the unborn child "in all its aspects is inherently, and primarily, a medical decision." In a more recent decision, the court has acknowledged that "abortion raises moral and spiritual questions over which honorable persons can disagree sincerely and profoundly." I welcome this shift in perspective.

What steps lie ahead for the Catholic Church as a community of faith and conscience—and for individual Catholics? Three areas call for both attention and action.

First, Catholics must continue to strive for legal protection for the unborn. This has been the church's consistent position, and it is based on Christian teaching about the dignity and value of every human person. As I have intimated, the *Webster* decision makes room for important dialogue at the state level on the politically divisive topic of abortion. And the Catholic Church will contribute to this discussion.

However, Catholics will not be ultimately successful in their defense of the life of the unborn unless they also strive for social and economic justice for women and children. The Supreme Court has made it clear that states may choose to make childbirth

an attractive alternative to abortion. Catholics must go beyond
that by helping indigent mothers raise their children, expanding
adoption services, and improving access to health care for needy
women and children, for example.

Second, Catholics must be more effective educators about
what abortion entails and why it is morally wrong. I recently came
across a disturbing statistic: 30 percent of the women who obtain
abortions are Catholic. True, it is difficult to get accurate statistics about abortion: many hospitals and clinics as well as women
refuse to cooperate; and when a woman identifies herself as a
Catholic, it is impossible to know to what extent she participates
in the life of the church. Nevertheless, this statistic remains profoundly disturbing. I am prolife and will do everything possible
to eliminate the evil of abortion. But I wonder if the Catholic
Church's preoccupation with the national debate on the legal di-
mension of this extraordinarily important issue had not blinded
us to the need *within* our own community to educate, to form, and
to encourage people on life issues, especially the right of the unborn to life.

While this right of the unborn surely demands legal protection and we Catholics must insist on this, I wonder whether we
have stepped back from the legal debate enough so that we can
really *hear* the issues, the struggles, and the anguish of women
who face life issues in a way that we bishops and priests—and husbands and boyfriends—never will? I wonder whether we have adequately spoken a word of faith to them? I wonder whether we
have inspired the community to help carry the burdens of our sisters in faith?

And this brings us to the third area of concern: our pastoral
outreach and ministry to pregnant women. Less than 20 percent
of women who have abortions are married. Only 7 percent have
abortions because of their own health, and 1 percent because of
rape or incest. Forty-three percent have had a previous abortion.
And is it really freedom of choice when poverty causes one to conclude that the only way to cope with pregnancy is an abortion?

Most women who have abortions are not callous child-haters.
They do not approach an abortionist easily. Any priest or counselor who has talked with them about their experience can verify
that most often they are frightened, very depressed, and overwhelmed. Some feel they are too young to be mothers. Others

say they are too poor. Still others, who may be older and even wealthy, cannot accept the change in lifestyle and career that rearing a child would entail. Seldom does anyone make such a decision lightly. They frequently feel that they simply have no choice but to have an abortion.

It is significant that many make their decision in relative isolation from those who should be expected to help and support a woman with an unwanted pregnancy—family, husband or boyfriend, close friends, pastors. Isolation leads to desperation.

We Catholics cannot truly be prolife if we shut these women out of our lives and ministry. We've got to do better—and more for them. And we need to continue and expand our ministries of healing and reconciliation for those who have gone through the pain and anguish of an abortion, for they are our sisters in the faith.

Bella Abzug is reported to have said recently that "Abortion is the Vietnam of this generation." If so, I hope that we have learned something from the bitterness, polarization, and confrontational tactics of that divisive period in our life as a nation. If we are going to build up, not tear down, our society, we need to learn how to talk with one another about our differences with civility and mutual respect. I stand prepared to participate in such a dialogue.

AFTER ROE[4]

Justice Harry Blackmun has said that *Roe* v. *Wade* might fall this term. Maybe he just wanted to provoke pro-choice forces to intensify their efforts. But there is no doubt that the new debate has begun: What comes after *Roe* v. *Wade* is gone? In *The New Republic*, Harvard law professor Mary Ann Glendon suggests we might have to learn from the way the Western Europeans deal with abortion. In a new book, *Science and the Unborn*, biologist Clifford Grobstein says that science might give us a basis for com-

[4]Reprint of an article by *National Review* religion editor Richard John Neuhaus. *National Review*, 41:38–40+. Ap 7 '89. Copyright © 1989 by National Review, Inc., 150 East 35th St., New York, NY 10016. Reprinted by permission.

promising on what is "truly human." George Will pulls the pertinent considerations together in a recent column (*Newsweek*, Feb. 13).

Will correctly notes the incoherence and "anti-constitutional nonreasoning" of the Supreme Court's abortion rulings. He also recognizes that the abortion debate is not really over the question of when human life begins. "The indisputable fact," he observes, "is that a fetus is alive and biologically human. . . . Biology does not allow the abortion argument to be about when human life begins. The argument . . . is about the moral significance and hence the proper legal status of life in its early stages."

George Will is skeptical about the other George's conversion to a pro-life position (no abortions except in cases of rape, incest, and direct threat to the mother's life). But he says that Bush is stuck with it. Will assumes that the pro-life position is a political albatross. He writes, "Many millions of voters who would recoil from enactment of the [abortion] policy embraced by Bush and the GOP platform vote Republican anyway because for 16 years abortion has been largely a subject of litigation rather than legislation." But, Will says, if *Roe* v. *Wade* is reversed the abortion issue will be brought to "an instant boil" in fifty state legislatures, and then the Republicans, if they stick with the pro-life position, are in for it. The Republican position, he says, goes against the grain of the culture, which was moving in a liberal direction on abortion before *Roe* v. *Wade*. Will's political judgment is unequivocal: "If *Roe* is reversed, either the Republican Party must retreat from its nearly categorical opposition to abortion or it will suffer severe reverses in state legislative contests—and hence in its party-building efforts and its hope of someday capturing the House of Representatives."

The argument about what comes after *Roe* is of considerable interest at four levels, each entangled with the others: the moral, the legal, the cultural, and the political. No doubt the question of the "legal status" of unborn life will depend upon a democratic judgment about the "moral significance" of that life. Will thinks some differences can be split "if the argument is not about when in pregnancy life begins but when in pregnancy abortions should stop." That may sound attractive, until it is seen that it redirects the argument to one of the rocks on which *Roe* was dashed. Will himself admits that *Roe*'s differentiations into trimesters—based upon notions such as "viability," and the distinction between "potential" and "meaningful" life—were logically incoherent and contrary to biological fact.

His proposed recasting of the question is no recasting at all. It simply replays the widely recognized illogic of *Roe*. With respect to the unborn, the question is, What is this? Maybe the question is, Who is this? Most people readily recognize that the "what" is human life which, barring natural misfortune or deliberate attack, will become the "who" of a person possessing rights. Certainly the question is not "when." Time lines that allow life to be attacked at one point but not at a later point cannot help appearing to be arbitrary, because in fact they are arbitrary.

The abortion argument has been up and down the chronological road for years, indeed for centuries. The effort to determine the point of "ensoulment," or of "quickening," or of when a human life becomes a "person" has been exhausted and discredited. In addition to the theological and ethical experience with such debates, contemporary science powerfully underscores the impossibility of making a rational determination of a "before" and "after" with respect to the "moral significance" and hence the "legal status" of unborn life. Of course there are purely emotive and subjective time differentiations that can be made. Grobstein speaks about the point at which we can "mobilize interest and concern" for the unborn. At, say, three weeks the life in the womb does not *seem* to many people to be a baby, whereas at, say, twenty weeks they have no doubt about the presence of a baby. But this is entirely subjective. It says nothing about what or who is there; it is only a comment on what or who many people *feel* is there. This is nothing more than an exercise in raw emotivism, which would also jeopardize the moral credibility of laws regarding persons and rights in connections other than abortion.

The debate is not over chronology but over the weighing of a human life against the reasons for terminating that life. The radical pro-choice position (i.e., the position of *Roe*) is that *any* consideration is sufficient to justify the decision to terminate. Indeed no reason need be given; the mere wish to terminate is sufficient reason. A more moderate pro-choice position is that at least *some* reason must be given, and the reason must not be trivial or willful. As the abortion debate comes to an "instant boil" in state legislatures, gradations of such pro-choice proposals will no doubt have considerable appeal.

Are we, then, facing the prospect of "splitting differences"? Yes and no. Post-*Roe* accommodations will be made in most, if not all, states. The accommodation already agreed to by most pro-life leadership is not on the "moral significance" of the unborn but on the limits of law. The distinction between the legal and the moral is firmly rooted in almost all traditions of ethical reflection, religious or otherwise. It is a distinction, not a separation. Laws must be legitimated by reference to morality, but if we try to translate all of morality into law, we overburden the law, with the result that law is brought into disrepute. The consistent pro-life position is that every unborn human life should be protected by law, without exception. The consensus in the pro-life leadership, however, is that there will be exceptions. The reluctant acceptance of that reality in no way implies approval of it. Nor does it indicate inconsistency with respect to the "moral significance" of unborn life. Rather, such acceptance is based upon a prudential judgment that combines considerations that are moral, legal, cultural, and political.

After *Roe*, it seems likely that every state will make exceptions for rape, incest, and direct threat to the life of the mother. The political fact is that most pro-life leaders and their political friends, including the Bush Administration, have decided that this is the most that is obtainable. There is also a matter of principle supporting the exception of direct threat to the life of the mother. No law can properly require heroic virtue. For a woman to surrender her life for the life of her unborn child is heroic virtue. One may argue that such self-surrendering love is morally mandated, but it cannot be legally mandated. Saints are produced by religious inspiration, not by edict of the state. Plus, there is a substantial Judaeo-Christian tradition that justifies the taking of human life in such extreme circumstances. Rape and incest do not constitute the same life-*versus*-life dilemma. Yet most pro-life thinkers have accepted the inevitability of these exceptions as well. To require a woman or girl to carry to term the child of a rapist or a drunken father would be politically unsustainable. Pro-abortionists would certainly exploit such cases in order to undermine the entire proposition that the state must protect the unborn. In addition, the argument can be made that the question of heroic virtue and the limits of law is engaged also in instances of pregnancy from rape or incest.

People of pro-life conviction are sometimes nervous about discussing the accommodations that may follow the reversal of *Roe*. Given our society's adversarial polity, some believe that not an inch should be given, and certainly not even a fraction of an inch should be given in advance. They contend that the pro-life movement should, state by state, go for broke. That viewpoint is understandable. By going for broke, however, they could wind up seeing the remarkable pro-life achievement of the last 16 years broken. It would not be the first time that insistence upon the best defeated the better and perpetuated the worst. In light of the inherent limits of law, it is also doubtful that an absolute prohibition of abortion is in fact "the best." What, then, is the best that the pro-life movement should work for? One answer would seem to be: The most comprehensive legal protection of unborn life that is culturally and politically sustainable.

Of course we can only discover what is sustainable by historical testing. What is sustainable may change over time. When the law's unlimited license to abort is withdrawn, when the "moral significance" of the unborn again finds support in law, popular attitudes are bound to change significantly. This is true not only of those seeking abortions but also of those doing abortions. For example, studies indicate that, with very few exceptions, abortionists say they would quit the business if what they are doing were no longer legal. We should not underestimate the pedagogical force of law. Common fatuities to the contrary, laws reflect moral judgments. Even when those judgments cannot be effectively enforced, they can be effectively taught, and the law is one of society's most potent teaching instruments.

No thoughtful person of pro-life persuasion believes that after *Roe* there will be no more abortions. In this instance too, where laws are made laws are broken. That is a truism, and has never been a valid argument for not making laws. It is a valid caution against making unnecessary laws. After 16 years of experiment with the abolition of abortion law, it is clear beyond reasonable doubt that a politically effective majority of the American people believes that laws protecting the unborn are necessary. But, if the restoration of abortion law will not eliminate abortions, what will it achieve? The hope is that it will effect two monumental changes.

First, it will effect a drastic reduction in the absolute number of innocent human lives unjustly terminated. It is quite possible that there will still be a hundred thousand or more abortions in America each year. And quite possibly, as some claim, there would be many fewer. Nobody knows. What we do know is that, even if we accept the high figure of two hundred thousand, that is 1.3 million fewer than the number of unborn children killed each year under *Roe*. If one believes that each of those unborn children is endowed by "Nature and Nature's God" with a life to live, such a change cannot help seeming a good beyond measure. Of course every abortion is a tragedy, but more than a million fewer tragedies each year is a monumental change for the better.

Hysterical propaganda to the contrary, this will not mean a return to the clothes-hanger and the back-alley perils of pregnant Pauline. As Dr. Bernard Nathanson has subsequently explained, the horror stories and statistics invoked to support liberalized abortion in the 1960s were frequently sheer inventions by himself and others. Moreover, the technology since developed by the abortion industry is relatively cheap, available, and medically safe (for the mother, not the fetus). Nor, despite the fumblings of the Bush Administration on this question, are we facing the post-*Roe* prospect of women being jailed for seeking or obtaining abortions. On the basis of long experience prior to *Roe*, it should be obvious that restored abortion law will carry criminal penalties aimed at the abortionist.

The second great change will be a return to an inclusive definition of membership in the community for which we accept public responsibility. Such a change is urgently needed, and for reasons that go beyond abortion. Witness current agitations for euthanasia and the elimination of categories of people who are, in the lethal logic of *Roe*, not living "meaningful human lives." The elimination of the useless aged, the hopelessly handicapped, and the persistently vegetative is not a matter of alarmist scenarios for the future. Such eliminations are being proposed and, to some extent, are being perpetrated now.

These developments have everything to do with the ominous turn that liberalism took early in the abortion debate. American-style liberalism is schizophrenic. On the one side, it is profoundly communitarian; on the other, radically individualistic. In the abortion debate, the pro-choice forces successfully seized the liberal banner for a radical individualism that, in the pursuit of self-actualization, acknowledges no bonds of community or duty to others. That is the individualism enshrined in *Roe*'s dubious dis-

covery of a constitutional "right to privacy." When communal
bonds are thus sundered, public protection is withdrawn not only
from the unborn. Proponents of euthanasia, of fetal farming and
experimentation, and of the eugenic elimination of the unfit (all
being people without "meaningful life") are entirely correct in appealing to the letter and spirit of *Roe*. The reversal of that decision, then, will dramatically reduce the incidence of abortion, and
will also apply the brakes to the extension of practices that are fully warranted by its reasoning.

So, what are we to say to George Will's argument that pro-
choice and pro-life advocates "can split some differences if the argument is not about when in pregnancy life begins but when in
pregnancy abortions should stop"? The pro-life movement has already made accommodations, but they are not accommodations
on the "when" or the "what" or the "who" of human life. They
are accommodations that recognize the limits of law in relation
to morality. As for splitting differences, one notes that the pro-
choice advocates have indicated not the slightest willingness to accommodate. The National Organization for Women, Planned
Parenthood, ACLU, et al. have adopted an unrelenting posture
of "not one inch." Sensing that they are on the losing side, they
fear that the smallest hint of willingness to accommodate would
precipitate the entire collapse of the victory they once thought
secured by the *Roe* decision.

In a democratic polity such as ours, it is generally best when
conflicts can be resolved without total winners and total losers.
After *Roe*, however, the pro-life position will hardly have a total
victory. There will be some abortions by legal exception, there
will be a substantial number of illegal abortions, and it is possible
that a few states will permit something close to abortion on demand. Such a situation is hardly satisfactory from the pro-life
viewpoint. The pro-life goal will be to continue to work toward
the most comprehensive sustainable legal protection for the unborn, and toward a more caring and sexually responsible society
that will reduce the felt need for abortion.

But, if the post-*Roe* situation will not be satisfactory to pro-
lifers, it will be much less satisfactory to pro-choicers. There is no
blinking the fact that in that situation they will be the losers. Mr.
Will correctly says, "This democratic nation needs a vigorous argument, not judicial fiat, about abortion." The pro-choicers won

a 16-year victory by judicial fiat in the *Roe* decision. It very quickly became evident, however, that they had lost the argument by their stubborn refusal even to acknowledge the question of the "moral significance and hence the proper legal status of life in its early stages." With that stubborn refusal, they set themselves against clear reason and scientific fact—and against the moral sensibilities and common sense of most Americans. On the most critical issue, the "vigorous argument" that Mr. Will calls for has taken place, and the pro-life position prevailed.

The analysis of George Will and others must be challenged also in connection with cultural directions and political consequences. Will writes, "The culture was moving [in a pro-abortion direction] before the Court moved." That was true of the elite culture of the knowledge class. On abortion, the elite culture took the more democratic culture by surprise. It was a while before the democratic culture was able to organize its response to the attack, but the last 16 years of the pro-life movement is the story of that stunningly effective response. Moreover, many in the elite culture who favored "abortion reform" in the 1960s were later repulsed by the reality of 1.5 million abortions per year. That, they began to say, was not what they had in mind at all.

The pro-life movement has benefited mightily by the recruitment or acquiescence of these "abortion reformers" of the 1960s who came to have second and third thoughts about abortion-as-contraception and the consequent debasement of human life and communal bonds. Witness today's changes in churches such as the Episcopal, United Methodist, and Presbyterian (U.S.A.). Once on the cutting edge of "abortion reform," they are now trying to make it clear that they are opposed to the present situation of "abortion on demand." Groups such as Presbyterians for Life and NOEL (National Organization of Episcopalians for Life), once marginal and barely tolerated in their church bodies, now have the initiative in changing their churches' positions on abortion. Then too, those churches that were "right from the start"—e.g., Roman Catholic, Missouri-Synod Lutheran, Southern Baptist—feel vindicated and possess a new confidence in the role that they have played and will play.

The elite culture, once solidly pro-abortion, has been fragmented as the actual consequences of *Roe* have become brutally apparent. These cultural and class differences in the abortion debate were brilliantly analyzed several years ago by Kristin Luker in her *Abortion and the Politics of Motherhood*. Changes since Miss Luker's research have all moved in a direction favorable to the pro-life position. An examination of survey-research data over the last two decades indicates that there now seems to be a fairly stable set of popular viewpoints on abortion. About 20 per cent of respondents favor prohibiting abortion in every circumstance, somewhat less than 20 per cent support the existing unlimited "right" to abortion, and about 60 per cent say that unborn life should be legally protected, with some exceptions for hard cases. Explore what respondents mean by "hard cases," and it turns out that the exceptions would be very limited indeed.

No doubt there would be powerful cultural resistance to legal changes protecting the unborn. But the resistance would come overwhelmingly from sectors of the elite culture that are bitterly disappointed that the"judicial fiat" of *Roe* did not carry the day. In legislative battles in all fifty states, the result will be an intensification of the class-based *Kulturkampf* in which our public life is now embroiled. To call it a *Kulturkampf* is no exaggeration: it is a war over the moral definition of American culture.

Finally, we should examine assumptions about the political consequences of the coming struggle. Mr. Will says Republicans must retreat from their pro-life position or abandon their hopes of controlling state legislatures and thus of capturing the House of Representatives. The fortunes of the Republican Party are not among our chief concerns, but we suspect that Mr. Will may be in error here as well. In the 1988 presidential election as many as one-third of the voters said that abortion was their number-one concern—and that one-third overwhelmingly voted Republican. (And maybe more. It is well known that people tend to avoid giving "controversial" answers to pollsters. To say that abortion is your primary concern is to risk being controversial.) No doubt, as Mr. Will says, some people voted Republican *despite* the pro-life position of Reagan and Bush. The evidence, however, is that a great many people voted for Reagan and Bush *because of*—or at least *also* because of—their promise to work for the protection of the unborn.

A common lament of Republicans is that they cannot do their presidential trick in congressional and state races because Democrats there are shielded from the ideological issues that win nationally, such as abortion. It is more than arguable that returning the abortion question to the states may be precisely what the Republicans need.

Far from being settled, the abortion debate may now explode as it never has before. If the question is returned to the states, it might be thought that the pro-choice proponents are pretty much in the position they were in back in the Sixties, pressing for the most "liberal" abortion laws they can get. But that will not be the case. Now they will no longer be the vanguard advocating what is new and progressive. They will be the old guard, urging a return to the discredited *status quo ante* under *Roe* v. *Wade*. The pro-life proponents, on the other hand, cannot now be taken by surprise. They are formidably organized, they have thousands of seasoned activists, and they possess the confidence that comes from having taken on the establishments and, against all odds, won. More than that, they are convinced that they are on the side of the angels, and they believe that most of the American people are too. To be sure, the pro-life movement could still snatch defeat from the jaws of victory, but it would have to work at it.

We are told that, after *Roe*, we will need a civil debate about splitting differences, and there is truth in that. But a civil debate about splitting differences can only happen on the basis of an acknowledgment that the chief difference has already been split. The difference between those who do and those who do not recognize "the moral significance and hence the proper legal status of life in its early stages" has already been split, and it has been split in favor of the pro-life position. The outcome of that split will, we expect, soon be ratified by the Supreme Court and then by the great majority of state legislatures. We cannot know precisely what this will mean for abortion law and other measures aimed at protecting vulnerable human life. We can be certain that there will be continuing argument and continuing conflict. Debate that is civil need not preclude passion, and the coming contests will be passionate. At stake is what we believe about the unborn, but also what we believe about ourselves and the communities of which we are part.

III. IF ABORTION WERE ILLEGAL

EDITOR'S INTRODUCTION

Suppose that the Supreme Court does indeed overturn *Roe v. Wade* and abortion is once again made illegal. What can we expect? No one thinks that abortions will cease entirely; many pregnant women, it is agreed, will seek out underground abortionists, just as they did before 1973. But many others will not want to risk an illegal abortion or will be unable to arrange or pay for one. The numbers of unwanted children born will increase, making it more likely (the argument goes) that the incidence of abandoned children, child abuse, juvenile crime, and dysfunctional families will rise also. In this view, we will all pay a price in social disruption for the existence of these children, and their mothers—especially poor and unmarried teenagers—will lose any chance of building good lives for themselves.

There is no agreement on the number of American women who obtained illegal abortions in the years preceding the *Roe v. Wade* decision. Some abortion advocates put the percentage as high as one in four. Some antiabortion activists estimate the figure as a few hundred thousand yearly. The first selection, an excerpt from the book *Back Rooms: Voices from the Illegal Abortion Era*, is by Ellen Messer and Kathryn E. May and contains first-person accounts by women who underwent illegal abortions. "Underground Abortion Remembered," by Diane Elze, is an interview with three women who were members of the Jane Collective, a group of women based in Chicago who arranged illegal abortions for pregnant women and eventually learned to perform abortions themselves—60 to 80 each week, they say. Were abortion to be recriminalized today, such groups would undoubtedly be formed again despite the risk of arrest and prosecution.

A similar point is made in Carl Djerassi's "Abortion in the United States: Politics or Policy?," with an important distinction: Djerassi believes that underground abortions would probably be controlled not by feminist activists but by organized crime. Djerassi, one of the synthesizers of the birth-control pill, cites the example of Rumania, where maternal deaths from illegal abortions increased tenfold after abortion was prohibited in 1965. In place of a blanket prohibition in the United States, he calls for a policy of better education about human sexuality, combined with more effective, easily obtainable, and subsidized contraception, to "make abortion unnecessary."

In anticipation of a day when abortion may become illegal, some women are already training one another to perform abortions using menstrual extraction, a vacuum-aspiration technique that can be used during the first eight weeks of pregnancy. Their efforts are described in the last selection in this section, "Abortion without Doctors," by Anastasia Toufexis.

THE BAD OLD DAYS[1]

Caroline

Caroline is a forty-four-year-old woman who is a librarian at a college in a small rural town.

For a long time I think I drank to avoid the feelings. And it wasn't until quite recently, five years ago, after I had stopped drinking for a while, that I went through a whole period of really reliving the terror of this experience. It was in the summer, between my junior and senior years of college. I was going to college in Cleveland, living there for the summer. And somehow I just knew I was pregnant.

It was the first and only time that I was ever sexually intimate with this man. He was a young artist whom I had been seeing for some time. I wasn't particularly physically attracted to him, but he was pressing me, and I just finally got to the point where I couldn't struggle with it anymore. So I gave in. Somehow I immediately had the sense that I was pregnant.

I really didn't know what to do. I knew, though, that having a baby would ruin my whole life. The man involved felt responsible and wanted to marry me, but I thought it was a very weak rea-

[1]Reprint of a magazine article by Ellen Messer and Kathryn E. May. *Ms.* 17:60-3. Jl '88. Excerpted from *Back Rooms: Voices from the Illegal Abortion Era*. St. Martin's Press, 1988. Copyright © 1988 by Ellen Messer and Kathryn E. May.

son for getting married. I spent a lot of time just seeing my life in a shambles. Things at that time in Cleveland were very tight. There had been several incidents reported in the paper. An abortion ring had been broken up. It was 1963, and when I followed up on the few leads there were, it seemed that it was absolutely the worst possible time in about five years to have an abortion in Cleveland.

In the meantime the weeks were going by and I was more pregnant all the time and it was really getting to the point that if I didn't do something soon it was going to be too late. Being raised a good Catholic girl, abortion was not a thing that I was very comfortable thinking about. But I didn't feel that I had any other option. I was getting pretty desperate by this time because I was nine weeks pregnant. I finally located an abortionist in Youngstown, Ohio.

This so-called doctor was a bookie and he was an abortionist. He was an elderly man in a ramshackle little house in a disreputable, shabby part of Youngstown. It in no way fit my image of a doctor's house and office. I think there was some actual gambling going on while we were waiting.

He had a room with a chair and stirrups set up. The money, one hundred dollars, had to be in cash, in certain denominations, and it had to be given to him in an envelope. He checked it very thoroughly to make sure it wasn't marked. He explained he was doing a saline injection and that there should be some cramping and the abortion would happen within twenty-four hours. Nothing happened.

I don't know how many days passed; I did a lot to block out this experience. But I do know that when I finally aborted I was alone in my room in the dormitory at school. I went through at least twelve hours of labor alone in my room.

It was more terrible than I ever imagined, partly because I was alone, partly because I was scared. I was timing the contractions and I just didn't think I could bear any more. I didn't feel I could cry out for help, and I just remember thinking, "I'm going to get through this." I remember noticing that the contractions were getting more and more frequent, five minutes, then four minutes, then three minutes, and then there was a lot of blood and there was a fetus. I was really beside myself, and terrified. I didn't know what to do. There was more blood than I ever imagined. I used one of these metal waste baskets we had in the dorm

rooms and I remember it being filled up. I think I had gone
through a whole night and it was now midmorning, and there
weren't many people around. I managed to get to the bathroom,
very surreptitiously. I was terrified of someone discovering me,
of being arrested.

I remember taking this fetus and not knowing what else to do
but flush it down the toilet. And I was terrified that it wasn't going to go down, that they'd have to call a plumber and then there
would be this hunt to find out who did this terrible thing in the
dorm, and I'd be tracked down and prosecuted. Somehow I
thought then it would be over, but it wasn't over. It went on and
on. I kept hemorrhaging and it just wouldn't stop.

I had become pregnant in August, and the abortion was in
early November. I remember going home for Thanksgiving and
my mother kept saying, "I think you're anemic." And I remember
being very drained and wiped out.

Early in December, I became friendly with a very gentle, brilliant but quite crazy college student who had been hospitalized
while he was suicidal. I found myself confiding in him that I'd had
this abortion, and was still bleeding. He talked to the rector of the
Episcopal Church in Shaker Heights, and the rector, to whom I
shall be forever grateful, called one of the doctors in his congre-
gation. He was so appalled at my condition that he said, "Do you
realize you could have killed yourself?" He admitted me to the
hospital.

After they built me up they did a D & C. I wasn't yet twenty-
one, so the doctor called and spoke to my mother and said there
was nothing to be concerned about; the D & C was just a routine
procedure and would help. He said that I was quite anemic.

I must have been in the hospital five days. The Episcopal
Church paid my hospital bill and the doctor never charged. I was
very thankful, and totally done in at the end of that ordeal.

I didn't feel guilty. I was determined once I made the decision
to go through with it, and I did.

Nora

Nora is a historian and educator.

There was a doctor who did surgical abortions in Virginia, in
the early fifties. He was ultimately arrested and, I believe, sent to
prison.

I went to him, to that place in Virginia, in the spring of '52. He was recommended by a doctor in Washington, D.C., who I think may have gotten a cut of the money.

Preparations for doing this were very complicated and anxiety-filled. I had to stand on a street corner in Washington, D.C., holding a copy of *Time* magazine. A woman was supposed to approach me and ask me if I had a problem, and I said, "Yes, I have a problem," and, "Can we discuss it?" She said, "No, this is only the first stage." Then I had to make a phone call and this time I was told to be in a hotel lobby with a copy of the Washington *Post*, which I thought was kind of funny, since most people carried the Washington *Post*. The next stage happened a week later. I was picked up by a car, on still another street corner, by someone who took me to a place where there was a long black limousine waiting. I think there were three or four other young women in the limousine when I got in. I can remember that the radio was on, and Rockefeller was trying to get the Presidential nomination, in preparation for the '52 election.

Then we left Washington, and the car stopped, and the driver said, "And now, for fun, we're going to put these little goggles over your eyes." And so we all wore masks. But the limousine had opaque windows, so no one could see that these people were sitting there wearing masks. And then we arrived at a farmhouse. It was very well staffed. There were a lot of guards, strong, tough-looking men. The limousine was put in a garage and we walked from there into the house. There were guards standing around with guns, three or four nurses, and a staff of maybe ten. The procedure itself was a D & C with local anesthesia, which meant that there was not too much pain, but it was scary as hell.

I couldn't see the doctor because he was all done up for surgery. He talked as he worked, because I think he sensed that I didn't want the routine: "Who are your favorite movie stars?" So he said, "You know, the things people talk about are interesting. I have had movie stars on this table, I've had doctors, lawyers . . . " The doctor did have a somewhat reassuring quality.

This cost four hundred dollars. It was well done. I had volunteered to be first, not wanting to see or hear anything else, but I found out later that I wouldn't have seen or heard anything because there were television sets all over the house, playing very loudly, and in addition, the toilets were calibrated to flush every half-minute or so, so there was a lot of noise. If anyone had freaked out and yelled, I don't think you would have heard it.

When it was over, I was taken into a bedroom and laid down with white sheets.

Lila

Lila is a successful businesswoman and has recently earned a doctoral degree.

I had been dating Joseph almost a year. I didn't want to be a married student with a baby trying to finish up college for two years. I really couldn't imagine having a baby by this guy. What I first did out of my own naiveté was to ask people, "What can I do?" I only remember one remedy—very hot baths and gin. To this day I can't stand the smell of gin. I must have tried that about three or four nights. It didn't work.

I decided to ask my stepmother in Des Moines if she could help me. Now, my stepmother's a real meddling and involved lady—she knows everything about everybody everyplace. So I told her I was pregnant and that I didn't want to have the baby, I wanted to finish school, and she says, "Come to Des Moines this weekend." I said, "How much will it be?" and I think she said one hundred dollars. I felt nothing. I didn't feel anxious. I think I was stupid. No, I was not stupid, I think I was overcontrolled. I just got on the train. Not only did I not think about the moral or ethical implications, but I didn't think about the physical possibilities. Maybe I didn't know. Maybe I knew and just blocked it out. But I said, "I'm going to go have this thing and I'll be back to school on Monday."

We must have done it on a Friday night. I think she picked me up from the train station. We went to the poor section of town. Now, I'm the daughter of a well-known man in our town, not to mention my stepmother. Whenever I saw these townspeople I saw them as my father's daughter. They were renters of his apartments and frequenters of his pool hall. So now that I'm going to this house where everybody knows there's an abortionist that has an apartment in the back, I was even more self-conscious. And my stepmother greeted everybody and she just walked me through the door.

It was a kitchen table, coat-hanger abortion. It took maybe six minutes. I got on the kitchen table. I think my stepmother gave me a drink of brandy or something, and she said, "Now this may hurt a little bit." She held my hand and this woman stuck a piece of coat hanger into my vagina. She stuck the coat hanger in, a piece that had been sterilized or whatever the hell she had done, and then my stepmother said, "Okay, now you get dressed." And what you were supposed to do was leave that in there until you started to abort. And then I left. I remember walking out with this coat hanger between my legs. I went back home to my father's house.

That evening I started bleeding and I remember I had cramps, and my stepmother put me to bed. I remember her giving me a drink, and giving me aspirin, and I went to sleep and to me it was fine, because it was better than I would do with my menstrual cramps. I got up very early in the morning and went to the bathroom and there was just this passage of blood and a clot that was slightly bigger than the clots I usually passed during my menstrual period. I realized that that was the fetus passing. I felt a little mixed then because it seemed like I should have done something at that moment. The next month my period came on time.

Heather

My first abortion was approximately one month before abortion became legal. I had become pregnant on what was called the sequential birth-control pill, which was given to me by a gynecologist because I was not ovulating.

When I went back to my gynecologist, who was the head of ob-gyn at a large metropolitan hospital, he yelled at me. He asked me what kind of birth control I was on, and I told him "sequential birth-control pills," and he said, "Who was the idiot who gave you those?" and it was him! So he tried to cover that whole thing up and dragged my husband into it. We were young kids in our twenties, and newly married, and he said he wanted one thousand dollars cash—to "pay off the hospital board"—in a paper bag! So I had to go take the money out of the bank and pay him cash, and see two psychiatrists that he gave me the names of and pay them each one hundred dollars in cash to get them to type a letter saying that I was suicidal. It was as if my husband and this doctor were on the phone like cronies, consulting each other and that sort of thing. My husband's screaming, "We can't have this child . . . " It was like a full moon or something, and I was the victim.

I should also mention that my husband was checking places for me to go. He had me ready to go to Haiti when the revolution broke out in Haiti, so I couldn't get an abortion there. He was going to fly me to England, because you could obtain an abortion there. So the process was something that seemed to take weeks of the most incredible and ridiculous effort involved in booking flights and travel agents and everything else, just to do what people now go to a local clinic for.

Finally, I went to the hospital and had the abortion. It was just a terrible mess. I was just there overnight—I got home and went into labor! I had terrible pain, and tried to call the doctor. We finally tracked him down at a restaurant. He told my husband that I was just being a big baby, but he agreed to give me a prescription. John went to get it, and while he was gone, a fetus came out of my body, which freaked me out. It was one thing to have an abortion and go through all this process, but to have to deal with the fetus! It was supposed to be a D & C, but he did not remove the fetus. Later he insisted that I must have had twins and he had missed one. It really affected my mind, and the doctor just tried to cover it up, and he didn't recommend that I receive any help, and was constantly saying to my husband, "Oh, she's just being crazy."

During the follow-up examination, this doctor was on the phone with one of his colleagues and said, "Oh, hi, yeah, I'm here with all the girls with their legs up. You know me, I'm just a glorified plumber." I just got up off the table, and put my clothes on and walked out the door and went home. He called my house and wanted to know why I had left, and I said, "Look, I just decided I'm not a glorified sink," and I just would never go back.

Margot

Margot is a registered nurse who has written several books on pregnancy and birth, and has worked as a Lamaze instructor.

I had three abortions, but the first one was the most hardhitting. I was nineteen. I had gone to one year of college, and I didn't like it, and I didn't want to go back. My main ambition was to get married and be taken care of. My father said, "While you're waiting for a husband, you're not just going to sit at home—you're going to get yourself a career, so what do you want to do?" And having absolutely no sense of myself as a person at all, I said, "Well, what do women do?" They're either secretaries, nurses, or teachers, and I didn't want to do the other two, so I chose nursing.

I was going out with a guy who was at an Ivy League college on the G.I. Bill. He was twenty-seven. He'd been in the Navy during the Second World War. We used to screw on the front seat of his car. And it was really, for me, a way of being held and getting attention. And he would interrupt intercourse. And I felt like I was getting my love interrupted, so I asked him not to do that, and so I got pregnant.

In the middle of being overwhelmed and frightened, there was another part of me that was tremendously excited—I mean very happy. I was elated. And I begged Tom to get married. I said, "We're engaged—let's just get married." I would quit nursing school. By this time he was working as a traveling salesman. Tom said to me he absolutely could not get married this way because it would kill his parents.

Then he had to track down an abortionist. He did all these little things in code. He talked to a pharmacist that he knew and he'd say, "You know, I have a ship that is now full of cargo. Do you know any way to . . . " Finally, Tom found a genuine M.D. who did abortions, who had this whole rigmarole set up. One of the weekends that I was off, Tom came and picked me up, and we drove to Boston. We had to drive very fast because we had to get there at a certain hour. This doctor had said, "If you're not there on the dot of seven I'm leaving, and don't bother to try to make another appointment with me." We went to a hotel in Boston. This doctor came up to the room at a certain hour, examined me, and said, "Yes, you are pregnant." He explained to me that we were going to go to a residential neighborhood where there were houses very close together on both sides of the street. We were going to park in a place which would be empty—right in front of a house—he was going to go in. I was to look at my watch, or the clock in the car—and in exactly six and a half minutes, or some set time, I was to get out of the car exactly as though I lived there—again purposefully—walk right up the walk, open the door and go in.

It was somebody's home, lower class but comfortable and cozy. A woman came out of the room directly on the left and she rather brusquely said, "Come with me"—and I walked down the hall to a bathroom. There was a douche bag hanging on the closet door, which stank to me of Clorox—and she said, "I want you to douch with this and then come directly into the room." I went into the bedroom, with a double bed in it. There was a rubber sheet on it. I was asked to lie down and bring my rear end to the edge of the bed and the doctor then put this sling on me—like a belt that goes around your neck and on the outside of your legs and under your knees and back. And you can relax and this thing supports you. I was kind of interested in what he was going to do and wanted to be cooperative and congenial and somewhat sophisticated; being a nurse I would know these things—except I didn't know anything, and I really wasn't a nurse. And he brought up a pail—a great metal pail that clanked. And pulled the edge of this rubber sheet down into it. And the woman sat down on the bed to my right. Then he started scraping and I got really bad cramps, you know, it really hurt. And he said to me, "You must not move. Don't you dare move," because obviously if I moved he would slip and cut me.

It hurt me so much I started to say the Lord's Prayer out loud. And that threw him. I knew that he was thinking, "What the fuck have I got here; God damn, sitting there saying the Lord's Prayer." Anyway, I just said it over and over and, oh, the woman held my hand. I must have squeezed her fingers into nothing. She gave me strength that way.

Well, afterward, I had to walk really straight to the car and act as if nothing had happened.

Dr. White

Dr. White's medical practice has spanned more than forty years.

Early on in my practice, a friend's sister found out she was pregnant. At the time she was unmarried, in her mid-thirties, and already had two children. She became so desperate that she jumped in front of a subway train at Forty-Second Street and Broadway in an effort to commit suicide. She survived the accident with a fractured skull, fractured shoulder bones, and fractured pelvis, and spent four months in the hospital. Her child was delivered about three months later—a perfectly normal child. I thought if a woman was willing to go to that length to avoid a pregnancy she didn't want, then something really ought to be done, and I became an active advocate of abortion from that time on.

After that, when a woman came to me for help, and she was a patient I knew, I would be willing to go out on a limb. What I did was to examine her and try to initiate bleeding. This was done by gently inserting the instrument that I would normally use for taking endometrial biopsies. And then after starting a little bleeding I'd tell her to go home and call me back within twenty-four hours to let me know if the bleeding continued. If it did, which I expected that it would, I would then admit her as a threatened abortion and complete the process in a legitimate way. In reality, I was performing an illegal abortion. But it was under controlled circumstances, in a hospital with proper backup, anesthesia, and so forth.

I recall what happened to me when I was an intern. I was very much in love with a nurse, and she became pregnant. And when it happened, we looked at each other and I said, "This can't be, I'm earning twelve dollars a month." She was doing a little better—something like fifty or seventy-five a month. And we agreed that we should have an elective abortion. I was referred to a doctor whose office was on West End Avenue, and I remember to this day—that was the summer of 1940—going to West End Avenue, on the subway from Brooklyn where we both were working. We walked into this office and an older gentleman, surely in his sixties at the time, greeted us, took my nurse friend into the office. I sat in the waiting room like any other anxious partner. About an hour later, he came out and said that she would be all right, and I could take her home. I shall never forget that ride on the subway going back to Brooklyn, because of my concern that she might have been harmed in some way. She was feeling kind of beat from the ether, and she was obviously exhausted and upset by the whole experience. And that personal experience was enough to make me think women shouldn't have to carry children they don't want.

UNDERGROUND ABORTION REMEMBERED[2]

They called themselves "the service." Their home was Chicago, though they never settled in just one place. They were a women's collec-

[2]Reprint of an interview by journalist Diane Elze. *Sojourner: The Women's Forum*, 1050 Commonwealth Ave., Boston, MA 02215. 14:14+. Ap '88. This interview first appeared in *Our Paper*, Vol. 5, No. 2, December 1987. Reprinted by permission of the author.

tive, their membership averaging 20–25. Mostly white, a few black and Hispanic, from very young to very old, they were homemakers, students, mothers, hippies, and professional women. They called themselves the Jane Collective. In fact, everyone went by the name of Jane. These women performed illegal abortions during the late '60s and early '70s. Last summer, as Robert Bork's nomination to the U.S. Supreme Court putrefied before the Senate Judiciary Committee, and as I contemplated committing civil disobedience with other lesbians and gay men during the March on Washington activities, I had the opportunity to interview three former members of the Jane Collective. And as the police dragged me away on October 13, I thought of many things, among them my conversation with these three women one July evening around a kitchen table over steaming cups of tea.

In the spirit of Jane, all three women chose to use the name "Jane" for the interview.

Jane 1, 34, a former family planning counselor and now a health educator specializing in gay and lesbian health, and reproductive and sexual health, lives in coastal Maine. She started with Jane as, she says, "an unofficial member" in 1971 and stayed with the collective until it folded in 1973.

Jane 2, 38, a nurse for the last ten years, lives in midcoast Maine but grew up and lived most of her life in Chicago. With Jane the longest of the three women, Jane 2 joined the collective before the members performed the actual abortions themselves, though they controlled all other aspects of the process. Jane 2 was one of seven women arrested in the 1972 bust.

Jane 3, 40, now living in Albany, New York, has been a community organizer for, she says, "more years than I care to remember," dating back to her activist days in Chicago in 1971, the year she joined Jane.

By the time Jane folded, the collective was receiving 300 calls and performing 60–80 abortions weekly, though sometimes they'd perform as many as 100.

I wanted these women's words recorded because those of us working for gay and lesbian rights, particularly on AIDS issues, can learn much from the Jane Collective. We have not paid close enough attention to the women's health movement. We cannot afford to waste that wealth of knowledge and experience.

In the spirit of taking the law—and our lives—into our own hands . . .

Diane Elze: What was Jane, and when were you each involved?

Jane 1: It was a group—it called itself a collective—that provided women with abortions that weren't legal at the time in Illinois. It sometimes referred women to New York or California or other locations where abortions could be obtained legally, but basically the collective performed abortions and provided some counseling and education.

Jane 3: The group really evolved from being a counseling and referral service—of which there were thousands all over the country during that period of time—to a place where not only did the women in the group control the operation, but they did everything in the operation.

Jane 2: When I joined the group, women would call a tape and the tape would say, "This is Jane from Women's Liberation. Please leave your name and number, and someone will call you back."

Jane 3: The tape always said that for its entire life.

Jane 2: It would change voices sometimes. Then someone would pick up all the names from the tape and call the people back and collect a little bit of information on the woman—her name, address, age, phone number, how many weeks pregnant she was, if she had any medical problems, history of twins, history of bleeding—and we'd tell her how much it might cost.

This information was put on an index card, and these cards were distributed to counselors. When anyone entered the group, she would enter as a counselor. You'd get your little pile of cards at a meeting and you'd counsel women for abortions [in your home] either in a group or individually, as the particular counselor felt comfortable or as it seemed appropriate for the woman involved.

The woman, at the time of the counseling, would be told when she would be having her abortion, the date, and the time. She'd be given an address of where she would be going, "the front." She was encouraged to bring a friend or family member with her. She'd go to this place where there would be lots of women and their friends, male or female friends, and kids. Counselors would be there to facilitate, help people feel comfortable, and answer questions.

From this place, the woman, without her friends, would be driven to what we called "the place"—the place where the abortion occurred. At the place, there would be women from the group assisting in the abortions and being with the woman, sitting and holding her hand, making it as comfortable a situation as possible. But at that time the abortionist was a man. That was when I joined the group.

[After the abortion] the woman would be driven back to the front, given medication and instructions, and sent on her merry way. The counselor would be in touch with her afterwards.

DE: Was the male abortionist a physician?

Jane 1: No. There was a whole art of illegal abortion which I sometimes worry has been lost, though I feel it can be regained. Many different kinds of illegal abortionists were out there. We were working with some pretty sophisticated people who actually did D&C's. We learned from them.

Jane 3: But there was a period when there was either an assumption or people were told outright that this particular person was a doctor.

Jane 1: He told us he was a doctor when he first started. I don't know how he hooked up with the abortion referral group, but he did. I don't know if he heard about us and then sought us out for business, or the other way around, but we thought, at first, he was a doctor. My impression is that when people found out he wasn't a doctor, they said, "Well, the hell with it. If he can do them, we can do them."

Jane 2: At the point I entered the group, everyone knew very well he wasn't a doctor. And shortly thereafter one of the women learned how to do the abortion. It was always kind of a fluid thing—assisting the abortionist and doing the abortion. There are steps. You learn one step; then you learn the next. Before you know it, you know the whole thing.

DE: How does the group make the leap to doing abortions? Could you say more about the evolution?

Jane 2: Abortion is a simple procedure. Not that it doesn't have risks and complications and things that can go wrong, but basically it's a pretty simple procedure.

Jane 1: There are no incisions, no sharp instruments used. It's a matter of learning how to do a lot of simple things altogether.

Jane 2: A woman had the opportunity to learn and took it.

Jane 3: There was a personal relationship between one of the women in the group and this guy, and he was really torn. On the one hand, he was real into teaching it. On the other hand, he knew his little cushy gig—and it was real cushy for him—was going to be over if he did it. With cajoling, he showed her.

Jane 2: We were so happy. The first thing we did was cut prices way down. Prices dropped from $375 to $100 because we didn't have to pay him anymore. Before, all the money went to that guy except $25 per procedure to pay the phone bills, the medications. So we lowered the prices to practically nothing. In fact, women paid nothing if they couldn't afford it. We got an average of $40 per person.

Jane 3: No one got paid in the group at that point.

Jane 2: And right away things lifted. No more blindfolds.

Jane 1: No more man.

DE: At that time in your lives, why did you get involved in Jane?

Jane 1: I heard about the group from a friend who was in it. I wasn't sure what she was doing. I thought she was doing abortion referrals. I came back to Chicago after a brief stay in New York and didn't really have anything else to do. This friend was calling the out-of-towners who didn't get counseling beforehand. They got their counseling at the front. She had to call those women and tell them where to go. Sometimes she needed help calling, so she'd ask me, and she'd split her fee with me. I needed some money. That's why I said I wasn't an official member right away. I actually started doing counseling first, and I didn't go to meetings.

For me, it was something to do. I was ready to do something interesting. Because of being friends with her, I met all these other interesting women who were doing this work and it became a social focus for me. I was only 18 at the time. I had dropped out of college. Once I started doing it, though, I never thought about not doing it. It was very satisfying. I probably always had a bent towards medical activity and technical skills, and that was another way to do it.

Jane 2: I had a legal abortion in California—what they called a therapeutic abortion. I had to see two psychiatrists who would say I wasn't fit to become a mother, essentially, and a gynecologist who would say the same thing and agree to do the procedure. All three had to submit letters to a hospital board which would then approve my having the abortion.

For the abortion, I was in a semiprivate room on the psychiatric ward of the hospital. I had the abortion under general anesthesia. I had all my pubic hair shaved off. It was really a terrible experience.

I lived in California for about a year. When I returned to Chicago, I lived on the South Side, and I went to a talk about abortion. Different people gave presentations, all in very general terms, but it made me reflect back on the abortion I had had and I decided I wanted to do something. I had never been involved in the women's movement or thought about it very much. I came across information about Jane. I called the tape and left a message saying that I wanted to do counseling. I was contacted. I sounded like a sincere person, not like a cop.

I wanted to emphasize that I got a lot of training to do counseling. Then I had a buddy counselor. I immediately felt very close to the other women in the group. This was really important to me as far as my personal growth and moving into being real involved in the women's movement. I feel it really was just so pivotal in my life.

Jane 3: When you say, Jane 2, that you hadn't been involved in the women's movement before Jane, there was no women's movement before. The present part of the women's movement that we know really didn't start until 1970.

Jane 2: Well then, I guess I was on the cutting edge . . .

Jane 3: You are one of the mothers! We have to take credit for this stuff.

My very good friend got pregnant with no money and went to the local free clinic and they said, "Call 643-3844 and they can help you." And she did. And she had an abortion at the time when the man was still being used. She was blindfolded, but she had a wonderful experience. In fact, Jane 1 remembers her from that day. She was my only friend from college days, and we're still very close. She took me to meet her counselor, and I voiced interest. I went to the next training session.

I moved to Chicago in the fall of 1971. I had gotten my consciousness raised in late 1969 to 1970. That was a very different time. There was a lot going on, a lot of new information, new ways of looking at the world that most of us had never thought about before. I remember feeling like I had my eyes open for the first time, that I had never seen the world before.

I really wanted to get involved in women's health. I had a chronic health problem and had gotten very fucked over by health practitioners in New York City, one after another. And I knew I wanted to do political work, women's health work. I came from New York where abortions were legal. It was no big thing. Abortion wasn't the first thing on my mind.

But I moved to Chicago and my friend had her abortion and I hooked into the abortion service. It was very weird at first: here are these women doing this outrageous thing and they're all real sweet and real nice; I was very used to New York aggressive, strong, assertive women, and it was real confusing to me. How could anybody so sweet do anything so gutsy?! Some had kids and husbands and everybody had long hair.

Jane 2 was my buddy, my big sister who trained me. I remember taking copious notes at all the counselor-training sessions. I wrote down everything that was said, and I practiced.

Jane 2: People were entrusting us with their lives. We felt we'd better give them some good information. They were in totally desperate situations. They couldn't hop a plane and go to New York. They were doing everything they could to scrape together the money they had. They were desperate not to be pregnant.

DE: Who were the women in Jane?

Jane 1: I was younger than most of the people in the group, and I was attracted to all these people who seemed to be more mature and experienced in life than I was. Unlike Jane 2 and Jane 3, I had actually been a feminist in high school. I remember very clearly when *The Feminine Mystique* came out, and I remember shoplifting it from the local dime store, but to this day I have not read the book.

Quite a few women in Jane were housewives and mothers. There were also quite a few college students, especially from around the University of Chicago because the core group, as I recall, was on the South Side in Hyde Park. There were many women in the group I never knew very well. There were some professional women, some women in social services, some women like me who were kind of like hippies, actually—we were a little different. We didn't have the same financial or family commitments or professional commitments that a lot of the other women had, and we were a little younger.

DE: What was the age range and racial composition of the group?

Jane 1: It was almost all white. Occasionally there was a black woman in the group. It was a real difficult issue if you were the only black counselor in a group of 30 white women.

Jane 2: I think there were more black counselors towards the end, and some Hispanic women. The women were in their twenties, thirties, some in their forties, fifties. One woman was in her sixties.

Jane 3: The real age concentration was early to mid-twenties to around thirty.

DE: What was the structure of the group?

Jane 3: Every ten days we got together—we all groaned about having to get together every ten days—but now, when I think about it, every ten days wasn't very much for a group doing illegal abortions.

Jane 2: All we dealt with were work issues. We did not talk politics.

Jane 3: This was not the kind of group where everybody obsessed about decisions.

Jane 1: We didn't even talk about group dynamics.

Jane 2: We didn't talk about how somebody feels about this or that. We passed around cards with the names of the women who needed abortions over and over again until all of them were gone. We'd fill up pill boxes with tetracycline, figure out where the next front would be, deal with concrete problems.

Jane 1: Other work assignments, too. Who's working the front? Who's a driver? Who's assisting? Whose car are we going to borrow? Does anyone know an apartment we can use?

Jane 3: A lot of the problems with the group didn't get handled up front. In some ways, that was really good. We didn't have the luxury of a lot of time to obsess or hassle about things at meetings. But it left people feeling like decisions were being made that they weren't really a part of; yet, we were all equally responsible in some ways. That was a tricky dynamic. But none of us really wanted to go to meetings. A lot of things got discussed when small groups got together or at the workplaces afterwards.

Jane 2: Nobody talked about taking care of themselves. There was no room for that. You went to a meeting once every ten days. You did counseling groups in your home two or three nights a week. And then you worked at places and fronts for two days a week.

Jane 1: And your phone rang any time of the day or night.

Jane 3: And you answered it, no matter what you were doing. What if it was somebody hemorrhaging and you were too busy doing something more fun?

A lot of us left for periods, from a couple of weeks to a month, to go someplace to get away. Even though we were so strong in what we were doing, the stress level was exceptionally high.

DE: How did being a part of Jane change your perception of women and your feeling about yourselves as women at that time?

Jane 2: I felt myself become a stronger, more powerful person. I never had a vision of myself doing things that would affect people's lives, doing life and death kinds of things. And I ended up in that situation not because I thought it all out ahead of time, but because there was a need. You had to do it. These things just had to be done because who else was going to do it? You just rose to the occasion. We were ordinary women who did what had to be done.

Jane 3: And I think the times were extraordinary.

Jane 2: Yes. There was such a feeling of optimism. I felt the world was never going to be the same. I felt the world was changing so much.

Jane 3: And it gave us the right to be more extraordinary in our actions and activism. One of the thrills was that I watched my friends change and get stronger and more assertive. Necessity is a mother.

We saw this as something that had to be done. We were not the group that was going to beat on the doors of the state capitol and say, "Please, boys, won't you do this for us?" We never thought that was a stupid thing to do. It would have been a stupid thing for *us* to do. It wasn't our style. We would do what had to be done because the situation demanded it.

The timing was right. The times called extraordinary strengths out of us and changed us all. But we weren't by any means superwomen. We were lucky because we got a chance to put our politics into practice. The late 1960s and early 1970s were a river of action. I think all of us were exceptionally lucky that we got to be involved and participate in that action.

ABORTION IN THE UNITED STATES:
POLITICS OR POLICY?[3]

Single-issue politics is a relatively recent phenomenon in the United States. Its terrible consequence is that we trade policy for politics. The best example I know of to illustrate the worst aspects of single-issue politics is that of abortion in America. Therefore, I wish to focus on the policy issue of abortion—that part of the equation that seems to be almost completely unnoticed by the present Administration.

Many of the key policy-makers in Washington act as if we were still in the early twentieth century, rather than approaching its end. In my own lifetime the world population has increased from 1.9 to 4.7 billion and will reach 8.0 billion by my hundredth birthday. Control of human fertility is an indispensable, though not the only, approach to ameliorating the consequences of the population explosion which, by the end of the twentieth century, will have resulted in a tripling in the number of inhabitants. If this sounds serious, consider the fact that the population of the poorest continent, Africa, will triple—not over a century, but in only 35 years.

For most women who have abortions it is a choice of last resort. But whether we like it or not, of the various means of birth control, abortion is, worldwide, one of the most frequently practiced methods; approximately 50 million are performed each year. Only the contraceptive pill and sterilization are more widely used. Except in China, most abortions are the result of individual decisions by women, rather than by governments. Virtually all current abortions in the United States are performed under legal sanction, in contrast to the situation up to the late 1960s, when most such procedures were illegal.

The legal status of abortion is relevant to my argument. Thirty-nine percent of the world's people live in countries where

[3]Expanded version of a speech before the Commonwealth Club of California, August 1985, by Carl Djerassi, professor of chemistry at Stanford University and contributor to the synthesis of the first oral contraceptive. *The Bulletin of the Atomic Scientists*. 42:38–41. Ap '86. Reprinted by permission of *The Bulletin of the Atomic Scientists*. Copyright © 1986 by the Educational Foundation for Nuclear Science, 6042 S. Kimbark Ave., Chicago, IL 60637, USA.

there are virtually no restrictions on first-trimester abortions. These range from the United States and the Netherlands, to Catholic countries like Italy and France, Muslim countries like Tunisia, and officially atheist countries like China and the Soviet Union. In another 25 percent of the world—in nations as diverse as India, Great Britain, Japan, and most East European countries—permission for abortion is granted almost as liberally, since social factors such as inadequate income and unmarried status are taken into consideration. Among another 10 percent of the world's population, broader medical grounds—fetal damage, rape, and incest—are accepted as reasons for abortion.

Therefore, only a quarter of the world's population lives in countries where abortion is still either totally illegal or permitted only to save the life of a pregnant woman. These include most of the Muslim nations in Asia, the majority of Africa, four West European countries (Ireland, Spain, Portugal, and Belgium), and two-thirds of Latin American countries. It is in these Latin American states that the largest number of illegal abortions (and deaths associated with them) occur.

Pressure in Washington and elsewhere in the United States is building up to change the legal status of abortion. But before taking this step we ought to consider carefully the experience of other countries. Two examples should suffice.

Ireland, by world standards, is an affluent country inhabited by educated people, yet until 1984 even the importation of condoms was illegal. Abortion, of course, is also illegal, and the attitude of the Irish government is that it is simply not a problem. In apparent support of this assumption, one can point to the absence of any hard evidence for noticeable rates of illegal abortion in Ireland. Thus President Reagan might point to that nation as an example that the United States should emulate: make abortion illegal and it will disappear.

But if he really examined the Irish case, the president would be in for a shock. Consider the number of legal abortions performed in neighboring Great Britain on nonresidents of that country. In 1969, shortly after abortion was made legal in Britain, 100 Irish women sought abortions there. This number increased every year until 1981 (the last year for which I have been able to secure statistics), when 3,600 Irish women had legal abortions in Great Britain. To convert this figure into its U.S. equivalent we need to multiply by 70, since there are 70 times as many people in the United States as in Ireland. We then arrive at the staggering conclusion that all-Catholic Ireland has an abortion rate comparable to over 250,000 abortions per year among American women. Clearly, Ireland has an abortion problem, even though the procedure is, and always has been, illegal. Incidentally, during the same period the number of Spanish women who made the long journey to Great Britain for abortions rose from 100 annually to the present level of 20,500 annually.

In Ireland and Spain abortion has always been illegal, and the problem is simply ignored. What about a country where abortion was legal (as it is now in the United States), but where almost overnight it was declared illegal—a country which accomplished what our present Administration would like to achieve? The time was 1965, the country Romania, and abortion was legal and virtually free. As in many other East European countries following a pronatalist policy with concomitant poor contraception, abortion became the main vehicle for fertility control. The Romanian government was not so much concerned about the number of abortions as it was about its falling birth rate at a time of relatively rapid economic growth.

Overnight, the government instituted a very restrictive abortion law, with the result, unprecedented anywhere in the world, that Romania's birth rate skyrocketed in one year from 13 to 34 per 1,000. One can almost see the men in Bucharest—and I am using the word "men" with full gender implications—congratulating themselves on the spectacular success of their anti-abortion policy.

Admittedly, this was policy, not politics, but the results were an almost unmitigated disaster. By 1968, the birth rate underwent an equally dramatic drop—from 34 back to 19 per 1,000! Because there was no evidence that the quality or prevalence of contraceptive services had improved, we must conclude that it simply took a couple of years for the abortion system to move underground.

What the men in Bucharest did not take into consideration, but could have been easily predicted, was the increase in deaths associated with illegal abortions. By the time 10 years had passed, this death rate had increased by a factor of 10: but the birth rate has not changed since 1972. Washington can, and should, learn from Bucharest.

The current U.S. birth rate is not the issue. But this bland, factual statement hides some shocking realities which are unique to this country:

• A teenage pregnancy occurs every 30 seconds in the United States.

• Of the total number of abortions—about 1.3 to 1.5 million per year—nearly a third are performed on teenagers, and another third on women between the ages of 20 and 24.

• Over 70 percent of U.S. abortions are sought by unmarried women. By contrast, over 90 percent of abortions in India, China, or Japan, and over 70 percent in East European socialist countries, such as Hungary or Czechoslovakia, occur among married women.

Suppose that the anti-abortionists' wishes are realized and, following the Romanian example, abortions are declared illegal overnight. Will this stop abortions? According to a recent *Newsweek* poll, 88 percent of Americans believe that it will not.

President Reagan disagrees. During the 1984 presidential campaign, he said: "There are a million and a half people out there . . . waiting to adopt children they can't have any other way." The source of this seemingly authoritative statement is the born-again anti-abortionist Bernard Nathanson, star of *The Silent Scream*, a film which the president recommended to every member of Congress. Among numerous unsupported or discredited claims, Nathanson states in his book, *The Abortion Papers*, that before 1967 there were annually only 98,000 illegal abortions in America, compared to the present figure of 1.3 to 1.5 million legal ones. He concluded that "it is inescapable that 1.4 million of those women would probably have opted to have their children in a less permissive era, and 1.4 million children would have been spared."

How many illegal abortions per year were there really before 1967? Nobody knows precisely. Published estimates range from 200,000 to as high as two million. The best guess is approximately one million until the early 1960s. By 1967, it may have dropped to half this number, due to improved contraception. Nathanson's estimate of 98,000, however, is based on the totally discredited figures of one Thomas H. Hilger, who has become the laughingstock of statisticians in this field.

Hilger's illegal abortion estimates are based on grossly exaggerated maternal mortality figures which one critic, Willard

Cates, equated to stating that a woman jumping off a 40-story building is at very little risk of dying by the time she passes the twentieth floor. Nevertheless, this is where President Reagan found his 1.5 million extra babies each year—assuming abortion again became illegal—and why he assumed that an equal number of adoptive parents would be waiting in line. Let me debunk this statement before it also becomes part of U.S. dogma, and let me do it through official California statistics.

Briefly, they show that in California, in the early 1980s, approximately 2,500 approved adoptive parents were waiting for children, and that approximately 500 obtained such children in any three-month period. Therefore, during an entire year, approximately 2,000 children were adopted through public and private agencies, and an additional, though smaller, number through other channels. In each three-month period, there were approximately 66,000 abortions. Two-thirds of them were performed on women below age 24, a group which also constitutes 72 percent of all mothers who offer their children for adoption. Women above age 24 are responsible for the remaining one-third of abortions, but only for 28 percent of the children who are put up for adoption.

Now let us accept Reagan's assumption that, once abortion becomes illegal again, all 66,000 women would choose to carry their pregnancies to term. Let us also assume that the same percentage of mothers would offer their babies for adoption as is the case now. California would end up with a minimum of 37,300 baby adoption candidates every three months! But remember that at present, there are only 2,500 prospective parents who actually qualify. This number might double or even triple, but how could it suddenly multiply by a factor of 15, and continue to do so annually thereafter? Where is that line of prospective parents who would adopt 37,300 children—77 percent of whom are classified as "hard-to-place," that is, not white, young, and healthy—every three months?

Will a return to hundreds of thousands of illegal abortions increase maternal death rates? Of course, but probably not as much as many people fear; certainly not as much as it did in Romania in the 1960s or 1970s. Why? Because the criminal community will be prepared to bridge the gap.

Having had safe abortions for well over a decade, it is unlikely that American women will return to the bent-coat-hanger days if abortion should become illegal. Well over a million women will initially look for illegal but relatively safe abortions; and these will be offered, but for a price. That underground price will make illegal abortions a most attractive target, and I am convinced that much of it will then be taken over by organized crime. Surely the lesson from prohibition days should not be lost, nor that of the present drug abuse problem. Unless we address ourselves to the underlying causes of such problems, declaring them illegal is almost pointless, even though we may feel virtuous in doing so.

Abortion, however, should not be equated with alcohol and drug abuse problems. Drug laws are designed to protect the users, but no anti-abortion law has ever been introduced anywhere for the protection of women. On occasion, as was the case in 1965 in Romania, it is done for blatant demographic reasons. In most countries, including the United States, these laws were used to enforce a standard of sexual morality. And again today, the underlying objection to abortion reflects certain attitudes toward sex. But if a segment of the society wishes to make a case against premarital or extramarital sex, it should not do so by punishing the woman, and frequently the baby. Remember that it takes two to conceive a child.

The pointlessness of seeking legal palliatives is best seen by looking at the terribly high teenage abortion rate in the United States—higher than anywhere else in the world. The pious will cite Sodom and Gomorrah; to them, it bespeaks lax sexual standards, greatly increased sexual activity at an increasingly early age, the breakdown of the American family. But making abortion illegal will hardly bring American families together again. And the argument about teenage sex is at least partly a specious one. A recent study of teenage sexual conduct and abortion in the United States, as compared with other affluent countries such as Sweden, Holland, and France, shows that their teenage abortion rates are just a fraction of our own. Holland's, for instance, is almost one-tenth of ours. Yet by age 17, just about as high a proportion of Dutch or French girls have become sexually active as have American ones. In Sweden, every age group shows a considerably higher percentage of sexually experienced females than pertains in the United States, but the Swedish abortion rate is less than half of ours.

Why does a woman get an abortion? For few is this a matter of first choice. For most the unwanted pregnancy is the outcome of unavailable contraceptives or inadequate contraception. Our long-term objective clearly ought to be that every pregnancy be a deliberate one, every born child a wanted one.

How can we approach the ideal of wanted births and intelligent birth control? In the medium term, through the beginning of the twenty-first century, we have only two choices:

• First and foremost is improved education—about human sexuality, with education about birth control as a logical appendix. Such education must start early, and given the fact that parents are doing such an abysmal job (no more than 20 percent of American youngsters learn about sex and birth control from their parents, and among Asians it is even less), the schools are the obvious location. Yet because American schools are decentralized, curricula are often left to the decision of individual administrators, and are sometimes subject to vetoes by a few vociferous parents. This situation could and must be reversed. The Reagan Administration, together with a group of senators from both parties, however, is going in precisely the opposite direction by reducing and even eliminating funds for this purpose.

• Better utilization of existing, effective birth control devices is needed because we cannot realistically expect any major advances in birth control methods for the balance of this century, at least not in terms of something new and usable by millions of people.

In many states, condom dispensers are illegal. The contraceptive sponge, a recent development which has been approved for over-the-counter sales and has been advertised in newspapers and family magazines, cannot be sold in dispensers in California. But I would argue that such dispensers should be in all high schools and that the price should be very low. The easy and private availability of safe contraceptives would be a great societal and economic bargain, but I am fully aware that American parent-teacher associations would never stand for such a suggestion. Hundreds of thousands of abortions a year among teenagers—two teenage pregnancies every minute—are tolerated; subsidized, or even nonsubsidized, over-the-counter contraceptives in high schools are not.

Technologically, Americans are the first to push into the twenty-first century. In terms of sexual morality, however, we are pretending that we still live in the days of the puritans. Last July 31, CBS and ABC refused to air a two-minute public service announcement prepared and paid for by the American College of Obstetricians and Gynecologists. The announcement was to discuss briefly various contraceptive options and to announce a toll-free number that teenagers could call to obtain a free pamphlet on birth control. CBS stated that "contraception is an unacceptable subject for public service announcements." Yet the network has no difficulty rationalizing a daily TV fare for teenagers replete with brutality, killing, and overt sexual behavior.

What about a long-term policy, or a policy that will at least respond to the deficiencies—both at home and in the schools—of American education in dealing with sexuality and birth control? Everybody's answer would be to develop better and more acceptable methods of birth control than we currently have. But what kind?

I believe that such research should focus primarily on postcoital contraception. The pill, condoms, intrauterine devices, diaphragms, and sponges are all precoital methods. If they were used consistently, abortion would rarely be necessary. But what if a contraceptive is not used, did not work, or was not available? For those who believe that life starts at conception, and that any interference with a fertilized egg—even one minute after fertilization—is immoral, there is no answer other than to bear the inevitable consequences. But for the tens and hundreds of millions of women in this world—the silent but overwhelming majority—there could be other options.

With respect to postcoital contraception, I am not referring to the "morning-after pill." Rather, I am referring to a pill that a woman would take once a month—and only in those months when she has had unprotected intercourse and when she expects a normal period. The agent would be a menses-inducer, and the woman would not know, as no woman knows now, whether her menstrual flow included a recently fertilized or unfertilized egg.

I do not suggest that this be the only form of birth control, or even that it is the ideal one, because no single method can be ideal for all people. But in my opinion, no other *new* birth control method will have as great an effect in reducing abortions as such a postcoital, once-a-month pill.

What's wrong with it? For one thing the present policy in Washington, subscribed to by the majority of anti-abortionists, is that no research dealing with postcoital birth control should be supported. No wonder that, with a few exceptions, the bulk of such research is now conducted in Europe.

The second problem is that even under ideal conditions, such a new agent, whether developed by a European or an American pharmaceutical firm, is not likely to be available in this country before the turn of the century.

So far, I have dealt only with the legal and geopolitical implications of abortion, its present inevitability, the difficulties in reaching the day when it will be largely unnecessary. But what about the morality of the issue? It is not that I consider it unimportant—on the contrary. Whenever we think about sex and procreation, moral issues are central. But whose morality?

The anti-abortionists like to call themselves pro-lifers. Their view is that abortion is clearly immoral because it is pure and simple killing. But is it that simple? The vast majority of anti-abortionists make exceptions in cases of incest or rape. But if an abortion is an act of killing, how does the criminal act of rape justify "killing" the fetus? Possibly, the answer is that the anti-abortionists consider a raped woman innocent and hence eligible for an abortion, while a woman who indulges in voluntary intercourse is judged guilty, and hence doomed to an unwanted pregnancy.

Take the issue of killing in general: One of the most common moral edicts is "thou shalt not kill." But even priests, ministers, rabbis, and ayatollahs find ways of justifying some killing—most commonly in wars. Of all wars, religiously justified ones are usually the most murderous. In the end, morality is a totally private matter, and the morality of abortion is an issue that is hardly ever clear-cut.

There are those who side with Senator Jesse Helms in his goal to write into law that life begins at conception. I grant every person who believes this the right to do so, but only as long as they grant me the right to believe that this is not so. Reformed abortionists, like Dr. Bernard Nathanson, refer to a 12-week-old fetus as a "child." But I have not heard him call a one-month-old embryo a child, and he is even less likely to call a two-week-old fertilized egg a child. To paraphrase the ecologist Garett Hardin: If an embryo or fetus is a human being, then an acorn is an oak tree, and an egg a chicken. Scrambling an egg is then gallicide, and crushing acorns, deforestation.

In the thirteenth century, Dante, in *The Divine Comedy*, suggested that life only starts when the brain is sufficiently developed to accept a soul. But even Dante could not tell the precise moment when life begins; nor can Senator Helms, President Reagan, the Pope, you, or I. The immorality of the issue arises when one person decides, on her or his own authority, what all of us should think.

To me the question is not whether abortion is moral or immoral. To make abortion illegal, without considering the consequences of declaring it so, is not an act of morality; it is an act of irresponsibility or cruelty. It is politics at its worst. We need a national policy—not single-issue politics—on which all of us could agree. My proposal for such a policy can be enunciated in three words: Make abortion unnecessary.

ABORTIONS WITHOUT DOCTORS[4]

The Supreme Court decision to throw the abortion issue back to the states has thrown pro-choice supporters into turmoil. If, as many fear, abortion becomes tightly restricted or banned, what are women to do about unwanted pregnancies? Some feminists are proposing a radical remedy: women should master abortion techniques and perform the procedure for one another.

That idea is being widely discussed by women's groups and has already drawn sharp criticism not only from right-to-lifers but from medical authorities and some pro-choice supporters. Promoters of self-help abortions are looking at several methods, including RU 486, the controversial French pill not yet available in the U.S. But most of the attention is focusing on menstrual extraction, a technique that can be used to end a pregnancy through the eighth week. At a recent meeting in Dallas, sponsored by the

[4]Reprint of an article by *Time* associate editor Anastasia Toufexis. *Time*. 134:66. Ag 28 '89. Copyright © 1989 The Time Inc. Magazine Company. Reprinted by permission.

local unit of the National Organization for Women, more than 100 women saw a 30-minute videotape that showed how the procedure is performed with a $90 kit containing a glass jar, plastic tubing and a special syringe. "We're being realistic," says Charlotte Taft, an abortion-clinic director who spoke at the meeting. "When abortion becomes illegal, not many physicians will risk losing their licenses. If I have a choice between going to a group of caring women I trust or a stranger, then I'll take the women."

Advocates think the lessons will keep women from seeking back-alley butchers or resorting to the horrifying home measures, such as inserting coat hangers and douching with Lysol or Coca-Cola, that were common before *Roe v. Wade* made abortion legal nationwide in 1973. NOW's national headquarters in Washington takes no position on self-help abortions but has not discouraged its local affiliates.

First championed by women's groups in the early 1970s, when abortion was illegal in most states, menstrual extraction is a variation of the vacuum aspirations used in medical clinics. A thin plastic tube is first inserted through the cervix into the uterus. Then the uterine lining, along with an embedded fertilized egg, is suctioned out by pumping a syringe attached to the tubing. Proponents of the procedure insist that it is safe.

But medical experts are skeptical. Warns Dr. E. Hakim Elahi, medical director of Planned Parenthood: "It's a wrong notion that abortion is very easy." He and others fear that cursory instruction will lead to medical complications. "There's no way that watching a video and seeing someone demonstrate this is going to make self-help procedures safe," declares gynecologist Michael Burnhill of the Robert Wood Johnson Medical School in New Brunswick, N.J. Possible dangers: missing the tiny fertilized egg, lacerating the cervix, perforating the uterus, and spreading bacterial infection.

Many feminists call the effort politically misguided. They argue that it gives the wrong impression that abortion is already illegal and unobtainable. They are also concerned that it diverts attention from their battle to keep abortion legal. Whether that battle is won or lost, the pursuit of self-help abortions makes one thing clear, warns Patricia Ireland of NOW: "The demand for abortion will continue and will be met one way or another."

IV. ETHICAL DEBATES

EDITOR'S INTRODUCTION

Each side of the abortion issue claims that its position is morally superior to the other's; yet neither one can be sustained without trivializing, to some extent, the suffering and the humanity of either the mother or the developing baby. Antiabortion advocates tend either to dismiss or to ridicule the pregnant woman's dilemma (as Neuhaus does, in Section II of this book, when he speaks of "the perils of pregnant Pauline"), or to ennoble the idea of maternal self-sacrifice. Many proabortion advocates define the developing baby in the embryonic stage as a kind of vermin that can properly be exterminated, at later stages as a subhuman entity whose unique identity and consciousness of pain need not be seriously considered. The first article in this section, "The Hardest Question," by Kenneth L. Woodward with Mark D. Uehling, considers some of the ramifications of these views and the cultural and philosophical assumptions they mirror.

The next two selections, "Should Medicine Use the Unborn?" by Matt Clark with Mariana Gosnell, Mary Hager, and other *Newsweek* staff writers, and John Leo's "Baby Boys, to Order," take up two of the most disturbing consequences of abortion: the "harvesting" of tissue from the partially formed bodies of aborted fetuses to use in medical research and treatment, and the selective elimination of children because of their gender. An expert panel convened by the National Institutes of Health voted in 1988 to recommend that the federal government lift a ban on the use of fetal tissue in medical research, but the Bush Administration sided with the panel's dissenters and retained it. The extent of abortion for purposes of gender selection in the United States is not known, but the practice is perfectly legal. It is commonly used in India and Asia to eliminate girls, with the result that India, for example, now has 23 million more males than females. As Leo points out, gender selection poses a dilemma for feminists, because in this case women as a group suffer as a result of abortion decisions made by individual women.

The ethics of abortion have been a much-discussed subject among religious groups, and though most members of the antiabortion movement are motivated by religious concerns, many equally religious people are active in the proabortion movement. Even the Catholic Church, a stronghold of consistent opposition to abortion, counts among its adherents a number of organized dissenters who call themselves Catholics for a Free Choice. Christine Dubois compares the positions of various religious bodies in "What Different Christian Churches Believe about Abortion." Her article is followed by Jason DeParle's "Beyond the Legal Right," subtitled "Why liberals and feminists don't like to talk about the morality of abortion." DeParle, himself a liberal with an obvious sympathy for feminist goals in general, wrestles with the moral dilemmas of unwanted pregnancy with a directness rarely exhibited by people who follow the "party line" on either side of the issue.

THE HARDEST QUESTION[1]

For all the years that have passed since *Roe v. Wade*, the problem of abortion—at once moral and medical, personal and social, political and religious—is no nearer a solution. And while technology has brought a terrifying reality to the procedure—through sonography, a mother can now see the image of the fetus she may choose to abort—it has nonetheless become an American routine. Three abortions are performed every minute. Some concerned thinkers in both the pro-life and pro-choice camps believe that there are too many abortions, and too little attention paid to finding ways to care for the victims of the process, both born and unborn. "There's more agreement than most activists imagine," report philosopher Daniel Callahan and his wife, Sidney, a psychologist, who hold divergent but not incompatible views themselves. Yet in the world outside the seminar room, society seems to be drifting toward a brave new world where the techniques of control over life are developing much faster than the wisdom to guide them.

Moral analysis of abortion generally follows one of three lines. Pro-life morality, as enunciated by advocates such as New York Archbishop John J. O'Connor, tends to subordinate all other considerations to the fetus's right to life. The direct taking of innocent life is always evil, in this view. The fetus is innocent life, hence abortion is always a wrong—even, in its strictest version, when a mother's life is at risk in childbirth.

Balancing Rights

The second and opposite argument, often explicitly feminist, holds that the mother's rights are prior to all other considerations. In this view, a woman's freedom rests finally on her control of her own reproductive processes. Since she alone loses independence by giving birth, she alone has the right to decide to abort. The third position belongs to all those who weigh each case and try to balance the relative rights of mother and fetus.

The gap between the two absolutist camps extends to the language they use. Most arguments about abortion turn on the status of the fetus. If, as some extreme pro-choicers insist, a fetus is merely a collection of cells, or tissue, or a "conceptus"—language that in itself denies any humanity to fetal life—then abortion is a morally neutral surgical procedure. If, on the other hand, it is "a baby," then abortion is a form of killing—though not necessarily the crime of murder pro-life extremists claim it to be. In most serious debates, however, it is taken as a biological fact that a fetus is alive, human and unique—a developing human being. "If anyone seriously doubts that," says Jesuit moralist Richard McCormick of the Kennedy Institute of Ethics at Georgetown University, "they need only wait 266 days to see what they get."

It is one thing for the born to recognize the unborn as human, however, and quite another for society to vest them with moral or legal rights as persons. "I don't think abortion is ever wrong," argues psychiatrist and anthropologist Virginia Abernethy of Vanderbilt University's School of Medicine. "As long as an individual is completely dependent upon the mother, it's not a person." In this view, which is shared by other pro-choice theorists, an individual becomes a person only when he or she becomes a responsible moral agent—around age three or four, in Abernethy's judgment. Until then, she thinks, infants—like fetuses—are nonpersons; defective children, such as those with

Down's syndrome, may never become persons. The claim they have on persons, she says, is compassion, not a moral right to life: "Compassion is always very important, but [it] loses when weighed against the rights of a person."

Lurking not far below the surface of this analysis is a leap from abortion to euthanasia for severely handicapped newborns—in short, infanticide. "I got into the abortion debate two years ago after listening to doctors tell me that perhaps parents ought to have a 30-day period—a sort of one-month guarantee—in which to see whether their newborn babies have any disabling defects," says civil-libertarian writer Nat Hentoff. "I know of women who have had abortions because their fetuses were the wrong gender. If fetuses have no rights, handicapped infants have no rights, can the aged and infirm be far behind?"

To be sure, most pro-choice partisans are interested only in preserving a woman's legal right to medically safe abortions. But by framing the abortion issue solely in terms of personal rights, pro-choice ideologues have absolutized the principle of freedom at the expense of the principle of obligation and the reality of human interdependence. "The argument that abortion is a right necessary to the control over one's self," argues Jean Bethke Elshtain, professor of political science at the University of Massachusetts at Amherst and herself a feminist, "is based on a social-contract model of society which presupposes that only independent, rational adults have rights, or needs to be met. Such a society is nothing more than a network of freely negotiated contracts between isolated Robinson Crusoes, a marketplace where we choose what we want, goaded by consumerism." In such a society, she says, "we enter parenthood with a shopping list of qualities we want in a child. So infanticide becomes both possible and permissible. But this model leaves out the bonds of caring and dependency you get in traditional family life. And it ignores the human life cycle, which all of us enter as dependents and most of us leave in the same condition."

Roles Threatened

Indeed, there is a growing body of literature amply demonstrating that a woman's attitude toward abortion has less to do with morality than with one's position in the marketplace society that Elshtain describes. In a recent study of pro-choice and prolife activists in California, sociologist Kristin Luker found that the former tended to be highly educated, well-paid careerists with few children, almost no ties to formal religion and a strong vested interest in their work roles. The pro-lifers, by contrast, tended to be practicing Roman Catholics with large families and low-paying or no outside jobs, whose self-esteem derived from their maternal roles. For the first group, loss of the right to abortion would threaten their place in the world of work, hence their self-identities. For the second, the very notion of abortion called the value of their self-defining role into question. For the first, motherhood is an option and children a project. For the second, motherhood is a calling and children a gift.

In short, abortion remains an intractable issue because it is not just a conflict between ethical theories or choices. It is primarily a clash between radically different understandings of the self and of the world, shaped by divergent social and economic expectations. Abortion will remain an answer to problems so long as society itself refuses to supply its victims—born and unborn—with realistic alternatives.

SHOULD MEDICINE USE THE UNBORN?[2]

No one thinks twice these days about whether it's proper to transplant hearts, kidneys, livers and other organs "harvested" from the recently deceased. But there is another source of human tissue, little used so far but already explosively controversial— human fetuses. Researchers hope that by implanting certain tissues of dead fetuses, which have been removed from the womb during abortions, they could dramatically improve the treatment of a score or more intractable afflictions, ranging from Parkinson's disease and diabetes to sickle-cell anemia, some forms of cancer and even stroke. Dr. Abraham Lieberman of New York University Medical Center says of brain transplants using fetal tissue, "This is to medicine what superconductivity is to physics."

[2]Reprint of an article by Matt Clark with Mariana Gosnell, Mary Hager, and other Newsweek staff writers. From Newsweek, S 14 '87. Copyright © 1987, Newsweek, Inc. All rights reserved. Reprinted by permission.

But physicists don't face the ethical problem that medical researchers do. Right-to-lifers paint a Brave New World scenario of embryos fertilized and growing on racks like hothouse plants in commercial laboratories. They raise the specter of white-suited entrepreneurs recruiting indigent Third World women to become pregnant so their fetuses can be sold to the highest bidder. National Right to Life Committee president Dr. John Willke worries that fetuses already are being shipped to laboratories in somewhat the same way stray dogs and cats have been rounded up for research. "We are now destroying tiny lives and using their tissues," he says.

His views are being voiced with greater urgency because of recent experiments in treating Parkinson's disease, a neurological disorder that afflicts at least 1 million Americans. Surgeons in Sweden, Mexico and the United States have been removing adrenal glands from Parkinson's victims, then implanting adrenal cells onto the brain's basal ganglia. The hope is that the implants will secrete dopamine, a chemical these patients lack and which is needed to control tremors and permit normal body movement. It's too early to say yet how well the adrenal transplants will work, if they will, but some experts think fetal transplants would work better, for two important reasons. For one thing, they would spare the patient the abdominal operation required to remove the adrenal tissue. For another, fetal cells, in theory at least, would be more likely to make new nerve connections.

This possibility has created a surge of interest in fetal-tissue implantation, and research both here and abroad is beginning to offer an exciting glimpse at treatments that could lie ahead. An estimated 20 percent of the U.S. population suffers from neurological problems—from strokes to Alzheimer's to epilepsy and Huntington's disease—and researchers are optimistic that fetal tissue could repair some of the defects. Dr. George S. Allen at Nashville's Vanderbilt University, one of the surgeons doing adrenal operations on Parkinson's patients, is conducting animal experiments to see if fetal tissue could be useful in treating Huntington's disease; so far the results have been encouraging. At the University of California, San Diego, Dr. Fred Gage has implanted fetal cells that generate the chemical acetylcholine into the brains of aging rats; the rats' memory and learning improved significantly, which suggests that something similar might be useful in treating Alzheimer's, a disease that afflicts up to 3 million Americans. In other animal work, neurobiologist Raymond Lund of the University of Pittsburgh has shown that fetal brain cells can establish new connections in the optical system, raising the possibility that implants could someday restore sight in the blind.

Nuclear disaster: A few doctors have already begun using fetal tissue in humans. Dr. Robert Gale of the University of California, Los Angeles, implanted liver cells from aborted fetuses into three of the victims he treated after the Chernobyl nuclear-plant disaster in the U.S.S.R. Gale hoped the cells would multiply and replace the bone marrow that had been destroyed by high doses of radiation, restoring the patients' ability to produce blood cells. But all three died from burns before the results of the therapy could be determined. Still, Gale believes that fetal liver cells will prove better than adult bone marrow for transplantation, to treat not only radiation sickness but also leukemia—a cancer of the blood-forming bone-marrow tissues. Bone-marrow transplants are particularly tricky because of the threat of rejection. But because fetal tissues are immature, their cells seem less likely to trigger an immune response, eliminating the need to find a closely matched donor.

Gale is doing more testing in animals before he tries again to implant fetal cells in humans. But Dr. Kevin Lafferty of the University of Colorado is currently implanting pre-insulin-producing cells from fetal pancreases under the skin of the groin in patients to treat diabetes. Five have shown a "significant" reduction in their need for insulin, and one may soon be off it altogether.

Fetal tissue might also be used to restore the health of other fetuses; liver-cell implants, Gale thinks, would be a good way to give an unborn child found to have a genetic defect like sickle-cell anemia, hemophilia or Tay-Sachs disease a normal set of genes. And whole organs from fetuses could also be transplanted. In West Germany, surgeons have recently transplanted fetal kidneys into three patients.

Research with fetal tissue is hindered somewhat because it is unavoidably linked to the highly emotional debate over abortion. Right to Life and other opponents of abortion argue that the use of fetal tissue lends legitimacy to a procedure that they expressly and devoutly abhor. But, replies the University of Colorado's Lafferty, "A fetal cadaver shouldn't be treated any differently from another cadaver, as long as society agrees that we can use cadaveric tissue." Gale of UCLA points out that abortion in the

United States is legal, and thus research on fetal tissue should be allowed, as long as it is carefully done.

No sale: But even the most partisan researchers and ethicists agree that there *are* measures worth taking to keep fetal research from becoming barbarous. One would be a ban on the sale of fetal tissue—something that already applies to major transplant organs. Another would be to prohibit women from choosing who would receive tissue from their aborted fetuses. (One woman proposed to get pregnant so that she could give tissue from the embryo to her father who suffered from Alzheimer's; another wanted to use her own fetal tissue to treat her diabetes.) "The worst possible ethical evil of all this," says Arthur Caplan, director of the Center for Biomedical Ethics at the University of Minnesota, "would be to create lives simply to end them and take the parts."

Ethicists like Caplan would also confine the use of fetal tissue to medical "centers of excellence," noted for their expertise in both basic and clinical research. This would discourage the exploitation of desperately ill patients and their families by entrepreneurs promising "cures" for such diseases as Alzheimer's. It took the medical profession nearly two centuries to live down the stigma of the grave robbers who supplied human bodies for anatomical study. Today's scientists hope it won't take that long to resolve the issues surrounding this emotional debate—the desperately ill can't afford the wait.

BABY BOYS, TO ORDER[3]

Back in the 1970s, many pro-abortion doctors used to call attention to their thoughtfulness by harrumphing now and then about the need not to take abortion lightly. In practice, this meant saying yes to abortion 99 percent of the time but no in cases where the fetus happened to disappoint the mother-to-be by being male or, more typically, by being female when she felt under pressure to produce a son.

[3]Reprint of an article by senior staffwriter John Leo. *U.S. News & World Report*, 106:59. Ja 9 '89. Copyright © 1989, U.S. News & World Report.

But time marches on, as Yogi Berra once observed, and the number of doctors wishing to take abortion lightly appears to be on the rise. In 1973, the year of *Roe v. Wade*, medical geneticists were surveyed to find out how many approved of prenatal diagnosis for sex selection, i.e., for the purpose of planning an abortion if the fetus had the effrontery to be the wrong sex. Only 1 percent said they did. Last week, the *New York Times* reported a new poll showing that nearly 20 percent of such geneticists now approve of the practice.

This is one of those news stories that manage to be both surprising and obvious at the same time. First reaction: This is surely the most frivolous use of abortion yet invented. How can a fifth of all medical geneticists possibly go along with it? Second reaction: How could they not? Since abortion on demand is the law of the land, on what grounds could they logically and legally withhold test results? An overwhelming majority, of course, still refuse to go along if they suspect sex selection is the real aim of the test, but their stance already seems hopeless and rear guard. The woman can always get the test done somewhere else. Still, the fact that nearly 20 percent of diagnosticians consider this practice morally acceptable is astonishing. Apparently many doctors are tailoring their own ethical standards to fit the sweeping permission of *Roe v. Wade*. As Dr. Mitchell Golbus of the University of California at San Francisco told the *Times*: It is very hard to make a moral argument about terminations for sex when you can have abortions for any reason.

Higher laws. Actually, it's not that hard at all. Not everything legal is moral, and this ranges from racist jokes to designer abortions. When these operations are not plainly sexist (aimed at reducing the number of females born), they are manifestations of the custom-made-child syndrome. These days, some adopting parents return their child to the agency after finding a medical flaw, just as some pregnant women abort fetuses that would be born only marginally disabled. This search for the perfect baby now extends to getting rid of a fetus for being the wrong sex. If technology allowed it, presumably some would abort for insufficiently high intelligence or the wrong ultimate height. If we do this, what kind of society do we become?

The good news is that opposition to sex selection is likely to cut across the usual battle lines on the abortion issue. Some demographers and feminists, for instance, are likely to oppose the practice. Looked at as a worldwide phenomenon, sex selection is the natural successor to female infanticide as a method of increasing the ratio of males to females. Tens of thousands of fetuses, perhaps hundreds of thousands, have already been destroyed in Third World countries for the offense of being female. A few feminists are gingerly using the term *femicide*, a rare appearance of the suffix *-cide* in a movement that tends to regard abortion as the simple shedding of an unnecessary body part, such as an appendix or a hangnail. In the Netherlands, feminists staged a symposium on the subject under the title "Death of the Female."

The search for the designer baby, feminists argue, is likely to bring back the image of women as brood mares tied to biological tasks. Fewer females also means more competition for mates and less political influence. The argument goes like this: "If we can't win equality when we are 51 percent of the population, what are our chances when we drop to 45 percent or lower?" There is also a small anti-female grenade in the studies suggesting (not always convincingly) that firstborn children have heavy social advantages over chidren born second or third. Since surveys show that about two thirds of American couples would like their first child to be male, designer abortions could create a pattern of the favored older son and the not-so-favored younger daughter.

This is only the second time that feminists have come out from behind the official and totally unnuanced prochoice position in reproductive matters. (The first was in the Mary Beth Whitehead rent-a-womb case, when feminists first produced the usual rhetoric about choice, then had second thoughts when they noticed that there were enough poor women around to constitute a semipermanent caste of breeders for the childless rich.) Some feminists are now willing to say, in effect, that prochoice is a laissez-faire system that does not automatically advance the common good or even the interests of women.

The reason demographers should be concerned is that no one really knows how far the male-to-female ratio might tilt if designer abortions become routine. Studies in the early 1970s suggested a 7 percent increase in males. But there are some signs that this figure may be too low. In Seoul, South Korea, in the early 1980s, obstetricians began to notice a rise in the number of young males and found that, at select Seoul hospitals, 109 boys were born in 1983 for every 100 girls. The next year, the male figure was 110, and in 1985, just before South Korea banned testing for the sex

of fetuses as a result of the findings, it went to 117. These parents
were not backward peasants who needed sons to avoid ostracism
and abandonment in old age; they were the sophisticated, well-
educated urban elite of a burgeoning economy. A change of 15
to 20 percent in the sex ratio would be a social disaster, and it
could happen here, too.

WHAT DIFFERENT CHRISTIAN CHURCHES BELIEVE ABOUT ABORTION[4]

Twelve years and 15 million abortions after the 1973 Supreme Court decision that made the controversial procedure legal, abortion is still a red-flag issue. Feelings run high: debates
degenerate into inflammatory rhetoric; abortion clinics are
bombed or "torched"; increasing numbers of protesters march on
state capitals; medical experts passionately debate the point at
which life begins.

The issue has split the Christian community as well; the Catholic Church and evangelical/fundamentalist Protestant Churches take a prolife stand; mainline Protestant Churches defend a
prochoice position. Why don't Christians agree about abortion?

Many prolife Christians maintain there is only one Christian
position on abortion: theirs.

"We'll embrace anybody who's against abortion," says the
Rev. John Decker, Seattle-area director of the Continental
Broadcasting Network (formerly the Christian Broadcasting Network) and an ordained minister in the evangelical Foursquare
Church. "Abortion is killing; and we're trying to let the public
know that as Christians, whether you're Catholic, Protestant, or
whatever, it's against God's will. It's against the Bible."

Another Seattle evangelical says bluntly, "I just don't see how
people can call themselves Christians and stand irrevocably for
any length of time for abortion, not when they've been presented
with the facts."

[4]Reprint of an article by Christine Dubois. *U.S. Catholic*, 50:33–8. Ag '85. Reprinted with permission from *U.S. Catholic*, published by Claretian Publications, 205
West Monroe, Chicago, IL 60606. Copyright © 1985 by Claretian Publications. All
rights reserved.

But the fact is, many Christians do take a prochoice stand.

Carol Van Buren is a policy-council member and former chair of the Washington State chapter of the Religious Coalition for Abortion Rights, an organization of Protestant, Jewish, and other religious groups working "to safeguard the option of legal abortion." She believes abortion can be a moral choice for Christians.

"Any time the issue of abortion comes up, people always hear that the religious organizations are the ones that are giving people flak. What the general public comes to believe is that all religious organizations are against abortion. That's not true."

Van Buren spreads the word through displays at street fairs and other public events. She says many people are surprised to learn of the organization. "They kind of look at you and say, 'You mean there are religious groups that are prochoice?'"

Many of the "mainline" Protestant churches (American Baptist, Episcopal, United Methodist, United Presbyterian, Lutheran Church in America, Church of the Brethren, United Church of Christ, Disciples of Christ) have gone on record as opposing any legislation that would prohibit abortion. Their positions vary from a belief that abortion is morally justified only under extreme conditions—such as rape, incest, or danger to the mother's health—to a more liberal position that a woman may choose an abortion for economic or personal reasons. All express a regard for the sanctity of life and urge that any decision be a matter of deliberate thought and prayer.

That's not to say mainline Protestants think abortion is a good thing, only that they consider it a necessary option in a sinful world.

The Rev. Mitchell Jones, pastor of St. Paul's Lutheran Church in Seattle and chair of the Lutheran Church in America's Mission Commission of the local synod, describes abortion as "an unacceptable option that needs to be there. The difficulty with abortion or carrying the child to actual birth is that sometimes neither of these are good solutions. It takes a lot of really well-thought-out medical, spiritual, moral, and family counseling and advice to decide which one of the two unacceptable options may be the one you have to go with."

A Personal Choice?

Many mainline Protestants emphasize that the decision to have an abortion is a personal decision that shouldn't be controlled by legislation. "I would never take the position that abortion is murder," says Lois Selmar, a former social-justice staff member of a committee representing the Disciples of Christ, United Church of Christ, and Church of the Brethren. "From a theological point of view, I think every case has to be looked at individually to determine whether abortion is allowable or whether it is a sin. And the only way you can do that is when you don't make sweeping statements or legislation that says abortion is murder."

"Part of our faith is responsibility to make your own choices, to find God on your own and find your own values," says an active member of the United Church of Christ. "I don't want to see any one religion imposing its values on others. It's fine for people who are Catholic to say 'We do not choose abortion.' But why should they impose that on other parts of the pluralistic society?"

Other prochoice Protestants base their position on the potential harm that the developing life of the fetus could cause the already-developed life of the woman or family. The Rev. Rebecca Beyer, a United Methodist minister, calls it "a conflict of life with life. I interpret it in the broader meaning of life, which I think is faithful to the Christian tradition. When a pregnancy would prevent a woman's life from unfolding in the direction of life, I consider that a conflict of life with life."

An Episcopal dental assistant, who admits she doesn't really know where she stands on abortion, raised a common prochoice argument when she says, "I'm concerned about women who would get an abortion anyway, even if it were illegal. In a society like ours, the problem's not going to go away. Maybe (outlawing abortion) would just make it worse."

Although they believe abortion should be a legal option, mainline Protestants denounce it as a form of birth control. A prochoice Protestant woman says, "If I had made no effort to protect myself from getting pregnant and then said, 'Well, I'll get an abortion because this is inconvenient for me,' I would not find that morally defensible."

Prochoice Christians usually couch their arguments in terms of religious freedom, quality of life for the mother and child, or the dangers of prohibition. Prolife Christians base theirs on the sanctity of life and the protection of the innocent. Both sides buttress their arguments with Scripture.

John Black, a middle-aged man who at different times in his life belonged to the Presbyterian, Methodist, Lutheran, and Episcopal Churches before settling into a "middle-of-the-road, evangelical denomination,"says he bases his prolife stand solely on the Bible.

"Deuteronomy 5:17, 'Thou shalt not kill.' Period. Enough said. Killing is killing, whether it's a fetus or a person." He also cites Psalm 127:3 ("Children are a heritage of the Lord, and the fruit of the womb is his reward") and Psalm 113:9 ("He maketh the barren woman . . . a joyful mother of children") as proof that abortion is against God's will. "People who really search the Bible will find the answers, but they try to overlook it to satisfy their own stand."

John believes the mainline Protestant Churches' position on abortion reflects their general spiritual malaise. "People who truly have the Spirit of God residing inside them and are living with a scripturally based or biblically based foundation in their lives are the ones that are against abortion."

But Marianne Craft Norton, a Lutheran and former director of the Washington State Women's Council, disagrees. "I think there is nothing in Scripture that talks about abortion. It talks about life. It talks about beginning and end. But I have found no example of specific fact or verse in the Bible which speaks accurately and directly to abortion."

Heated Debate

Since neither Scripture nor theology nor medical science seems able to provide conclusive answers, prolife and prochoice Christians often fall into heated rhetoric that leaves few capable of coming to a rational decision.

"I'm anti-abortion, but one thing about the prolife movement that really bugs me is the emotionalism which they use to present their case," says a Seattle mother. "I don't think that because on some level we are kind of aesthetically offended by the fact that an abortion is gory and fetuses look like babies—that doesn't have anything to do with whether it's right or wrong. It just distracts and gets people utterly hysterical."

For Karen Crabtree, however, 15 million abortions are cause for some emotion. "We're talking about life and death," says the Washington State Director of Women Exploited by Abortion. "If anybody has seen an abortion, seen pictures of an aborted baby, and if they realize that every day in this country there are over 4000 babies being aborted, I would ask you to be emotional too. Until people are convinced of the sin and the horror of this issue, we're going to find a lot of people sitting home being opposed to abortion but tolerating it; and I don't think God would look fondly on those of us who tolerated it."

Despite flaming rhetoric on the extremes, leaders on both sides admit there's a lot of apathy in the middle.

Prochoice advocate Van Buren says that despite their churches' prochoice stands, it's hard to get mainline church people involved in the abortion struggle: now that abortion is legal, everyone assumes it's settled. "For religious organizations, it's a very difficult issue. If they could, they'd rather not deal with it at all. That's why it's important for the Religious Coalition on Abortion Rights to exist, to say, 'We do have to deal with it.'"

Things are no better for prolifers. Although most mainline Protestant denominations have small prolife groups working within them, their influence has not been great. Since these churches have democratic forms of church government, the denominations could not hold a prochoice stand if the majority of the members—or even an organized minority—were opposed to it.

Rev. Dan Bloomquist, secretary of the Northwest Chapter of Lutherans for Life, admits that pushing the abortion issue in the Lutheran Church in America right now is "like butting our heads against a concrete wall. For a lot of our Lutheran leadership, this is just not a front-burner issue. This isn't even an issue that is talked about."

Bloomquist says the prochoice position of his own LCA reflects the more liberal bias of the clergy rather than the opinion of the people in the pew. "I think there are a lot of people, myself included, who are indeed very distressed that our church doesn't take a stronger prolife stand."

"Frankly, I don't know if people are afraid, or apathetic, or what," says Linda Nathan, a member of the National Organization of Episcopalians for Life. "I've seen people get all riled up; then when you say, 'Why don't we meet together and pray about this?' they say, 'I'm not ready for that,' or 'I haven't got time.'"

Nathan says she hasn't always been opposed to abortion. A supernatural healing of cancer she received seven years ago helped change her mind. Previously, she had been told she would never be able to have children. After her healing, however, she conceived. The joy of carrying and bearing her son Eric convinced her that "life was from God, and it was not ours to take."

Nathan and her husband, Richard, who has studied medical ethics, have tried to organize seminars and study groups at their parish but have been disappointed with the results. "It's been really hard, and it hasn't been terribly fruitful either. But it's between me and the Lord. I just have to keep doing something about it."

Scarlet Letter

Presbyterian Laura Glessner says she was prochoice when she attended college in the late 70s. But she began to feel uncomfortable with prochoice "rhetoric," especially suggestions that the birth of handicapped children be prevented through abortion. Since she is a teacher of the severely mentally retarded, that idea disturbed her.

She studied the issue, which led her to become a staunch prolifer and convinced her of the need for alternatives to abortion. Today she is a board member of the Crisis Pregnancy Center in Seattle, an organization that counsels pregnant young women and provides them with medical care, maternity clothing, and career guidance if needed. She and her husband, Tom, speak in churches of all denominations on the need for alternatives to abortion.

"People are very interested in changing their old attitudes," she says. "There used to be a real stigma of being pregnant and single. People are seeing that the 'scarlet letter' attitude isn't right. These women need to be cared for and supported; and their children—both born and unborn—need to be cared for and supported. (Christians) are really called to care for these women, not put them down or condemn them."

Karen Crabtree says her abortion, and the guilt she later felt, led her to a conversion to Christianity. An evangelical Christian, she now seeks to "warn" women about abortion.

Crabtree believes abortion is not the "quick fix" it is often portrayed as, but rather a sin; a woman who has had an abortion will never know peace until she seeks God's forgiveness. "I was deceived," she says bitterly. "My child has died because I was sold a lie.

"Women do not know the truth about abortion. What we're trying to do is to warn women about abortion, to tell them what it's really all about. To tell them what the baby's really all about. That the baby really feels pain. That they really could be rendered sterile. That they really may miscarry in the future. That their lives may never be the same."

A Lutheran pastor who has been a professional counselor for 15 years agrees that many women choose abortions without proper counseling. "I've seen some of the abortion counseling that goes on, and it's hardly counseling. Sometimes the counseling consists of 'Which week do you want to have (the abortion)?' or 'Which doctor do you want to go with?' They don't really deal with the issues in an awful lot of these cases. A lot of people involved in abortion counseling are so caught up in the proabortion movement that they fail to recognize some of the very serious possibilities."

Many Christian women who have faced the question of abortion and who have considered all the options nevertheless decide abortion is the best alternative.

"Sometimes I think it's the best choice," says the wife of an Episcopal priest. When she became pregnant at 38, she underwent amniocentesis and determined that if the fetus were missing a chromosome she would have an abortion. "My reasoning was that in a younger woman, a fetus with that defect would abort spontaneously. It was hard for my husband, but he finally said it was my decision." Fortunately, the test revealed no abnormalities; and today her baby is a healthy, rambunctious 2-year-old.

A 44-year-old mother of two expresses concern over the cost to society when teenage mothers are forced to have children they don't want and aren't prepared to care for. "The children are malnourished, abused, abandoned; then we're left as a society with tremendous social problems. The answer is not to say to these young girls, 'You got yourself into this; you have to go through with it.'"

What about the Man?

A Protestant woman who taught English at a Catholic seminary says she became so fed up with the simplistic, moralistic tone of her students' essays on abortion that she decided to expose them to a case from real life. She told the class about a young Chicano woman her daughter had befriended in a Colorado bluejeans factory. The woman was her family's sole support; her husband was chronically unemployed. She already had several children, and her husband said he would leave her if she became pregnant again. A devout Catholic, she refused to use birth control yet lived in terror of becoming pregnant. When she slept on the couch, her husband threatened to find another woman.

"If she gets pregnant, what is her choice?" the teacher asked the class. "This is the kind of situation you're going to be faced with."

The future priests' response? "That's not a fair case."

The question of men's responsibility in unwanted pregnancies is often raised by prochoice advocates.

"Very often, prolife people don't recognize women's concern about the way their lives have literally been shaped by biology and the oppression that results," says the Rev. Rebecca Beyer. She points out that though women are condemned for having abortions, nothing is said about the responsibility of the men involved. "I've never heard an anti-abortionist saying that if men took more responsibility in their relationships with women, there wouldn't be so much abortion. When I've counseled with women making that choice, a major factor is almost always a lack of commitment from the man to help parent."

Some theologians have gone so far as to suggest that one undercurrent of the prolife movement is anti-feminism. In an article in *The Christian Century*, Catholic theologian Dr. Daniel McGuire writes: "Is there no sexist bias in the new Catholic Code of Canon Law? Is that code *for* life or *against* women's control of their reproductivity? After all, canon law excommunicates a person for aborting a fertilized egg, but not for killing a baby after birth. A person could push the nuclear button and blow the ozone lid off the earth or assassinate the president—but not the pope—without being excommunicated. But aborting a five-week-old precerebrate, prepersonal fetus would excommunicate him or her. May we uncritically allow such an embarrassing position to posture as 'prolife?' Does it not assume that women cannot be trusted to make honorable decisions, and that only male-made laws and male-controlled funding can make women responsible and moral about their reproductivity?"

"I am still a believer in the old moral principle: where life is concerned, the choice must be in favor of life," says Father Gregory Kenny, C.M.F. "Perhaps excommunication is the wrong means of dealing with a serious problem, in view of the other terrible ways human beings can destroy one another that are not equally penalized. Yet because the church hasn't chosen to act as seriously against war and murder doesn't mean the moral principles governing abortion are wrong. A seamless garment is just that."

Perhaps the church is institutionally antifeminist, says Kenny, but it is far-fetched to call it so because of the excommunication it legislates for abortion. In fact, he says, the majority of the seven automatic excommunications seem to affect men.

"Even in the case of abortion, it seems that the man would more likely incur the excommunication than the woman. In every case without exception where a woman confessed abortion to me, I found it impossible to judge her subjectively guilty of mortal sin. Each had such tremendous fear, psychological and even physical isolation, or self-destructive guilt feelings that sufficient freedom was not present, in my opinion, to make the person guilty of mortal sin. And if there were no mortal sin, no excommunication was incurred because the automatic excommunication is effective only on one who is accountable for her actions. I do wonder, however, if the male in those cases did not more likely incur excommunication by his irresponsibility prior to the sexual encounter and his positive efforts to effect an abortion to get himself off the hook."

Of course, there are aspects of the abortion issue that all Christians agree on: responsible counseling, better education, and support for adoption and other alternatives. No Christians are *for* abortion. All look forward to a world without the social and economic pressures that produce unwanted pregnancies.

It's another rainy Seattle morning, and Carol Van Buren is handing out brochures from the Religious Coalition for Abortion Rights. "You wish you could be dealing with something else," she says candidly. "There are a lot of other things I would rather put my energy into."

Prolife activists don't like standing in the rain, either. But for them, in the midst of all the pamphlets, brochures, and tracts, the issue remains one of life and death. "We've learned a lot after ten years of unlimited human abortions," says Juli Loesch, a prolife activist, "and it turns out that abortion is not good for women—and other living things."

BEYOND THE LEGAL RIGHT[5]

We are going to watch a child being torn apart . . . " promises Dr. Bernard Nathanson, "by the unfeeling steel instruments of the abortionist." But the promise isn't really kept. What we see in *The Silent Scream*, Nathanson's famous anti-abortion film, isn't red dismemberment but flickering gray chaos. I stopped the video tape three times to examine the fuzzy image that Nathanson calls a child's mouth emitting its silent scream. But what I saw looked more like a satellite photo of a Manitoba blizzard, an undifferentiated swirl.

Several years ago as the film's influence spread—Ronald Reagan showed it at the White House—Planned Parenthood released a handsome brochure of rebuttal, entitled "The Facts Speak Louder." Whereas *The Silent Scream* claimed the fetal head was too big for a suction tube and had to be crushed first with forceps, the brochure said the doctor could have used a larger tube. Whereas *The Silent Scream* said the invasion of the uterus raised the fetal heart throb from 140 beats per minute to 200, the brochure said a rate of 200 is normal. The lines of inquiry remained the same on the "CBS Morning News," where dueling experts speculated on whether a 12-week-old fetus possesses enough cortex to feel pain, and what, in fact, we mean by pain—something understood or merely reflexive? "We know that the fetus spends lots of time with its mouth open," said one Yale physician, so what looked like a scream might have been "a chance random finding."

[5]Reprint of an article by Jason DeParle, an editor of *The Washington Monthly*. Reprinted with permission from *The Washington Monthly*. 21:28-9+. Ap. '89. Copyright © 1989 by The Washington Monthly Co., 1611 Connecticut Ave., N.W., Washington, D.C. 20009.

While these facts may, as Planned Parenthood says, speak loudly, it's unlikely that they say what the prochoice groups hope, since they put the fetus, even a televised facsimile, on center stage, precisely where prochoice groups don't want it. Assume the film is wrong and the Planned Parenthood brochure is right. Assume that was a fetal yawn and not a scream. None of the experts contested that it was a fetal mouth, and that it was part of a fetal head, attached to a fetal spine, and that it had arms and legs, fingers and eyes. Nathanson was certainly wrong to suggest that the 12-week-old fetus was "indistinguishable in every way from any of us"; a rather important difference, one would think, is that the rest of us aren't enveloped in the living flesh of another human being with needs and rights of her own. But if the film's scientific and rhetorical claims are extravagant, it nonetheless succeeded in directing all eyes toward—take your pick—the "fetus" or "unborn child."

Writing in *Ms.* magazine, Barbara Ehrenreich argued that the film's failure to mention the woman having the abortion, "not even as a sinner or a murderer," was the "eeriest thing" about it. "Abortions, after all, have to take place *somewhere*," she wrote, "i.e., in the uterus of an actual human being." Ehrenreich's point is well-taken: much of the right-to-life movement does act as if abortions took place in an abstract neutral setting, rather than within a woman whose life may begin to unravel with an unwanted pregnancy. But I don't think I'd call that the "eeriest thing" about *The Silent Scream*; as eeriness goes, the image, clear in mind if fuzzy on screen, of tiny bits of head, shoulders, ribs, and thighs being fed to a suction tube is formidable.

It's hard to hold these two images—the dismembered body of the fetus and the enveloping body of the mother, each begging the allegiance of our conscience—in mind at the same time. One of the biggest problems with the abortion debate is how rarely we do it, at least in public discourse. While contentious issues naturally produce one-dimensional positions, the remarkable thing about abortion is that many otherwise sensitive, nuanced thinkers hold them. To one side, visions only of women in crisis, terrified and imperilled by an invasive growth; to the other, only legions of innocent children, chased by the steely needle.

The inhumanity that issues from baronies within the right-to-life movement is well known: the craziness of a crusade against birth control; the view of women as second-class citizens; even the

descent into bomb-throwing madness. The insistence that an unborn child must always be saved, no matter the cost, isn't compassion but a compassionate mask, and it obscures a face of cruelty.

But what ought to be equally if not more disturbing to feminists, liberals, and others on the Left is the extent to which prominent prochoice intellectuals mirror that dishonesty and denial.
One-and-a-half million abortions each year is not the moral
equivalent of the Holocaust, precisely because of the way in which
fetuses *are* distinguishable: growing inside women, they can
wreck the lives of mothers and of others, including her children,
who depend upon her. But the fact that three of 10 pregnancies
end in abortion poses moral questions that much of the Left, especially abortion's most vocal defenders, refuses to acknowledge.
This lowering of intellectual standards offers a useful way of looking at the reflexes of liberals in general, and also reveals much
about the passions—many of them just—that underpin contemporary feminism.

What the Suction Machine Sucks

The declaration of a legal right to an abortion doesn't end the
discussion of what our attitude toward it should be, it merely begins it. Ehrenreich, like many of the prochoice movement's writers and intellectuals, would have us believe that the early fetus
(and 90 percent of abortions take place in the first three months)
is nothing more than a dewy piece of tissue, to be excised without
regret. To speak of abortion as a moral dilemma, she has written,
is to use "a mealy-mouthed vocabulary of evasion," to be compro-
mised by a "strange and cabalistic question."

Yet everything we know—not just from science and religion
but from experience, intuition, and compassion—suggests otherwise. A pregnant woman, even talking to her doctor, doesn't call
the growth inside her an embryo or fetus. She calls it a *baby*. And
she is admonished, by fellow feminists among others, to hold it
in trust: Don't drink. Don't smoke. Eat well, counsels the feminist
manual, *Our Bodies, Ourselves*: "think of it as eating for three—
you, your baby, and the placenta. . . . " Is it protoplasm that
she's feeding? Or is it protoplasm only if she's feeding it to the
forceps?

Grant for a moment that it is; agree that what the suction machine sucks is nothing more than tissue. Why then the feminist

fuss over abortions for purposes of sex selection? If a couple wants a boy and nature hands them the makings of a girl, why not abort and start again? All that matters—no?—is "choice."

It wasn't sex selection but nuclear power that got a feminist named Juli Loesch rethinking her own contradictory views of fetuses. As an organizer attempting to stop the construction of Three Mile Island, she had schooled herself on what leaked radiation can do to prenatal development. At a meeting one day, she says, a group of women issued an unexpected challenge: "If you're so concerned about what Plutonium 239 might do to the child's arm bud you should go see what a suction machine does to his whole body."

In fact, we need neither *The Silent Scream* nor a degree in fetal physiology to tell us what we already know: that abortion is the eradication of human life and should be avoided whenever possible. Should it be legal? Yes, since the alternatives are worse. Is it moral? Perhaps, depending on what's at stake. Fetal life exists along a continuum; our obligations to it grow as it grows, but they must be weighed against other demands.

The number of liberals, feminists, and other defenders of abortion eager to simplify the moral questions is, at the very least, deeply ironic. One of the animating spirits of liberalism and other factions on the Left, and proudly so, is the concern for the most vulnerable. But what could be more vulnerable than the unborn? And how can liberalism hope to regain the glory of standing for humanity and morality while finding nothing inhumane or immoral in the extermination of so much life?

The problem with much prochoice thinking is suggested by the movement's chief slogan, "a woman's right to control her body," which fails to acknowledge that the great moral and biological conundrum is precisely that another body is involved. Slogans are slogans, not dissertations; but this one is revealing in that it mirrors so much of the prochoice tendency to ignore the conflict in an unwanted pregnancy between two competing interests, mother and embryo, and insist that only one is worthy of consideration. Daniel Callahan, a moral philosopher, has written of the need, upon securing the right to a legal abortion, to preserve the "moral tension" implicit in an unwanted pregnancy. This is something that too few members of the prochoice movement are willing to do.

One fine example of preserving the moral tension appeared several years ago in a *Harper's* piece by Sallie Tisdale, an abortion clinic nurse with a grudging acceptance of her work. First the mothers: "A twenty-one-year-old woman, unemployed, uneducated, without family, in the fifth month of her fifth pregnancy. A forty-two-year-old mother of teenagers, shocked by her condition, refusing to tell her husband. A twenty-three-year-old mother of two having her seventh abortion, and many women in their thirties having their first. . . . Oh, the ignorance. . . . Some swear they have not had sex, many do not know what a uterus is, how sperm and egg meet, how sex makes babies. . . . They come so young, snapping gum, sockless and sneakered, and their shakily applied eyeliner smears when they cry. . . . I cannot imagine them as mothers."

Then the fetus: "I am speaking in a matter-of-fact voice about 'the tissue' and 'the contents' when the woman suddenly catches my eye and asks, 'How big is the baby now?' . . . I gauge, and sometimes lie a little, weaseling around its infantile features until its clinging power slackens. But when I look in the basin, among the curdlike blood clots, I see an elfin thorax, attenuated, its pencilline ribs all in parallel rows with tiny knobs of spine rounding upwards. A translucent arm and hand swim beside. . . . I have fetus dreams, we all do here: dreams of abortions one after the other; of buckets of blood splashed on the walls; trees full of crawling fetuses. . . . "

It's not surprising that the defenders of abortion don't like pictures of fetuses; General Westmoreland didn't like the cameras in Vietnam either. Fetuses aren't babies, and the photos don't end the discussion. But they make it a more sober one, as it should be. Fetuses aren't just *their* image but our image too, anyone's image who is going to confront abortion.

If the prochoice movement doesn't like the way *The Silent Scream* depicts the fetus, turn to an early edition of *Our Bodies, Ourselves*. Describing an abortion at 16 weeks by means of saline injection, the feminist handbook explains: "Contractions will start some hours later. Generally they will be as strong as those of a full-term pregnancy. . . . The longest and most difficult part will be the labor. The breathing techniques taught in the childbirth section of this book might help make the contractions more bearable. After eight to fifteen hours of labor, the fetus is expelled in a bedpan in the patient's bed."

Heil Mary

When Suzannah Lessard wrote about abortion in *The Washington Monthly* in 1972 ("Aborting a Fetus: the Legal Right, the Personal Choice"), a year before *Roe v. Wade*, she described what she called a "reaction formation along ideological lines . . . of the new feminist movement" as it related to abortion. This was a time when Gloria Steinem was insisting that a fetus was nothing more than "mass of dependent protoplasm" and aborting it the moral equivalent of a tonsillectomy. "I think a lot of women need to go fanatically ideological for a while because they can't in any other way overthrow the insidious sense of themselves as inferior," Lessard wrote, "nor otherwise live with the rage that comes to the surface when the realize how they have been psychically mauled." This is an observation about the psychology of oppression that could be applied to any number of righteous rebellions; the path to autonomy tends to pass, by necessity perhaps, through stages of angry defiance. "But I don't think that state of mind—hopefully temporary—is the strength of the movement," Lessard wrote. "It has very little to do with working out a new, undamaging way of living as women."

But to judge by much contemporary prochoice writing, the mere-protoplasm camp still thrives. Certainly, there are exceptions, Mario Cuomo's 1984 speech at Notre Dame perhaps being the most famous: "A fetus is different from an appendix or set of tonsils. At the very least . . . the full potential of human life is indisputably there. That—to my less subtle mind—by itself should demand respect, caution, indeed . . . reverence . . . [But] I have concluded that the approach of a constitutional amendment is not the best way for us to seek to deal with abortion." And others on the Left have gone even further: Nat Hentoff, who supports a legal ban, has written a number of attacks on abortion in the *Village Voice*; Mary Meehan, a former antiwar activist, published an article in *The Progressive* that attacked the magazine's own editorial stance in favor of legal abortion.

But these are the exceptions. Pick up the past 10 years of *The Nation*, *Mother Jones*, or *Ms*. Read liberals and feminists on the oped pages of *The Washington Post* or *The New York Times*—you're likely to find more concern about the snail darter than the 1.6 million fetuses aborted each year.

Consider:

• Barbara Ehrenreich in a "Hers" column for *The New York Times*: "I cannot speak for other women, of course, but the one regret I have about my own abortions is that they cost money that might otherwise have been spent on something more pleasurable, like taking the kids to movies and theme parks. . . . "

• The Yale University women's center, pledged to be "a place for all women—of every race, ethnicity, age, ability, class, sexual orientation, religion . . . ," barred a group called Yale Students for Life. After the prolife group applied for space, the women's center amended its rules to specify that its members support "reproductive freedom." Similar banishment of prolife groups from women's studies centers has occurred on a number of college campuses.

Mother Jones published a note on Catholic schools that amended the Pledge of Allegiance to read, "with liberty and justice for all, born and unborn." The magazine headlined it, "Heil Mary."

• Linda Gordon, a leading feminist historian, in *Harper's*: "I'm not sure, by the way, that we should spend our time debating the ethical points of abortion. . . . Abstract ethical arguments over when life begins are not very illuminating. They inevitably become moralistic—and they inevitably carry the implication that people who support abortion are less moral than other people.

"When women are able to be self-assertive, that to me is a step toward moral, emotional, and intellectual growth. When I had an abortion, that's what it represented to me."

• Ellen Willis, a senior editor at the *Village Voice*, in the same issue of *Harper's*: "I think it is a *good* thing to have an abortion rather than to have a child that you don't want. Women *should* feel good about it. . . . "

• Katha Pollitt, a poet and critic, writing in *The Nation*: "When I first heard that an antiabortion demonstrator had stationed himself outside of the building in which *The Nation* has its offices—a building that houses, among other businesses and concerns, a gynecological clinic that performs abortions—I had an immediate image of what he would look like. He would be pale and rawboned and strained, a hungry fanatic in a cheap suit, like a street-corner preacher in a Flannery O'Connor story. . . .

"I was wrong about the details. The demonstrator—perhaps harasser is a better word for what he does—wears his hair in a long ponytail and, in his blue jeans and parka, looks like a pudgy

hippie. . . . I was right about the main thing though: he is a religious fanatic. . . .

"There was a certain elation, I admit, at having my beliefs
about the antiabortion movement so neatly confirmed in a single
person: that it is a reactionary religious crusade, opposed to non-
procreative sex and contraception, indifferent to the health and
individual circumstances of women, bone-ignorant. . . . "

• Katha Pollitt again, this time in a "Hers" column for *The
New York Times*: "Moralists, including some who are prochoice,
like to say that abortion isn't or shouldn't be a method of birth
control. But that's just what abortion is—a bloody, clumsy method of birth control."

Ms. in 1989, naming Anne Archer, an actress and prochoice
activist, Woman of the Year: "Cut to a scene at last summer's Republican National Convention. We're in that part of Schlaflyland
where reproductive reactionaries who feel free to thrust bottled
fetuses in your face are assured a place on the party platform. The
audience . . . contains some of those elements who wouldn't
mind frying Betty Ford at the stake for being a radical feminist. . . . "

Archer says: "I don't care [about the anti-choice women].
They're a minority. They're vocal, but it's not really based on intelligent thinking or caring. . . . Once you take a step back and
deny women privacy and choice, you put them back in the kitch-
en; you put them back in an inferior position. If they cannot
control their reproductive systems, they cannot control their personal destiny."

"The anti-choice, anti-privacy forces," *Ms.* says, "would seem
to prefer things that way. . . . "

And when it comes to dissent, even dissent of the mildest sort?

• In 1985 *The North Carolina Independent*, a biweekly alternative paper with a history of support for left-liberal and feminist
causes, put a fetus on the front page, labeled with the blandest
caption: "Controversial, magnified images like this one . . . are
credited with winning converts to the antiabortion camp."

The phone calls and letters poured in. "The enmity that it
aroused was just unbelievable," said Katherine Fulton, the paper's editor. "It was perceived as antifeminist." The graphic
seemed like "the other side's image. We didn't couch it enough."

• Fetuses again, this time in *The Progressive*: In 1985, the magazine ran an *advertisement* from a group called Feminists for Life.

"This Little Girl Needs Protection . . . " it claimed, presenting an embryo at eight weeks.

The Funding Exchange, a New York philanthropy that had supported the magazine, wrote to say it was "greatly offended," was canceling its subscription, and would henceforth find it "difficult for our staff to lobby for funding for your publication."

Michael Ratner of the Center for Constitutional Rights, a civil liberties group, weighed in as well: "Happily I am not a subscriber so I needn't cancel my subscription," he wrote. "I would surely do so after seeing the antiabortion ad. . . . "

Liberal Precincts

The list could continue, but the point is clear: questioning abortion—not only the legal right but also the moral choice—is often viewed, even by otherwise sensitive and thoughtful activists, as a betrayal of the highest order. (Except, at times, for Catholics, whose antiabortion views are usually dismissed as a quaint if unfortunate quirk of faith.)

A great irony about this public demonstration of zeal is that there may be more ambivalence on the Left than is usually acknowledged. When *The Progressive* published Mary Meehan's prolife piece in 1980, it drew more mail than any article save the famous guide to the workings of the H-bomb. About half were predictable: "your knees buckle at the mere thought of taking a forthright stand for women's rights," "prolife is only a code word representing the neo-fascist absolutist thinking." Etc, etc.

But the others: "I support most of the positions of the women's movement, but I part company with those who insist on abortion as a 'right of women to control their own bodies.' There's a lot more than just one body that is being controlled here." "I have no religious objection to abortion, but I do oppose it from a humanitarian point of view." "I was awfully glad to see a liberal publication printing an antiabortion article."

Why aren't there more voices like these heard in liberal precincts? The answers come in two general sets, one pertaining to liberal and progressive values generally and the other connected more specifically to the passions of contemporary feminism.

Right or wrong, abortion helps further values that liberals and progressives generally hold in esteem. Among them is public health. Even those with qualms about abortion tend to back the legal right, if for no other reason than to stem the mutilation that a return to back alleys would surely entail. There's also an equity-between-the-classes argument: if abortion is banned all women may experience trouble getting one, but the poor will have the most trouble of all. For others, there are always planes to Sweden.

Beyond questions of abortion's legality, the Left tends to hold values that encourage the acceptance of abortion's morality too. There's the civil liberties perspective, which argues that the state should "stay out of the bedroom." There's a population control argument; without abortion, wrote one *Progressive* reader, "there will be a more intense scramble for food and all the world's natural resources." There's a help-the-poor strand of thinking; what, liberals constantly ask, about the welfare mother who can't afford another child? And there's a fairness-in-the-marketplace argument, which maintains that without absolute control of their fertility, women cannot compete with men: if two Arnold & Porter associates conceive a child at a Christmas party tryst, bringing it into the world, whether she keeps it or not, will penalize her career much more than his.

These principles—a thirst for fairness between genders and classes, for civil liberties, for economic opportunity—are honorable ones. And they speak well of those who hold them as caring not only for life itself but also for its quality.

Careful, though. Quality-of-life arguments sometimes stop focusing on quality and start frowning on life. Concerns about population control have their place; but whether abortion is a fit means of seeking it raises questions that go well beyond environmental impact studies. One of the most troubling prochoice arguments is the what-kind-of-life-will-the-child-have line. Yes, poverty may appropriately enter the moral calculus if an additional child will truly tumble the family into chaos and despair, and those situations exist. (And there is little cruelty purer than child abuse, which afflicts unwanted children of all classes.) But liberal talk about the quality of life can quickly devolve into a form of cardboard compassion that assumes life for the poor doesn't mean much anyway. That sentiment says to an unborn child of poverty: life is tough, so you should die. Compassionate, that.

Polyester Clothes

Abortion's neat fit with other liberal concerns creates a package-politics tug. The right-to-life movement looms as the Great Beast in the mind of the Left: "Schlaflyland." "Reproductive reactionaries." (Do opponents of abortion like Nat Hentoff or the Berrigans live in Schlaflyland? Does Christopher Hitchens?) One is inclined to take Katha Pollitt very much at her word, when she confesses to "a certain elation, I admit, at having all my beliefs about the antiabortion movement so neatly confirmed. . . . " That kind of confirmation lulls us into avoiding the issues right-to-lifers pose.

Let's be clear: much of the right-to-life movement *is* antipoor and antiwoman. This tends to be particularly true of the movement's political spokesmen, like Jesse Helms. And beneath the debate on the moral status of the unborn, lies a debate on how career, family, sex, birth control, and control in general should shape our lives—all of which are important, but none of which finally answer the question of our obligations to prenatal life. Hunkering down for the great defense of other values, the defenders of abortion tend to miss the ways in which their own concerns can wend back to the womb.

Juli Loesch, the antinuclear activist at Three Mile Island, said a social discomfort with the antiabortion people she knew initially closed her mind to their arguments. "They weren't my set," she said. "They liked Lawrence Welk; I liked the Rolling Stones. They wore polyester clothes; I wore natural cotton. They were pro-inhibition; I was anti-inhibition." But in reconsidering her protests against the Vietnam war, Loesch said she found herself being "inconsistent to the point of incoherence. We were saying that killing was not an acceptable solution to conflict situations, yet when we had our own conflict situation we were willing to go straight to killing as a technical fix."

Another obvious link, made too seldom, concerns abortion and executions. If killing criminals is wrong, then what about fetuses? (At least the criminals have done something wrong.) The issues, of course, aren't synonymous; there are thoughtful arguments to be made to permit abortion and ban capital punishment, and the other way around. But one of the real ironies of contemporary politics is that the Left and Right tend to split that ticket in exactly opposite ways, and each often invokes the word "sanctity."

Perhaps if liberals and progressives weren't so besieged in general, more ambivalence about abortion would bubble to the top. In my talks with Katha Pollitt and Barbara Ehrenreich, they, like others, found it particularly troubling that moral objections to abortion would be raised be someone who, to use Ehrenreich's phrase, "had been on the right side of the barricades." When I asked why, she said, "that kind of thing always cuts the legitimacy of our [legal] right; it's the kind of wedge used to threaten us."

The Christmas Party Tryst

While the values of the Left in general provide one set of explanations for the contours of the abortion debate, the specific passions and experiences of feminists provide another. These concerns don't, finally, answer the question of what our personal, as opposed to legal, obligations toward fetal life need to be. But they do underline the history of injustice that women have inherited.

In rough outline, one persuasive feminist argument for keeping abortion *legal*—an argument I accept—goes something like this: Without the option of abortion, women cannot be as free as men. Not just socially and economically but psychologically as well. And not just those with unwanted pregnancies. As Ellen Willis of the *Voice* has put it, "Criminalizing abortion doesn't just harm individual women with unwanted pregnancies, it affects all women's sense of themselves. Without control of our fertility we can never envision ourselves as free, for our biology makes us constantly vulnerable." Vulnerable to failed birth control. To rape or other coercive sex. Or simply to passion. Vulnerable in a way that men are not. And in a society that rightly prizes liberty as much as ours, it's unacceptable for one half of its members to be less free, at an essential level, than the other. Therefore the legal right.

Of course, having the legal right to do something doesn't tell us whether it's a desirable thing to do. Women have the legal right to smoke and drink heavily during pregnancy, but few of us would hesitate to dissuade them from doing so. Why don't more feminists take the same view toward abortion—defending the right, but urging women to incline against it whenever possible? The feminist defenders of abortion I spoke with reacted to that proposal with a litany of past and present injustices against women—economic, social, political, and cultural, all of them quite real. "You can sit around all day talking about what's the morally right thing to do—rights and sacrifices and the sanctity of life and all that—but I don't think it can be divorced from women's lives in this society," Pollitt said.

Leaving aside for a moment the wrenching emotional issues, one obvious burden is economics. Having a child—even one put up for adoption—costs not only trauma but time and money, and takes them from women, not men. The financial burden is one reason why poor women are more likely to have abortions than others.

But the same inequity is true among professional women. To return to the Arnold & Porter Christmas party tryst, what would happen if the female associate does the right thing by prolife standards and decides to have the child? At $65,000 a year, she can certainly afford to do it, and her insurance is probably blue chip. But in the eyes of some senior partners, the luster of her earlier promise begins to fade. They may be reluctant to keep her on certain accounts, for fear of offending the clients. What's more, even if the clients understand, she'll be missing at least six to eight weeks of work—just, as fate would have it, when she's needed in court on an important case. The long-term penalties may be overestimated—good employees are in short demand in most professions; it's the marginal who will suffer the most—but the fears are nonetheless real. What's more, the burden is unequally shared. Her tryst-ee suffers no such repercussions. The clients love him, he shines in court, and his future seems assured. Unfair? Yes, extremely.

These inequities are one reason why the right-to-life movement has the obligation, often shirked, to support measures that would make it easier for women of all incomes to go through pregnancy—health care, maternity leave, parental leave, day care, protections against employment discrimination. But even if all these things were provided—as they should be—it's unlikely that the strength of feminist feeling on abortion would recede. Economic opportunity is an important facet of the abortion debate, but it's not, finally, at its core. Of all the women I spoke with, the one I most expected to forward an economic argument was Barbara Ehrenreich—since she is co-chair of Democratic Socialists of America—but she never mentioned it. When I finally asked her about it she said that no amount of money or servants would change the essential moral equation, which centers, in her mind, on female autonomy. "The moral issue has to do with female personhood," she said.

Cruel Choices

What surprised me in my talks with the female defenders of abortion, was how many of them seemed to view the abortion debate as some sort of referendum by which society judged women's deepest levels of self. Words like *guilt* and *sin*, *punishment* and *shame* kept issuing forth. They did so both about abortion and about sex in general. "The whole debate is more about the value of women's lives and the respect we have for women than it is about the act of abortion itself," said Kate Michelman, the head of the National Abortion Rights Action League.

A few days before my scheduled meeting with Michelman, I got a phone call from her press secretary. "We hear a nasty rumor," she said, "that you're writing something that says abortion is immoral." I mentioned the rumor when I sat down to speak with Michelman, who quickly told me about the very difficult circumstances surrounding her own abortion. Her first husband had walked out on her and her three small children when she was destitute, ill, and pregnant. She had to make a difficult moral judgment, she said, weighing her responsibilities to her family against those to the fetus. Then, this being 1970, she couldn't even make the decision herself but had to obtain the consent of a panel of doctors and then, to further the pain, get her ex-husband's signature. Call me immoral, she seemed to say, in an I-dare-you way.

But it seemed to me that Michelman's decision, like those, certainly, of a great number of women, had involved a thoughtful handling of difficult questions—as she herself was underlining. "Sure the fetus has interests, absolutely," she said, as do other things, like a woman's commitments to her family and her health. It was only when I began asking why those leading the prochoice movement didn't discuss these moral tensions more often that her reasoning turned curious and defensive.

"The ethical questions are being raised," she said. "And if [a woman] makes a decision [to have an abortion] then she's made the right decision."

I asked her how she knew. With 1.6 million abortions a year, there seems to be a lot of room for error.

Merely asking the question, she said, implied that women had abortions for frivolous reasons. "To even raise the question of when it's immoral," she said, "is to say that women can't make moral decisions."

In considering the way a legacy of injustice fuels the adamance over abortion, it is helpful to consider three generations of women: those who preceded the feminist movement of the late sixties and early seventies; those who soldiered in it; and those who inherited its gains. Each has faced the tyranny of a man's world in a way that primes passions about abortion, but each has done so in a different way.

Women who became sexually active outside of marriage in the days of blanket abortion bans faced a world prepared to hand them the cruelest choice: the life-wrecking stigma of pregnancy out-of-wedlock or the back alley; a "ruined" life or a potentially lethal trip through a netherworld. Men, meanwhile, made the decisions that crafted that world while escaping the brunt of its cruelty. That *was* an unjust life, and the triumph over it is among feminism's proudest achievements.

Feeling Accused

The following account from a woman identified simply as Kathleen comes from *Back Rooms*, a recent collection of oral histories, and is worth quoting at length. It speaks for a tremendous number of women.

"It was the first and only time I was ever sexually intimate with this man. . . . He offered me a ring. . . . But I did not want to do that. . . . I thought about going to a home for unwed mothers and I thought about how my family would deal with it, how it would affect my college career, my scholarships, my job. . . . I couldn't even imagine telling my parents. . . . It was just unthinkable. . . . I just really couldn't put my family through the shame. . . .

"Things at that time in Cleveland were very tight. . . . I finally located an abortionist in Youngstown, Ohio. It was going to cost one hundred dollars. . . . This so called doctor—this man who called himself a doctor—had two businesses. He was a bookie and he was an abortionist. He was an elderly man in a ramshackle little house in a disreputable, shabby section of Youngstown. . . . I don't recall seeing any medical certificates on the walls. I don't think anyone who was a doctor would also be a bookie. I think there was some actual gambling going on while we were waiting. . . .

"He had a room with a chair and stirrups set up. I went in and it was all very, very secretive. The money had to be in cash, in certain denominations. . . . He checked it very thoroughly to make sure it wasn't marked. . . . He explained that he was doing a saline injection and that there should be some cramping and that abortion would happen within 24 hours. . . . I don't know how many days passed. . . . But I do know that when I finally aborted I was alone in my room in the dormitory at school. I went through at least 12 hours of labor alone in my room. . . .

"It was more terrible than I ever imagined. . . . I remember noticing that the contractions were getting more frequent and more frequent, five minutes, then four minutes, then three minutes, and then there was a lot of blood and there was a fetus. . . . I remember taking this fetus and not knowing what else to do but flush it down the toilet. And I was terrified that it wasn't going to go down, and that it would clog up the system, that somehow, some way, I would be found out. The whole system would be clogged up. They'd have to call a plumber and then there would be this hunt to find out who did this terrible thing in the dorm, and I'd be tracked down and prosecuted. I was really in shock and just terrified."

A second generation of women share the memories of illegal abortion, but their perspective has been honed even finer by roles as activists. For these women—in their late thirties to late forties, which includes Ehrenreich, Pollitt, Gordon, Willis, and Michelman—the fight for other forms of feminist freedoms was linked to abortion not only intellectually but through political experience. "My early involvement in the women's movement was involvement in the health movement," says Ehrenreich. Reproductive rights, including birth control, were at the center of the feminist movement of the late sixties and early seventies, and the battles to win them were hard fought. Such experiences aren't likely to lead to a lot of second-guessing.

Nor, for that matter, is the fact that so many women (of many different ages) have had abortions. According to the Alan Guttmacher Institute, 46 percent of American women will have an abortion before menopause, and more than a third of those will have had more than one. During my telephone conversation with

Barbara Ehrenreich I asked her why she thought there wasn't more discussion of whether abortion is an acceptable type of killing. She sounded incredulous. "That's a when-did-you-stop-beating-your-wife question," she said. "I've had two abortions—do you want to call me a murderer?"

In retrospect, I regretted my use of the word "killing." I hadn't meant it as an accusation, though, perhaps understandably, that's the way she heard it. I explained that I had in mind a great difference between the word "killing," which I regarded as neutral and descriptive, and "murder," a legal term meant to describe killing of a very narrow and wrongful sort. This is a problem that makes all discussion of abortion so difficult. I no more think Barbara Ehrenreich or other women who've had abortions are murderers than I think that of people who support capital punishment—there are people I respect and admire greatly in both groups. It's difficult to raise moral qualms about abortion, perhaps especially for a man, without a great number of women feeling accused of something quite serious, even if accusation is not one's intent at all.

Stallions and Diaphragms

Women my age—I'm 28—haven't had to worry about back rooms. To a significant extent, too, they no longer face a life-wrecking stigma from a pregnancy outside of marriage (though this still varies greatly with individual circumstance). They have inherited the gains—more economic opportunity, fewer social barriers—that earlier feminists helped secure, and while this is a very good thing there is at least one sense in which that legacy contains some ambiguity: to some extent women were the losers in the sexual revolution. This is true in at least two ways. For one, much of the culture still remains ambivalent about female sexuality, acknowledging it legitimacy while at the same time distrusting it. Secondly, while the legitimation of sex without commitment was sought by women as well as men, men pursue it more often, and women are more vulnerable to its effects.

I ran this theory past Kate Michelman, and she bought it without a blink: "Men want sex, require sex, they use sex to. . . . " Her thoughts outpaced her words. "Women are less needful of actual sexual intercourse. Women are more needful of intimacy and closeness, while men drive right in there, you know. They want *sex*. I don't know how men and women ever get together, you know. We're very different. But the ultimate impact really falls on women."

More evidence of the way men's sexual behavior feeds the feminist fervor on abortion comes from a Katha Pollitt piece in *Mother Jones*. Entitled [Nat] "Hentoff, Are You Listening?" it answers Hentoff's attacks in the *Voice* on women who have abortions after deciding that giving birth, in Hentoff's words, would be "just plain inconvenient."

"Rather than fulminate against women, about whose lives he seems to know little, " Pollitt wrote, "would it not be more seemly for Hentoff to direct his moral fervor toward his brothers?" To help him along, Pollitt composed a sample speech for Hentoff to take on the road. It's worth listening to in detail, for the list it offers of women's legitimate gripes:

"Men! Abortion is a terrible thing, and it behooves us to ensure that there are as few as possible. . . . That means no more extramarital affairs, no more sleeping with our students, no more one-night stands. Should the marriage fail, let's vow to cheerfully continue to support every child we father until that child is 21— we have a bad record there, what with three-fourths of divorced dads reneging on court-ordered child support. . . .

"Now comes the hard part. . . . It goes without saying that we're mounting a major campaign to make male birth control the chief medical priority of our time. . . . vasectomies for you guys who can't live with the conditions I've outlined above, and, for the rest of us—condoms! They're messy, they diminish pleasure, but so what? How can we blame women for having 'convenience abortions' if we won't put up with a little inconvenience to prevent unwanted pregnancy? In fact, since condoms have been known to break, let's wear two at a time!

"None of this will amount to anything, though, if we don't change our attitudes about sex as well. Face it men, we give women mixed messages. So from now on, let's never call a woman frigid if she won't sleep with us without commitment, or promiscuous if she takes a diaphragm with her when she goes out for a date. As for men who sleep around, let's think of them not as stallions bursting with vitality but as hit-and-run artists so irresponsible they don't even know how many fetuses they scatter about. . . . "

Accepting Female Sexuality

One could scarcely ask for a better example of the way the male "stallion" legacy makes feminists angry about abortion. And rightly so. But what's interesting about the observations of male irresponsibility, as it relates to abortion, is that both sides cite it. Prolife feminists, like Juli Loesch, argue that the acceptance of abortion actually *encourages* exploitation. The "hit and run" artist can pony up $200, send a woman off to a clinic, and imagine himself to have done the gallant thing. "The idea is that a man can use a woman, vaccum her out, and she's ready to be used again," Loesch says. "It's like a rent-a-car or something." (In such scenarios, Loesch argues, abortion has the same blame-the-victim effect that the Left is typically quick to condemn, with the victimized mother perpetrating the injustice through violence against the fetus.)

When I asked Katha Pollitt about this, she dismissed it with the argument that men will be just as irresponsible with or without abortion, and that the only difference will be the burden left to women. To some extent she's right: irresponsible sexual behavior—by men and women both—will no doubt continue under any imaginable scenario. Then again, it's not unreasonable to suspect that casual attitudes about abortion, particularly among men, could increase precisely the kind of "stallion" behavior that Pollitt rightly protests. And abortion can become a tool of male coercion in other ways as well. "He said that if I didn't have an abortion, the relationship would be over," a friend recently explained. Many women have experienced the same.

Of course, feminist emotion toward abortion isn't just a reaction to male sexuality but also an assertion that women's own sexual drive is equally legitimate. Feminists argue that antiabortion arguments reflect a larger cultural ambivalence, if not outright hostility, toward female sexuality. This is where words like *guilt* and *shame* and *punishment* continue to arise. I recently sat down with Katha Pollitt for a long conversation about abortion. She cited the many ways in which women (and the children antiabortionists want them to raise) are injured by society: poor health care, poor housing, economic discrimination, male abuse. We talked also about power, politics, religion, and the other forces that play into the abortion debate, like the unflagging responsibilities that come with parenthood. (She is a new, and proud, mother.) But when I asked her which, of the many justifications for abortion, she felt most deeply—what, in her mind, was the real core of the issue—her answer surprised me. "Deep down," she said, "what I believe is that children should not be a punishment for having sex."

Ellen Willis of the *Voice* advances a similar argument. Opposition to abortion, she's written, is cut of the same cloth as the more general "virginity fetishism, sexual guilt and panic and disgrace" foisted on women by a repressive society. The woman's fight for abortion without qualm, she says, is part of the fight for the "acceptance of the erotic impulse, and one's own erotic impulses, as fundamentally benign and necessary for human happiness."

Pollitt agreed. "The notion of female sexuality being expressed is something people have deeply contradictory feelings about," Pollitt said. And her example to Hentoff of diaphragms and dates—damned if you bring one, damned if you don't—shows she's right.

An Unspoken Assumption

Pollitt and other leading feminists are right about a lot of things—right to point to the terrible past of stigma and dirty needles; right to complain of sexual exploitation; of double standards; of economic discrimination; of a shortage of birth control; of a society that places them in too many binds. Only one question remains: what about the fetus?

Do we have any moral obligations to it? What are they? What happens after the birth control fails, the egg becomes fertilized and implanted, and human life begins to unfold?

• "Maybe I'm a cold and heartless person," said Pollitt, "but I find it hard to think of it as a moral question, the right to life of this thing the size of a fingernail."

• "Would I feel comfortable getting rid of a fetus in the first few months of its life? Yes, indeed," said Ehrenreich. "And I have done it without qualm."

• "To say, 'I support the legal right but I'm against it morally' is still to deny women's equality," said Willis. "If you have some inherent moral bias in favor of fetuses it becomes a moral bias against the woman. There's no way you can give the fetus a claim, even a relative claim, without denying the woman's selfhood. You make the woman a vessel."

At the risk of taking these women at less than their word, I can't help but wonder if they believe this—if they truly believe the moral questions are as simple as they say.

Katha Pollitt said, "It's hard for me to imagine circumstances in which I'd have an abortion at this time in my life," with this-time-in-her-life meaning at age 39, happily married, professionally established, and prosperous. But "not for moral reasons" she said. And she quickly insisted—twice—that she "would never condemn another woman for having an abortion."

Next, she conjured a hypothetical example. Picture a friend, five months pregnant. The friend's husband, Bob, runs off with a 19-year-old flame. The friend comes to Katha Pollitt for advice.

"I would tell her to go ahead and have it, I'll help you," Pollitt said.

Surprised, I interrupted her to ask why.

"A woman in the fifth month of pregnancy is going to have strong feelings," she said.

Again—why?

She mixed up her words. "The baby . . . the fetus . . . ." Then she paused and said she would tell her friend to have the abortion if she had a heart condition and would be bedridden or endangered by the pregnancy.

And if she didn't have a heart condition?

"Just because Bob is leaving—why shouldn't she have the child?" she said. "I'd say, 'Fuck you Bob, I'm going to go ahead and hire a lawyer and take you for everything you're worth.'"

When I asked her about this example a few weeks later—didn't her instinct to tell her friend to have the baby indicate the fetus had some innate worth?—Pollitt said there's been an unspoken assumption in the scenario: "What I was saying is that if she wanted to have the baby until this rat walked out—why should he stop her?" But there seemed to be another unspoken assumption as well, that the fetus had some interests of its own—not enough to overrule, say, the mother's heart condition, but not to be easily ignored either. And why—if abortion is so neutral—would Katha Pollitt herself now find it hard to imagine herself ever having one?

Biology and Destiny

What the argument for abortion-without-qualm comes down to is this: the fetus doesn't exist unless we want it to. But the whole crisis over abortion is that we know precisely the opposite to be true. It's there physically, feminists say, but not morally. But how could it be one without the other—there to nurture one day (remember, plenty of fresh vegetables, we're eating for three: you, baby, and placenta), but free to dismember the next? Qualm-less advocates argue that all that finally matters is whether the woman, for whatever reason, desires to bring it into the world. Yet the fetus is already there, no matter what we plan or desire. Forces may conspire against a woman and leave her *unable* to bring it into the world, or unable to do so without a great deal of harm to herself and others. That is, *other* moral obligations may overrule. But it is suspicious in the extreme to argue—as the qualmlessness position does—that our moral obligations are nothing more than what we want them to be, a wish-it-away view of the world. Inconveniently fetuses exist, quite outside our fluctuating emotions and desires.

Finally, Ellen Willis's argument that by giving fetuses any moral status at all we reduce women to vessels breaks down because women *are* vessels. They're not *just* vessels. They're much more than vessels. But the attempt to reconcile the just desire for full female autonomy with our moral obligations toward fetuses by insisting that we have none attempts to wish away a very real collision; it refuses to acknowledge a (so far) inalterable conflict buried in biology. Willis argues this is precisely the oppressive "biology equals destiny" argument that feminism has fought to overturn. Biology doesn't equal destiny; but it does affect destiny, and it leaves us with the extremely difficult fact that women, for any number of reasons, get burdened with unwanted pregnancies to which there are no easy moral solutions. Something important is lost—female autonomy or fetal life—in either event.

There are two highly imperfect ways of dealing with this conflict. The first is abstinence (since birth control fails). But not much chance of that. The second is adoption—another imperfect solution. The first argument against it is that there aren't enough parents to go around, particularly for minority and handicapped children. Ironically those quickest to point this out tend to be those for whom putting up a child for adoption really is a plausible option—white professionals. George Bush's "adoption not abortion" line brought quick ridicule by Pollitt in *The Nation* and Ehrenreich in *Mother Jones*. He's wrong to suggest it as a panacea—babies would quickly outstrip parents, as Pollitt insists—but right to encourage its wider use. The real challenge for liberals and progressives would be to turn the thought back toward Bush, and demand the governmental support, in health care and other ways, needed to get through pregnancy, and needed to raise a child.

The second argument against adoption focuses not on demand but supply: nine months of illness culminating in a "physiological crisis which is occasionally fatal and almost always excruciatingly painful," as Ehrenreich has written. And other worries follow; think of Lisa Steinberg. "It's almost unimaginable to me to think about giving up the baby," said Ehrenreich. "Talk about misery. Talk about 20 years of grief and ambivalence." The grief is real—particularly for people of conscience, like Ehrenreich. (And people of conscience are the targets of moral suasion in the first place.) But where does that argument lead? That in order to spare a child the risks of an adoptive life, we offer the kindness of a suction machine?

"A Very Scary Time"

A few years ago, I was sharing an apartment with a friend who became pregnant just before breaking up with her fiance. Like many men—like the hypothetical Bob—he just walked away, dealing with the dilemma through denial. My friend dealt with it with a lot of courage. I called her recently to see how the experience seemed in retrospect, and perhaps she should provide the coda, since her view complicates both Ehrenreich's position and my own. Though she said that putting her child up for adoption was "the right thing," she said she "would never, ever, pressure someone to go through the same thing."

It surprised me to hear her say that abortion "crossed my mind several thousand times," since that was the one option she had seemed to rule out from the start. When she realized she was pregnant, she said, she went riding her bicycle into potholes "trying to jar something loose. It was very, very easy for me to think of the sperm and the egg as having just joined. It was like a piece of mucous to me." She decided against abortion after about a week, "a very lonely, very scary time."

"At some point, I realized I was old enough, and mature enough, that I could do it [have the baby]," she said, but she emphasized that this calculus could have been altered easily by any number of factors—including less support from family and friends, a less understanding employer, or the lack of medical care. She spent months in counseling trying to decide whether to raise the child or put it up for adoption, and the decision to give the baby away "was the most difficult thing I've ever had to do." Since the baby was healthy and white the adoption market was on her side—"I could have dictated that I wanted two Finnish socialists," she said—and her certainty that the new parents would not only love the child but pass on certain shared values was an essential thing to know.

"When I think about her," she said, "just the miracle of being able to have brought her into this life, even if she's not here with me right now, she's with people who love her. It's a miracle."

"When she left to go to her adoptive parents, it was the most devastating and wonderful thing," she said. "I kept thinking this is my child, and I love her.

"It always kept coming back to that —I love her."

V. APPROACHES TO COMPROMISE

EDITOR'S INTRODUCTION

Can there ever be a resolution of the abortion issue? What does the American public want? Both sides claim to have the support of the majority, but public opinion polls show that the population as a whole has a highly nuanced and ambivalent attitude toward abortion, one that supports neither an outright ban nor total acceptance. In a Gallup Report published in July 1989, 58 percent of the respondents said that they did not want to see *Roe v. Wade* overturned; yet 41 percent favored prohibiting the use of abortions to choose the baby's gender, 52 percent favored pre-abortion testing to see if the baby could survive, and 67 percent favored laws requiring teenagers under 18 to get their parents' consent before having an abortion. A *Newsweek* poll from July 1989 showed that 54 percent of the respondents supported mandatory testing for possible survival, 75 percent supported mandatory parental permission for teenagers, and 88 percent supported mandatory counseling on the dangers of abortion and on alternatives to abortion before a pregnant woman could have it done.

These figures make it appear likely that legislators could fashion, nationwide or state by state, a compromise arrangement in which abortion is available during early pregnancy only, with exceptions in the later months for such cases as a medical complication that threatens the mother's life. A compromise of this kind would not be acceptable to those in the conservative camp who consider an abortion to be a murder or those in the feminist camp who want complete autonomy. How far apart the two groups are can be seen in the first article in this section, "Is Abortion the Issue?," the transcript of a forum on the subject held by *Harper's Magazine* in 1986.

But there is reason to believe that some of the partisans can envision a compromise and may be prepared to work for one. In "When (If) 'Roe' Falls," Daniel A. Degnan, a Catholic priest with antiabortion views, concludes that a compromise may well be morally permissible, especially since an absolute prohibition of abortion is unlikely. He suggests that "a new abortion debate in the states could lead to important legal restraints on abortion and support for budgetary and other measures to enhance the dignity of women and families, thereby reducing the pressures on women to opt for abortion." Larry Letich, in "Bad Choices," is mainly concerned with encouraging the proabortion movement to win more converts by articulating a moral position that the majority can accept, one that distinguishes between a zygote (fertilized egg) lacking the "neural equipment" to experience "consciousness of existence" and a second- or third-trimester baby who does have such a consciousness. Focusing public debate on this distinction, Letich says, allows us "to create possibilities other than the yes-or-no choice offered by absolutists on both sides." While their own feelings about abortion are in complete opposition, Degnan and Letich define a common ground on which a consensus of moderates could take place.

A compromise adopted by many Western European nations is described in the fourth selection, an interview with Mary Ann Glendon, whose book *Abortion and Divorce in Western Law* compares the policies of twenty nations. Europeans, Glendon notes, have "worked out systems that combine compassion and support for the pregnant woman with concern for the fetus, a concern that increases as it approaches term." Glendon emphasizes the importance of developing a sense of community responsibility for the nation's children and their families.

No compromise is possible unless enough people can bring themselves to discuss abortion with a degree of civility and mutual respect. An interesting example of this is contained in the fifth selection, an interview with social psychologist Sidney Callahan (the author of "Abortion & the Sexual Agenda," in Section I of this book) and her husband of 36 years, ethicist Daniel Callahan, who are on opposite sides of the issue.

The final selection in this anthology is "We Do Abortions Here," a memoir by a writer, Sallie Tisdale, who worked as a registered nurse in an abortion clinic. Her article is an extended meditation on what really happens in an abortion and why so many women see in abortion the solution to a dilemma that, in an ideal world, would never arise in the first place.

IS ABORTION THE ISSUE?[1]

Thirteen years after *Roe v. Wade*, the debate over legalized abortion continues. Some Americans view it as an essential right, others as an absolute evil. Many, perhaps most, apparently regard it as an unpleasant reality to which there is no acceptable alternative. The polls, as always, are ambiguous. A majority of Americans believe that abortion should be legal under at least some circumstances; a majority of Americans also believe that abortion can fairly be described as "murder." Perhaps W. H. Auden's lines on the Spanish Civil War convey something of the ambivalent attitude of many Americans toward legalized abortion: "Today the deliberate increase in the chances of death,/The conscious acceptance of guilt in the necessary murder."

But the absence in recent years of any significant shift in public opinion inevitably begs the question: Is the abortion debate still a debate? "Do you ever wonder," the Gallup Organization asked last year, "whether your own position on abortion is the right one or not?" Fifty-five percent answered no. Do our differences go too deep to permit rational discussion or political compromise? *Harper's Magazine* invited a panel of women to discuss the question of legalized abortion—and to speculate on the possibility of finding some common ground.

The following Forum is based on a discussion held at the New School for Social Research in New York City. Judy Woodruff served as moderator.

JUDY WOODRUFF is the anchor of the PBS documentary series *Frontline* and chief Washington correspondent of *The MacNeil/Lehrer NewsHour*.

LINDA GORDON is a professor of history at the University of Wisconsin and author of *Woman's Body, Woman's Right: A Social History of Birth Control in America*.

SIDNEY CALLAHAN is an associate professor of psychology at Mercy College and co-editor of *Abortion: Understanding Differences*.

ELLEN WILLIS is a senior editor of the *Village Voice* and author of *Beginning to See the Light: Pieces of a Decade*, a collection of essays.

ELLEN WILSON FIELDING is a contributing editor of the *Human Life Review* and author of *An Even Dozen*, a collection of essays.

---

[1]Reprint of a forum discussion moderated by television journalist Judy Woodruff, *Harper's Magazine*. 273:35–43. Jl '86. Copyright © 1986 by *Harper's Magazine*. All rights reserved. Reprinted from the July 1986 issue by special permission.

Judy Woodruff: Let's begin by trying to establish the main lines of the abortion debate. What are the fundamental differences between pro-life and pro-choice advocates? Are they primarily ethical? Religious? Legal? Political? Linda Gordon, what is the one thing that most sharply distinguishes your position from that of the pro-lifers?

Linda Gordon: My overall political outlook. Abortion is a political issue. Indeed, for more than two centuries, reproductive issues have continued to emerge cyclically as social and political problems. Now, I don't deny that individuals may have deeply felt ethical differences over abortion. But the *social* problem of abortion has always divided people into two political camps, which might reasonably be called pro- and anti-feminist.

I'm not sure, by the way, that we should spend our time debating the ethical points of abortion. A lot of political principles seem, to the people who hold them, extremely moral and ethical. So when I say "political," I mean simply that issues like abortion have to do with large social questions about who will have power and how power will be distributed. In this case, I'm thinking particularly of questions about what our policy should be toward the family, and what our policy should be in terms of the relations between men and women.

Sidney Callahan: What distinguishes my view on abortion from Linda's is that I am a pro-life feminist, and, as a feminist, I think the pro-life position is better for women. I can't see separating fetal liberation from women's liberation. Ultimately, I think the feminist movement made a serious mistake—politically, morally, and psychologically—by committing itself to a pro-choice stance, a stance which in effect pits women against their children.

Ellen Willis: As I see it, "pro-life feminism" is inherently contradictory. Women can never be free and equal unless they have control over their fertility and unless their right to sexual expression is recognized fully. I see the anti-abortion movement as coming out of a traditional Judeo-Christian conception of morality, a patriarchal morality based on the idea that repression is not only morally permissible but necessary, that what keeps the human community functioning is self-sacrifice and guilt. It's a morality that views sexual desire as basically dangerous and antisocial unless it's clearly subordinated to marriage and procreation. My own morality, on the other hand, is anti-patriarchal and anti-authoritarian. I see sexuality as a fundamental force of which procreation is a byproduct, not as a cosmic bribe to get us to reproduce. And support for sexual freedom, by which I mean not only the rejection of traditional patriarchal restrictions but acceptance of the erotic impulse, and one's own erotic impulses, as fundamentally benign and necessary for human happiness, is a very important part of that outlook. So my opposition to the anti-abortion movement is based on an essential philosophical difference of which feminism, crucial as it is, is only a part.

Ellen Wilson Fielding: I don't see abortion as that kind of issue. I approach the problem specifically from the standpoint of protecting the innocent life of the unborn, and I don't think that "practical" questions of inconvenience or hardship ought to enter into it. That's why having an abortion should not simply be the private decision of the mother. If the mother makes the wrong choice, there are repercussions for the society and for the state as well. The first duty of the state is to protect its citizens, and it is because the decision to have an abortion is so critical, because it affects a human life, that the state has the right to intervene.

Callahan: I think that the ideas of privacy and individual decision, which are so central to the pro-choice position, have been death to the feminist struggle for equality in the work force and in education. Women need social support in our society. But how are they going to get it if their attitude toward pregnancy is based on a cost-benefit analysis? "This baby is my private property," the pro-choice feminists say. "I have the choice to let it live or let it die." But if that's the case, why should a man support a child *he* doesn't want? And why should the society as a whole provide, say, day care? Or any of the other things that women need?

Willis: You're assuming that abortion is a totally selfish, totally individualistic act that has no socially positive meaning and is completely at odds with any kind of communitarian concern for children once they're born. I don't accept that at all. I see the right to have *wanted* pregnancies as part of a larger social transformation that entails a very different idea of how to deal with these problems.

Gordon: The ironic thing here, Sidney, is that the people who *oppose* abortion rights are in fact the people most firmly associated with what you call an individualistic attitude. Opponents of abortion rights are more likely to be against welfare, to support a military buildup, and to accept all of the political and economic implications of capitalism. It's the people who *support* abortion rights who are more likely to accept the communitarian philosophy you advocate. And it's been that way, I might add, since the late eighteenth century.

Callahan: Yes, there are many right-to-life supporters who are like that. But it doesn't have to be that way, and it shouldn't necessarily be that way. A historical accident brought abortion rights and feminism together.

Willis: That's not true. Your point of view implicitly devalues individual freedom in favor of a particular notion of community or collectivity. Certainly abortion is a social issue. It's not simply the business of the individual. But I also think that in a good society, a community has to be based on certain fundamental individual rights. Feminism, more than any other political movement, has consistently stood up for extending to women what were once very radical ideas about individual freedom.

Callahan: But the fetus is an individual, too.

Gordon: This is why I call abortion a political problem rather than an ethical one. Abstract ethical arguments over when life begins are not illuminating. They inevitably become moralistic— and they inevitably carry the implication that people who support abortion are less moral than other people. Pro-choice advocates feel equally strongly that women's reproductive freedom is a moral issue.

Fielding: It doesn't matter whether or not it's illuminating. You have to talk about when life begins. If you're pro-choice, either you don't think the unborn is a human being or you don't think its right to life should prevail over other considerations. These things *have* to be discussed. They're at the center of the dispute. We can talk all day about things like women's empowerment or communitarian versus individual rights, but it's not going to get us anywhere if we're carefully covering up what we think about the fetus.

Gordon: That kind of thinking—the idea that either a fetus is a human life or it is not—is exactly what I'm objecting to. What I'm suggesting is that a better way to understand this problem is to start by saying that life is a continuum. There is life in a stalk of grass, in an animal, in a cell. People, not God, attribute life to citizens. If we don't accept that premise, then we're arguing over essentially religious points of view. I can understand that there are people who think about it in that way, but within the context of a society without an established church, we have to assume that decisions about such matters should be made by the community—and that there are no absolutes.

Fielding: A state either allows or doesn't allow abortion. That's an absolute.

Gordon: That's not true. Generally, there are all kinds of intermediate positions.

Fielding: But it allows it in this case or that. *This* pregnant woman either can or cannot have an abortion. You may be talking about continuums, but you're also talking about the arguments on which the state makes its decisions.

Callahan: Yes, let's look more closely at this idea of life as a continuum. No infant has a sense of self, no child engages in rational decision-making until about the age of two. In that sense, no infant is a person.

Willis: You've never met my daughter!

Callahan: Well, perhaps one is a "person" for only a very brief period of time in one's life. Many philosophers interested in the meaning of "personhood" have set the standards for eligibility so high that half the human race couldn't meet them for half of its waking hours. Perhaps life is a continuum in that sense. But where does that continuum begin? How can you say, for instance, that eight weeks old is more human than seven weeks old?

Willis: My problem with this line of argument is that I don't believe your views about fetal personhood really determine your stand on abortion. I do have feelings and intuitions about the moral status of fetal life—I don't call them ideas because I don't think they're subject to rational proof or disproof. For me, a fertilized egg does not have the same moral value as a person. On the other hand, I feel that fetuses have more moral weight as they approach birth. Yet I wouldn't restrict late abortions. The crucial question is, can forced childbearing *ever* be condoned? It's a question of relative values. If you're going to have a society in which fetal life is absolutely sacrosanct, then women are going to be vulnerable to the biological process of procreation in a way that men are not. There will be no chance of changing society in such a way that women can be free and equal human beings or that both sexes can have sexual freedom. The alternative is subordination and oppression. And the abortion debate is ultimately over the importance of this kind of equality.

A lot of our confusion in talking about sex arises from the fact that the so-called sexual revolution has mostly had to do with lifting some of the traditional restrictions on sexual activity. People's sexual psychology hasn't changed much. So one unfortunate effect of sexual permissiveness has been to allow men for the first time to act out certain kinds of antisocial sexual feelings and fantasies with women of their own class. Many people react to this by saying, "Sexual freedom must be wrong. Traditional morality was right all along. Back to the drawing board." But I don't see it that way at all. With all the imperfections of our present-day attitudes, I'm still a lot better off in terms of the sexual choices I have than women of my mother's generation. I was a lot better off after the sixties than I was before them. What sexual freedom I now have has been very hard-won. I wouldn't give it up for anything.

Woodruff: So is it possible to be a feminist and pro-life at the same time?

Gordon: In individual cases, yes. Sidney is certainly a feminist. But her position will continue to be marginal in terms of the right-to-life movement as a whole. The right-to-life position emerged out of a fundamentally conservative, anti-feminist, anti-sexual alarm about certain kinds of changes that are going on in our society. These changes are irreversible. There's no way we're going to get women out of the labor force. There's no way we're going to reduce the number of abortions, even if we make abortion illegal again.

Fielding: How can you say that we wouldn't significantly reduce the number of abortions performed in the United States by making abortion illegal? Abortion was legalized in 1973, *after* most of the social changes you've been talking about had already occurred, and the rate immediately skyrocketed. The point is that there is a relationship between law and behavior. The law can be a teacher. Since 1973, the law has taught us that abortion is O.K. If abortion were illegal, the law would be teaching us that it is *not* O.K. There is an interaction between law and the conscience of a nation.

Gordon: Well, I don't believe that there was any widespread opinion that abortion was not O.K. in 1960—or 1950 or 1890, for that matter. Most people seem to have looked upon breaking the abortion laws in much the same way they look upon getting a parking ticket.

What is even more significant, though, is the fact that the right-to-life movement has been against contraception, child care services, child welfare—against the whole array of services that you, Sidney, would certainly agree that women need. We need to think in terms of the larger implications of that kind of social policy.

Callahan: Do you really think legalized abortion is going to get us day care? Legalized abortion *trivializes* conception and pregnancy.

Willis: But do you think criminalizing abortion is going to help us get day care, Sidney? I don't think so. The only way we're going to get all these things is through a women's liberation movement. And you can't have a strong women's liberation movement unless you fight for control of fertility. That's the cornerstone of women's freedom.

Fielding: You don't stop being a victim until you stop victimizing others. And if you're saying, "It's me or the fetus, so the fetus has to go," then that's just turning around and victimizing somebody else.

Callahan: Are young girls going to feel more self-esteem, more self-confidence, a greater willingness to take on a male-dominated society, simply through having abortions?

Gordon: Let's go back to the remark made earlier about the rise in the number of abortions following *Roe v. Wade*. It's true that the number of abortions went up, but so did the number of illegitimate children born to teenagers. What's more, an increase in abortions is not necessarily a bad thing—abortion has often been a woman's first step to self-assertion. And as someone who has spent some time counseling teenagers, I can tell you that the issues involved in the rate of teenage pregnancy are issues that involve the *overall* position of women, particularly very poor and very young women. What's at stake is much more important than the narrower issues of contraception or the legality of abortion.

Legal abortion and free contraceptives are not in themselves the answer—I agree with you there. But teenage pregnancy inevitably exacts great hardship and suffering. And I'm not talking about physical discomforts. I'm talking about never graduating from high school, never getting off welfare, never getting a decent-paying job. Unwanted teenage pregnancies lead to irreversible turns in a life course.

Callahan: But abortion just helps maintain the status quo. It's an easy, quick solution that isn't really going to change the condition of women. Abortion is going to help adolescent girls? Suddenly there's going to be a great change in society's attitudes? We're all going to start caring about these girls just because they can have abortions?

Fielding: If you see abortion as a solution for teenage girls, then you presumably see it as something that wipes out the pregnancy. Well, it doesn't. The pregnancy *happened*. That's the critical thing.

Gordon: Why is that?

Fielding: Because the girl knows that she became pregnant, that she had human life. And if you say to her, "No, it wasn't really life, it never existed," or "Yes, it was life, but you've wiped it out and can go on from there," then you change her in a harmful way. You give her an unreal way of looking at the world, one which she will carry with her throughout her life.

Gordon: You think a woman is worse off having an abortion and not having to go through a whole pregnancy that she doesn't want and have a child that she doesn't want? You think she's worse off?

Fielding: Yes. And I'm not just talking in terms of pain and suffering. I mean worse off intellectually, psychologically, morally.

Callahan: And in relation to men, too. She knows that the man who got her pregnant was not willing to support her child.

Willis: Perhaps the man was willing to support her and she didn't want to be supported by him. I totally disagree with what you're saying. I think it is a *good* thing to have an abortion rather than to have a child that you don't want. Women *should* feel good about it.

Gordon: What I think is involved here is a question of self-esteem as it affects the moral and emotional growth of women. I reject the dichotomy that women should be nurturing and self-sacrificing and that it's acceptable for men to be self-centered and aggressive. When women are able to be self-assertive, that to me is a step toward moral, emotional, and intellectual growth. When I had an abortion, that was what it represented to me. I don't see any evidence whatsoever that people who have had abortions are in any way diminished in their nurturing capacities.

Fielding: That's not what I'm talking about at all.

Gordon: Well, then, what exactly is the "damage" that you're referring to?

Fielding: The damage, among other things, is that you keep passing over the question of whether or not the unborn child is a human being.

Gordon: I'm not passing over it. I'm merely accepting that you and I can't agree about it.

Fielding: But that's the point.

Gordon: That's not what you said a while ago. You were talking about damages to the woman who has an abortion, and that's what I want you to explain.

Fielding: I didn't say that was why the abortion was wrong. Abortion is wrong to begin with. But you're advancing it as a solution to the pregnant teenager's problem.

Gordon: Well, it's a solution to her pregnancy if the pregnancy is part of her problem.

Willis: I don't think abortion is the solution to the problem of teenage pregnancy, and neither does Linda. There is a larger crisis, one that has to do with the tensions between feminism and the backlash against it. On the one hand, society is encouraging sexual freedom; on the other hand, it's punishing people for indulging in it and not emotionally preparing them for it. Both women in general and teenagers in particular are caught in the middle. Abortion by itself is obviously not going to solve this crisis. We need a much larger social movement to solve it. The question is whether legalizing abortion or criminalizing it is more likely to lead toward solving these problems.

Woodruff: What about the argument that if abortion is outlawed, only the rich will be able to afford it?

Callahan: The pro-choice position presupposes that the greatest good the poor can have is unrestricted access to abortion. Not only does that devalue pregnancy and maternity and childbearing; it is also a very arrogant way of imposing your values on the poor.

Fielding: I don't think for a minute that the criminalization of abortion would mean the end of abortion. Indeed, if abortion is criminalized, it will be the babies of the rich who are discriminated against. I mean that quite seriously. They are the ones who will be killed in the greatest numbers. But I don't believe that the only acceptable alternative to discrimination is the indiscriminate abortion of fetuses. You work to have the fewest number of abortions possible.

Willis: People have the glib idea that if abortion were illegal, you could always get a safe abortion if you had enough money. Well, that's just not true. When you have illegality, you have secrecy, you have unscrupulous people. You can't always get a safe abortion under those conditions. Besides, there are relatively few women who really have their own independent money. This kind of class argument strikes me as a red herring, one which has often been used to devalue abortion as a feminist issue by painting it as a class issue instead.

Woodruff: Let's turn to the area of new technology. Scientific changes, better contraceptives, earlier detection of pregnancy—does any of this change the way the debate is framed? Will it make any real difference if we are able to detect pregnancy after, say, one day?

Callahan: I think it will help the pro-life movement. Seeing a sonogram changes a pregnant woman's feeling about what is inside her. And the development of surrogate motherhood has upset many feminists. They worry about the depersonalization and devaluing of women. They talk about the woman as "baby machine"—well, surrogate motherhood makes women into *real* baby machines.

Gordon: Historically, technology has tended to *follow* social need and social demand. The development of hormonal birth control, for example, followed an enormous demand which had outstripped the methods that were then available. I think the same is true of abortion, and that's one of the reasons why I don't think criminalization would lead to a rapid drop in abortion rates. Economic conditions today are such that women have a greater need than ever before to control their fertility.

But one unexpected and disturbing development that has arisen from the new reproductive technologies is the appearance of complicated and exceptional cases that distract us from the general policy issues. For example, an embryo is created in a Petri dish and then the couple splits up. She wants the embryo destroyed. He wants a chance to have it implanted in another woman, arguing that it has a right to life.

Lawyers have to worry about these problems, I know, but I'm more interested in the general social policy that is going to affect the masses of people in this country. By and large, it seems to me that the best way to protect fetuses is to give the mother total control. On average, women have proved to be the best custodians of their own pregnancies. My *moral* position is that contraception is better than abortion, that the earlier you interfere with pregnancy, the better. But as a matter of state policy, the only reasonable compromise position is that until a child is born, the woman in whom that fetus is living should be able to control it.

Willis: How far do you go? Do you throw a woman in jail in order to protect her fetus? And if a fetus is considered a full human being, why stop at its right to life? What about its right to health? Or optimum nutrition? I think it leads in the direction of totalitarianism to have a social policy which monitors or regulates the behavior of pregnant women on their fetuses' behalf. And I see no middle ground. If you have one, let's hear it.

Woodruff: Well, *is* there any common ground here? Is any compromise possible? Or are we too distant, too separated in our initial assumptions?

Gordon: The Wisconsin state legislature recently passed a "pregnancy options" bill, which was made possible because of the collaboration of feminists and right-to-lifers. I admit that the right-to-life people involved were more progressive than the norm.

Callahan: Be patient, they're coming along.

Gordon: The purpose of the bill is to make it possible for teenagers to be openly presented with a variety of options—including abortion and adoption. Now, I'm no particular partisan of this bill. I want to wait and see if it will be useful. But it does suggest a kind of compromise position. If the right-to-lifers are really serious about helping women, then let's hear a lot more talk from them about support services and sex education and birth control—and a lot less of the punitive, victim-blaming attitude they tend to show toward women who want to have abortions.

Fielding: Most of the anti-abortionists I've known, people who are far more active in the movement than I am, have long been privately involved in the kinds of things you're talking about. Perhaps this goes back to your personality profile of the "typical" anti-abortionist as someone who tends to distrust government action. I know any number of women who for years have been involved in giving money and giving their homes to pregnant teenagers, in giving clothes and organizing drives and finding jobs for people. I think this kind of support has to be given. But I can't see how it has anything to do with finding common ground between the pro-abortionists and the anti-abortionists.

Woodruff: Is there any common ground?

Fielding: Not on the basic question. No.

Willis: There may be common ground among individuals. I certainly don't think there's any room for compromise. I feel that there should be no restriction of a woman's right to have an abortion, none whatsoever. I feel that any such restriction is anti-feminist and anti-woman.

Woodruff: So where does that leave us?

Willis: I think it leaves us with a bloody battle.

Callahan: No, I disagree with that. Most people in America are in the middle on the abortion question. That's why neither side has won. And I think there's a great deal of common ground. What do we want? We want women to be fully empowered and we want babies to be healthy. We want the workplace to change so that women can work and the family can be more important. Surely there are many ways that both sides can work on all of this. I also think we might move toward compromise. The way we change things in this country is by persuading people.

Fielding: Persuasion is different from compromise. If someone is persuaded, you're not splitting the difference.

Willis: Is a pragmatic compromise possible? Of course. We have one right now, actually, because *Roe v. Wade* is a compromise, as far as I'm concerned. But is there a compromise that would satisfy me? No. Is there a compromise that I would consider honorable? No. Is there a compromise that would make me feel I didn't need to keep fighting? No.

WHEN (IF) 'ROE' FALLS[2]

When the Supreme Court issued its judgment in the case of *Roe* v. *Wade* in 1973, the Catholic bishops, in an inspired comment, called it another Dred Scott decision. In Dred Scott (1857), the Court declared that under the Constitution blacks could not be citizens and could not be protected by federal laws such as the Missouri Compromise. In *Roe* v. *Wade*, the Court declared that

[2]Reprint of an article by Daniel A. Degnan, S.J., professor of law and jurisprudence of Seton Hall Law School. *Commonweal*. 116:267–9. My 5 '89. Copyright © 1989 by Commonweal Foundation.

prenatal human life could not be protected by state laws. The Constitution meant, the Court said, that a woman's right to abortion took precedence over the fetus's claim to life, even in the final three months of pregnancy.

Dred Scott was, in effect, overruled by the Civil War. It now appears that *Roe* v. *Wade* may be overruled by the Supreme Court itself, or, at least, that its reach will be reduced, if not in the Missouri case, then with one or two more appointments to the Court. Of itself, however, such an outcome will not settle the issue of legal protection for the fetus; more probably, it will define the parameters of future legislative struggles in all fifty states. Under the Constitution, the individual states, not the national government, have inherent power to protect life as part of their power to provide for the general welfare. The Court's 1973 declaration of a right to abortion grounded in a personal right of privacy deprived the states of any authority to exert control over abortion. The likely effect of a new decision overturning or narrowing *Roe* will be to restore to the states the power to prohibit or restrict abortions.

The question I want to address here, in anticipation of such a judgment by the Court, is a moral one. If, as I believe, human life, including unborn human life, cries out for legal protection, is it morally permissible to accept a compromise on abortion? Suppose, for example, that a proposed state law would prohibit abortion in the final six months of pregnancy except for grave reasons such as a threat to the life of the mother posed by her pregnancy, but would provide little or no protection to the fetus in the first three months of pregnancy (the first trimester). Can defenders of human life agree in good conscience to reduced legal protection for prenatal life? The question is important. Compromise may well be the only way to obtain some degree of protection for the fetus. Yet since human life is at stake in every abortion, the need for the law's protection would seem to be absolute.

What is the convergence between law and morals in abortion? One thinks of the prochoice marchers in Washington on April 9, chanting, "choice, choice, choice," and then of Pope John Paul II in the United States: "America, you must choose rightly." Whatever an individual person's claim to autonomy and the reasons and forces that would impel a person to choose an abortion, the moral question in abortion concerns the killing of the human fetus.

In early stages of pregnancy, the fetus is dismembered in the womb, in curettage by use of a sharp instrument, in suction abortion with a vacuum tube, with evacuation of the fetal remains. At a later stage, abortion is achieved by removal of the amniotic fluid in which the fetus swims, followed by injection of a saline solution to poison the fetus. The fetus dies of salt poisoning within an hour or two; labor and delivery of the dead fetus complete the procedure. In late abortions drugs can be used to induce labor; the baby will be delivered prematurely and, if breathing, will be left to die. An abortion by hysterotomy resembles birth by Caesarian section. The premature baby, often born alive, is left to die.

Under *Roe* (the most permissive abortion law among Western nations, according to Mary Ann Glendon's *Abortion and Divorce in Western Law* [Harvard, 1987]), timing does not matter; as a matter of the mother's constitutional right, prenatal human life can be taken at any point in the nine months of pregnancy. Even in the final trimester (24–36 weeks), all that is required is the desire of the mother and the concurrence of a single physician, if a medical facility can be found to accommodate them. (Many physicians, it appears, are reluctant to give full scope to this legal right in the third trimester.)

In fact and logic, and therefore in morals, whatever the Supreme Court has said, it has proved impossible to separate third-trimester abortions from infanticide (24 weeks being the lower end of viability). But what about abortions performed before the fetus is capable of living outside the womb, when it depends for life and nourishment on the placenta to which it is attached in the mother's womb? Every new understanding —biological, genetic, medical—shows a continuum in unborn human life. As early as eight weeks, the crucial features of development have been achieved and there is readable electrical activity coming from the brain. By twelve weeks, brain structure is complete and fetal heartbeat has been monitored. After the eighth week, what follows is principally growth.

In abortion, then, there is no avoiding the nature of the choice that is made and the action that is taken: It is the taking of a human life. It is here that the law has its foremost duty. Whatever the reasons offered and the needs asserted to justify abortions, the first function of law is to protect innocent human life. My argument is a Thomistic one, based on moral reasoning and not on faith, and on Thomas Aquinas's concepts of the relationship between morality and law. As Alasdair MacIntyre of Notre Dame and John Finnis of Oxford have noted, Aquinas relies on commonly known moral principles, beginning with respect for life, a principle that both directs individual moral action and requires community response in the form of law.

Both morals and law are about justice, right relationships among human beings, based upon what each of us owes to the other. At a first basic level, these demands of justice are expressed in the ten commandments (treated by Aquinas as ethical, not religious, propositions): Do not kill; do not steal; do not commit adultery (thus injuring another's spouse and children); do not injure another by false witness. Each of us, in other words, has a right, a moral claim on our fellow human beings, to have our human dignity respected: our lives first, and our family lives, reputations, friendships, property.

My moral claim to life is not only individual, it is social and common. In the moral community of human beings, each of us is related to every other. That my life is to be respected is a claim made upon everyone and a duty owed by all. Justice, therefore, expresses an equality of moral claims among human beings.

It is here that law and morals converge with respect to abortion. First, laws forbidding homicide are almost identical with morality in the acts they proscribe and in their source. Both law and moral principle spring from the judgment that it is wrong to take another's life, or, more fully, from the recognition that justice requires, as its most urgent demand, that the dignity of each human life be accorded an absolute respect and value.

Second, the legal prohibition of homicide expresses the common good of humanity itself. Each human being's claim to life represents a mutual, universal claim, an ordering of moral rule and law. In Aquinas's thought, the natural laws or rational moral principles forbidding killing and assaults and commanding, more generally, that harm be done to no one, express the primary, basic structure of the common good of society. Abortion, therefore, is twice a wrong: It violates a human being's claim to life, and it destroys the order of justice and the common good.

The convergence of law and morals with respect to abortion, in sum, is demanded by the dignity of human life. Abortion is a form of homicide, and this demands that law intervene to protect unborn human life. Not only does each unborn human life have a claim to absolute respect, but our common good, our common dignity as humans, demands that unborn life be reverenced and protected. It is a conclusion that rises out of the premises, and the premises are hard to deny or evade. Yet, in our society, a partial divergence of law and morals occurs, the consequence of two separate but related realities: the response of Americans, at this time in our history, to abortion as a moral and legal question, and the practical limitations of laws forbidding or restricting abortion.

Laws, however moral their subject matter, are enacted by the political community, through its representatives. What laws will Americans support? Mary Ann Glendon's book demonstrates that, contrary to impressions created by misrepresentation and misuse of opinion polls, Americans have never supported the Supreme Court's position in *Roe* sanctioning abortion on demand. Neither do Americans favor a legal prohibition of all abortions. Their position seems to be like the stance taken by their counterparts in other Western nations whose laws enact severe restrictions on late-term abortions, with lesser restrictions in the early months. Americans generally, even some who welcomed *Roe*, seem to have been shocked by the flood of abortions unleashed by that decision, an attitude reinforced as people have become more familiar with the nature of abortion. It follows that, if *Roe* is indeed modified, meaningful restrictions on abortion can be sought with genuine hope. It would be unrealistic, however, to expect that abortion laws in most states will prohibit all abortions.

Underlying this political reality is the response of Americans to the morality of abortions and, further, to their understanding of the relationship between law and morals in abortion. Here I want to argue that the moral principles relating to abortion are not equally evident to all Americans, or to modern people in general. There is a difference between moral truth and our knowledge of it. As Aquinas puts it, even natural law judgments can sometimes be "abolished from the hearts of men and women." The cause, he argues, is an ignorance and a misdirected will or love arising in a society or in individuals out of sin or corruption. The language may be considered quaint, but can we doubt that for many in our society (not excluding ourselves) moral judgments have been clouded? Even apart from cultural degradation, there is the contemporary drive for autonomy, for control of one's own life, which can lead to lessened concern for or disregard of human relationships, responsibilities, and loves. In this climate, the fetus's claim to life will be semi-deliberately or deliberately ignored by some and will hardly be grasped by many.

Apart from sin and pathology, the knowability of moral principle is affected by long-term intellectual, political, and religious trends. To name just one, most modern ethical thought rejects the idea of moral principles or natural laws expressing universal, objective moral claims. Moral reality is seen from the viewpoint of the thinking subject, with the result for the abortion debate that the fetus's claims do not weigh, or do not weigh heavily, against a woman's needs or her claim to reproductive freedom and autonomy.

In consequence, defenders of human life against abortion cannot rely on the force of their form of ethical reasoning, particularly in efforts to persuade those Americans who are all too well instructed in relativist, subjectivist, situationist modes of moral discernment. Even with the broader American public, what will count against abortion will be insistent attention to concrete specifics: a continuing flow of information on who and what the unborn is—a human being like ourselves; a steady insistence on the human unborn's right to life; a constant reminder of the truth that abortion is the killing of a vulnerable human being. The result of this approach is not likely to be a full expression in law of the injustice of abortion. It can, however, save many of the unborn, while affirming the principle of the dignity of human life.

Apart from the degree of public understanding of what abortion is, one must consider the enforceability of restrictive laws, which is dependent to some extent on the willingness or capacity of Americans to obey them. How many persons in our society, as an expression of individual will and moral belief, are likely to seek illegal abortions as a solution to a personal or social problem or need? Abortion advocates predict massive disobedience, with back-alley abortions injuring many and killing some women. It is now admitted that before 1973 these same advocates deliberately and grossly exaggerated the number of deaths from illegal abortions. Nevertheless, these new claims must be given consideration. It is true, as Mary Ann Glendon confirms, that American law and policy impose severe moral and social pressures on American women. Among Western nations the United States ranks lowest in its support of families, particularly of women and children; it holds the same rank in the adequacy of support payments required for the children of divorce. In perverse complement, this nation's abortion and divorce laws are more permissive than those of any other nations studied. With specific reference to abortion, Ms. Glendon writes, women (and their children) are isolated. In keeping with our extreme individualism, a woman may choose an abortion or she may decide to bear her child, but the responsibility is hers. In this harsh climate, the pressure to resolve problems of family life and child rearing through abortion can be overwhelming. Judicial and legislative "permissiveness" on abortion combined with social indifference to family welfare expressed through governmental budgets, is in many cases coercive rather than kindly, dismissive of a woman's rights rather than genuinely respectful of her autonomy. Ironically, however, for prochoice advocates the first solution remains the continuation of abortion on demand.

Those who support the "seamless garment" approach to the defense of life must learn and convey a different lesson. The effort to protect human life must be a double one. The effort to restore protection of human life in laws concerning abortion must be accompanied by a human understanding of the moral and social forces in this country that lead women to choose abortions. This second, concurrent effort must be a broad, continuing one, to enable Americans as a community to recognize and accept their moral responsibilities to one another, both in their personal lives and in their laws. As the Catholic bishops have asked in their pastoral on the economy, this country must grow out of the selfish individualism now proffered by so many as the American way, and even the Christian way. Our society's support of family life, of parents and children, is a basic demand of justice.

The protection of unborn life is also a fundamental demand. In our respect for life, our refusal to attack it, one finds the basic elements of justice. In Aquinas's words, the natural law injunction against killing expresses "the very order of justice and virtue," "the order in the common good." By building on this first understanding of justice and the common good we learn, through experience and moral insight, to broaden and deepen the structures of justice.

Still, the question remains: Is it morally permissible to accept compromise on abortion law? In other Western nations, society has learned to live with compromise, often after bitter struggles. Severe restrictions on abortion are successfully enforced in the later and middle stages of pregnancy. Less severe but still significant standards apply to earlier abortions. The message of many of these laws is that abortion involves human life and poses a grave moral and social problem. Obviously, the exceptions that are made mean that the protection of innocent human life is not seen as an absolute; concretely, each exception involves the killing of a human being. Yet from the viewpoint of objective morality the situation is better than in this country; not only better but more promising, in the sense that these societies take a more serious and responsible view of what abortion is, and may be better positioned to move still further toward reducing its incidence.

Judging what is politically feasible in the American context is a very different exercise from determining what is ethically acceptable, but the two kinds of analysis are both relevant. It will be argued that the mere entertaining of the possibility of compromise will weaken the case for banning abortion altogether. That may be true.

It may also be true that after a decade-and-a-half of legally sanctioned abortion on demand the enactment of an absolute prohibition of abortion is out of reach in all or most of the states. It may also be argued that the acceptance of any compromise on abortion law would necessarily constitute an immoral betrayal of principle. In my view such an all-or-nothing approach is not required and may not be prudent. It is beyond the purview of this article to propose specific tactics to be followed by defenders of life in the new abortion debate we are likely to witness. If, as I think likely, a total or near-total ban on abortion is not possible, it would seem that a new abortion debate in the states could lead to important legal restraints on abortion and support of budgetary and other measures to enhance the dignity of women and families, thereby reducing the pressures on women to opt for abortion.

BAD CHOICES[3]

Sixteen years after the right to a safe, legal abortion was granted to every woman in America by the Supreme Court, that right is in a battle for its life. By mid-July, when the Supreme Court will have rendered its decision in *Webster v. Reproductive Health Services*, there's a good chance that the constitutional right to a safe and legal abortion will be lost, to to be fought for all over again in the legislative houses of every state in the nation.

Hopefully that won't happen. It's possible that the Supreme Court will act to maintain the status quo on the legal basis of *stare decisis*, that is, on the basis that to overturn *Roe v.Wade* would be to ignore precedent. It's unclear whether an enormous outpouring of support for the right to abortion will affect the Supreme Court's decision, but for now it's the best chance supporters of abortion rights have.

Win or lose, the pro-choice movement must ask itself how it got to this awful and painful moment of truth, with no assurance of winning. How did legal abortion, something that over fifteen million American women have undergone, remain controversial enough to approach repeal?

Has there been a backlash against feminism? Perhaps, but backlash can't provide a full explanation for this turnaround. It's clear that the idea that women can and should be equal to men has permeated our culture. Typical middle-class fathers, even among conservatives, go to their daughters' Little League games and dream of their future careers. Pat Schroeder could think seriously about running for president. Our society has barely begun to institutionalize this new attitude, and we've yet to make any progress in valuing more traditionally feminine contributions to our society; but the momentum is toward more equality of the sexes, not less.

What about the usual suspects—Reagan, the Republicans, and the religious right, with their excellent political organizations? These people, so goes the theory, form a very loud and vocal minority that somehow drowns out the will of the majority.

[3]Reprint of an article by public relations consultant Larry Letich. *Tikkun*, 5100 Leona St., Oakland, CA 94619. 4:22–6. Jl/Ag '89. Copyright © 1989 by The Institute for Labor and Mental Health. Reprinted by permission of the author.

Some truth here, too. But it's also a sad refrain that progressive and liberal movements have used too often to avoid accepting responsibility for failing to capture the American political imagination.

The disturbing fact that the pro-choice movement must face is that it has failed to communicate effectively to middle Americans why women must keep the right to abortion.

According to a study done by the National Opinion Research Center, which has been polling Americans about abortion for over twenty years, there is a core of people—about 10 percent—who are deeply convinced that abortion is wrong in almost all circumstances. There is a larger group of Americans—30 percent—who are equally convinced that abortion is a right that must be protected. But the vast majority of Americans, including the majority of baby boomers, are ambivalent about the right to a legal abortion. This moral ambivalence has been strengthened by the anti-abortion movement's daily hammering and its ever more creative publicity tactics.

What has the pro-choice movement done in return? It has *ignored* this ambivalence. It has blinded itself to the need to develop a dialogue with the American people, to understand the roots of this ambivalence and respond to it. The pro-choice movement has focused (at least until recently) only on the superficial aspects of the polls—such as the fact that 69 to 73 percent of the population supports the right to an abortion. It has acted as if abortion rights were being hijacked from a complacent but totally supportive majority by a small band of right-wing religious fanatics. Over and over again, however, the public has shown its ambivalence about abortion. Thirty-six states have passed laws prohibiting public funds for abortions, and in some states, Colorado for instance, the restrictions were passed in statewide referenda.

Much of the American public believes that liberalism is amoral and that it has contributed to the ethical decay of our society. This attitude, of course, doesn't reflect the way most liberal and progressive people live or believe. But for a variety of reasons, some good (the value progressives place on tolerance) and some bad (a reaction against the hypocritical morality of the right wing, a holdover from the "I do my thing, you do your thing" attitudes of the late sixties), progressives have failed to articulate a clear moral, values-based vision of what they want for America. Without such a vision, Americans can be forgiven for feeling that progressives stand for no morality at all.

Moreover, the abortion issue is right at the core of the public debate between individual rights and old-fashioned moral obligations. It is especially threatening because it calls into question the nature of *women's* role, *women's* morality, and *women's* power in a society that has historically seen women as the "civilizers" of a world run by men.

What can the pro-choice movement do to reach the ambivalent majority? How can the pro-choice movement get off the defensive and begin influencing and molding American opinion?

First, it must understand to whom it speaks. The largest and most important segment of the population is the baby boomers. The fact is, the entire baby-boom generation has grown up. The youngest baby boomers are twenty-five, the oldest forty-three, and the vast majority have gotten past the point where an accidental pregnancy is a serious worry for them. On the contrary, they've been having kids—cute, precious, doted-on little Jennifers and Jasons and Jessicas. Or else they've been spending months with thermometers by their beds and dreams of the baby they're finally ready for. An estimated 1.5 million Americans want a child but can't have one. One can't open a magazine these days without reading about infertility, artificial insemination, in vitro fertilization—and adoption. Somewhere unspoken is the resentment against women who have had an abortion when either oneself or someone one is close to can't conceive and may end up spending thousands of dollars to adopt a child.

Second, the pro-choice movement must confront the ambivalence head on. The anti-abortion messages—"abortion is murder," "a fetus is an unborn baby"—are simple, emotionally powerful, and effective. Moreover, the anti-abortion activists are aided by the medical advances of the past twenty years, which have brought home more vividly than ever the miracle of prenatal development.

Nothing the pro-choice movement is saying or doing is powerful enough to counter these statements. It is focusing almost exclusively on "freedom of choice" and "privacy" arguments—and they're very important and effective arguments, certainly the most important ones from a legal perspective. But alone they're not enough. It's true that the pro-choice movement tested these messages and found that "rights" and "freedom of choice" have positive connotations. But these terms also remind people of all those sixties-liberal-ACLU rights that middle America loves to hate. To many people, compared with even the *possibility* that abortion is "murder," a woman's "rights" seem very unimportant.

The problem with an exclusive focus on the "right" to abortion is part of a bigger problem facing liberals and progressives. "Reproductive freedom" and "the right to choice" are rejected by many Americans because these slogans seem to emphasize the primacy of the individual and neglect other moral considerations. Sadly, these phrases conjure up a vision of self-indulgence and selfishness, which leads many Americans to think that those who favor choice are insensitive to other moral concerns.

Americans do not accept the philosophy that each person is an atomized owner of personal rights, a person unconnected to other human beings. Even as they have lived according to this philosophy, they have suffered and are so desperate for messages validating human community that they'll buy anything—cereal, soda, presidents—based upon commercials that deliver these messages. These "community commercials," with their picturesque farmhouses, smiling old people, and families gathered around a table, are one of the hottest trends in TV advertising. People are yearning for community. Liberals and feminists seem to be promising people exactly what most Americans don't want any more—a lonely and empty freedom.

For that reason, it is extremely important that the pro-choice movement begin to reframe its arguments in terms that underscore the fundamental moral vision from which its politics emerge. One way for the pro-choice movement to make its moral commitments more explicit is to focus on the experience of women with unwanted pregnancies. The most vulnerable aspect of the anti-abortionist message is the way it ignores women, treating them as if they were mere vessels for the fetus. The right-to-lifers' underlying assumption (one that fits right in with middle-class experience) is that pregnancy and childbirth are always positive (or at least not destructive) experiences. It is on this false assumption that the anti-abortion movement is most morally vulnerable.

The pro-choice movement should focus on the experience of a woman who is pregnant against her will. It should argue that forcing women to stay pregnant against their will is abusive. In this way, the difference between a wanted and unwanted pregnancy is similar to the difference between wanted and unwanted sex. In both cases, an experience that in one situation is beautiful and wonderful in another situation is horrific. As difficult as it may be morally for some people to accept abortion, there is a greater wrong—a greater immorality—in forcing a woman to undergo experiences as demanding, intimate, and at times life-threatening as pregnancy and childbirth.

It's fine in the rarefied atmosphere of East Coast intellectual circles to talk simply of a woman's "freedom of choice." But the right-to-life movement (and the right wing in general) has shifted the moral base. The message coming from the heartland is that there has to be a moral calculus involved in the decision about abortion. The argument that unwanted children will live miserable lives, or that nobody will take care of these children properly, or that they'll end up on the welfare rolls, is too easily manipulated into a charge that eugenics is the hidden agenda of the pro-choice movement. But the claim that forced pregnancy will cause extreme pain and suffering, so much so that some will risk and lose their lives by having back-alley abortions rather than carry the pregnancy to term, has the moral justification for abortion that Americans demand. What's more, it gets the anti-abortionists off their moral high horse and reveals the true lack of compassion in their stance.

This message must be articulated forcefully. Advertisements with words like "forced pregnancy," "suffering," and "violation" not only pack an emotional wallop, but also capture the moral issues that the anti-abortionists ignore. Furthermore, every woman has either had forced sex or else lives with the nightmare that someday it might happen. To link "unwanted pregnancy" to "unwanted sex" is to connect it to a universally hated and morally repulsive experience.

The pro-choice movement needs to focus on the pregnant woman in general. Until the recent outpouring of articles on abortion, we hadn't heard much about the women who get abortions. We mustn't forget that the people who would be forced to carry their pregnancies to term, who would be forced to endure immeasurable suffering, are precisely that—people, not mere statistics. More specifically, they are women, and only women can humanize the abortion issue. Women, and women's lives, must be heard—in magazines, on television, throughout the media. People must be made to confront the humanity of the pregnant woman.

People also need to be reminded that criminalizing abortion will kill women. Unfortunately, such poor statistics were kept about fatalities from illegal abortions (partially because these abortions *were* illegal) that there are no reliable figures about how many women died and who they were. Still, it would be worthwhile to go into the archives and find the story of *one* woman who died of an illegal abortion. Perhaps a huge funeral march could be organized in her memory, if only to remind Americans that women die from abortions—not nameless women, but women of flesh and blood, women with friends and loved ones, women whose lives were cut short while they were still young.

The next issue is the most difficult but most important one of all. The anti-abortionists have spent sixteen years and countless dollars telling America that "abortion is murder." Watch any anti-abortionist rally or listen to any abortion debate, and you will see that the anti-abortionists' entire argument rests on the idea that a fetus is an "unborn baby." In the latest twist, in a "National Town Meeting" debate on abortion rights televised by PBS on April 9, the anti-abortionists repeatedly referred to fetuses as "preborn babies." However, if one accepts that a fetus is a "preborn baby," one *has* to agree with the anti-abortionists. There is simply no argument.

So, what does the pro-choice movement say in response? On the question of the human status of the fetus, the pro-choice movement's reaction has been a resounding "no comment."

But the American people are *demanding* a forthright answer to this question from the pro-choice movement, and the movement's failure to respond lends tacit support to the anti-abortionist position. The last ten minutes of the hour-long debate was reserved for questions from the audience. Three out of the five questioners brought up the issue of when life begins. The first was a right-to-life woman who said, "Let's just get biological. I would like to ask . . . each of you to respond to the question, If it's not a baby at the moment of conception, what is it?" Then an older man—someone I would count as a member of the ambivalent majority leaning over to the anti-abortionist side—said, "There's a basic question that nobody has really answered on the pro-abortion side of the fence. *When does life begin?*"

OK, let's get biological. Most abortions take place between the eighth and twelfth weeks of gestation. At that time the fetus is two to three inches long and weighs less than 1.5 ounces. Its brain, still in the very early stages of development, weighs at most ten to fifteen grams, compared to 350 grams for a newborn infant's and 1200 to 1400 grams for an adult's. A fetus, especially a fetus in the first trimester, when 91 percent of all abortions are performed, is no more a baby than an egg is a chick.

The pro-choice debaters, good liberals that they were, kept saying that the point when human life begins is a religious issue that honest people can disagree about—that some people may feel that human life starts at conception. This answer sounds like—and frankly is—a wishy-washy cop-out. The question is not simply a religious question; it's a moral one as well. In any case, the pro-choicers' response is unnecessarily conciliatory. Of course "human life begins at conception"—just as a building begins when you lay a cornerstone. But the belief that a full human life exists at conception is simply nonsense, no more a question of differing opinions, religious or otherwise, than the statement that the world is flat or that the earth was created in the year 4004 B.C.E.

If human life is something more than a human body, a human form; if it entails a quality of consciousness of existence; then somewhere in the second trimester a human life begins. Before that a fetus is the potential for human life, absolutely precious as such, but without the neural equipment to experience anything we would recognize as a human life.

This is to claim that there's no moral component to abortion. Most women considering abortion do realize that a potential life must be treated seriously. Yet they also recognize that a zygote and an eight-month-old fetus are in no way morally equivalent. Still, Americans constantly hear the argument that there is no moral way to separate the two, and in light of the fact that the pro-choicers have been unwilling to address the question, these people are beginning to believe the anti-abortionists. The pro-choice movement must be willing to rise above euphemism and speak truth.

Especially if abortion again becomes a matter for each state to decide, the distinction between a zygote and an eight-month-old fetus may become pivotal in the battle to save abortion rights. The viability argument has always rested on shaky ethical ground. In essence, it says that as long as the fetus is totally dependent on its mother for survival, the mother has the right to terminate its existence. This is a hard position to defend morally; the right to survival should not be based on questions of dependence. But if we change the terms of the debate so that they deal with the fundamental question of when life begins, we start to create possibilities other than the yes-or-no choice offered by absolutists on both sides. Legislators, in an eager mood to compromise, will begin to negotiate cut-off dates for legal abortion. Some states' cut-offs will be very early, some will be late; but the overall effect will be to reduce the power of the fundamentalists to mold the debate.

This two-pronged campaign, focusing on women's *need for* (as opposed to *right to*) an abortion, and entailing a serious public inquiry into the human status of the fetus at various stages of development, is the fastest way to reach consensus about abortion, one that takes into account the moral issues most people feel. It might defuse the civil war that we seem to be approaching, and it would also isolate the extreme right wing and set the stage for acceptance of RU486, the pill that induces early abortions.

The communications problems of the pro-choice movement are only a reflection of the broader difficulties that liberal and progressive movements are having in America today. In many ways, liberals and progressives have given up trying to *persuade* the American people to agree with their point of view.

Back in the sixties, the right wing was as popular as—well, as the left wing is now. There's nothing mysterious about this change in political fortune. In the sixties, the right wing morally discredited itself through its opposition to civil rights. Right-wingers looked pretty venal to the average American; they argued for segregation while Blacks in suits and ties and Sunday dresses were shown on evening television getting attacked with police dogs and fire hoses. Then came abortion (along with pornography and the exaggerated evils of suspects' rights), and the right wing was truly born again as the protector of the good and the innocent against the wicked and the licentious. While progressive people offered legal and technocratic answers to America's ills, the right wing grabbed the moral high ground in America's debates.

Liberals and progressives have also experienced a strange failure of the imagination. They seem to be struck by a need to communicate their vision in only the most earnest and humorless way imaginable—a sort of homegrown "socialist realism." With depressingly few exceptions, their brochures, pamphlets, and advertisements fall into one of two categories. They're either bland, apolitical exhortations that self-consciously try to appeal to Yuppies, or they're tomes that seem to say, "Here is three times more information about this subject than you've ever wanted to know. Now that you know the Truth, you'll agree with us or you're a heartless idiot."

Americans *will* listen to a progressive movement willing to reach them. As a whole, Americans are a compassionate people with a deep sense of justice and a great deal of sympathy for the underdog—and, by and large, the American people have failed us because we have failed them. We've stopped listening to their concerns, and most of all *we've stopped speaking their language*. As in any relationship, all the love and goodwill in the world don't make up for an unwillingness to listen and communicate.

The moral vision that we progressives hold can be the most important weapon in our arsenal. We must not focus on narrow legal and procedural concerns; we need to be up front about our moral commitments, finding ways to articulate them and relate them to political concerns. Americans are most responsive to that which makes the most moral sense. For that reason, what is deepest and truest is also what is potentially most popular.

America has been talking to us all along. It's up to us to find the right words to say in return. If we can listen to what America is telling us, be humble enough to see what we have misunderstood, and express our ideals and our compassion in words that speak to the American heart, then a new political era may begin.

TALKING TO MARY ANN GLENDON[4]

Mary Ann Glendon, a professor of comparative law at Harvard University Law School, has been examining Americans' true feelings about the meaning of family. Her new book, *Abortion and Divorce in Western Law* (Harvard University Press), a study of family policies in twenty countries, will shock many women. The reproductive freedom and autonomy that women cherish may work against them, she says; when women in our soci-

[4]Reprint of an interview by Marion Asnes. *Vogue*. 177:238+. N '87. Courtesy *Vogue*. Copyright © 1987 by The Conde Nast Publications Inc.

ety do have children, they're on their own.

Glendon asks: How does a society convince itself to nurture its young? And, does the American attitude toward the decision to reproduce—which we consider a completely personal choice—lead us to ignore women and children in need? In the United States, there is less regulation of abortion than in most other countries. Women may be able to win more social support for motherhood, Glendon says, if they relinquish some of their reproductive rights—trading away, for example, the right to unquestioned second-trimester abortions for improved social assistance, child care, and child-support laws.

The question of abortion is particularly important now since the Supreme Court's newest proposed member, Robert Bork, has written that the right to choose an abortion is not really protected by the Constitution.

Q: How is abortion related to divorce?
A: There's a Catch-22 that runs through American family law: We do not protect the dependent fetus before birth; and we do not support either the economically dependent woman engaged in childrearing or the dependent children themselves. All over the world, other countries show more concern both for the life of the fetus and for the pregnant woman, whom we leave stranded!

One reason that we Americans have so much trouble with mothers and children is that compared with other countries', our population is very big and heterogeneous. We don't seem to be able to work up the feeling that, say, a Swede would have about other Swedes—that all children are our own. It is hard for a lot of people here to find the charity to provide for the needs of other Americans who may not be the same color or have the same kind of background.

Our current laws are the logical consequences of certain ideas that we're very attached to, such as individual freedom and self-reliance. It's as if our extreme love of individualism has created a disdain for the weak. Women are allowed—left alone—to make reproductive decisions, and to flourish or suffer from the results. We are not conscious of the way we have let our love of individual liberty trump everything else, such as our sense of community.

Q: How do Americans feel about the abortion rights we have now?
A: Only about 20 percent of the population believe that abortion should be available on demand throughout pregnancy; about 20 percent think that there should be no abortion except possibly to

save the mother's life. The majority of the population—the remaining 60 percent—feel uncomfortable with the idea that a woman could only have an abortion if her life were in danger, but feel equally uncomfortable with no restrictions on abortion at all.

Europeans have found that you don't have to opt for one extreme or the other. They've worked out systems that combine compassion and support for the pregnant woman with concern for the fetus, a concern that increases as it approaches term.

I believe that most Americans want a European-type compromise: an abortion would be easy to get in the first trimester, and progressively more difficult to get as the pregnancy went on. I also think that most Americans, if their attention is called to the matter, want to support maternity and child care. We're not as bad as our legal system makes us out to be.

Q: Would a European-style compromise dramatically alter women's behavior?
A: Well, 91 percent of abortions take place in the first trimester. But in the U.S. there is less regulation of abortion, even in the third trimester, than in any other country but India and China.

Q: How would Robert Bork's becoming a member of the Supreme Court affect future decisions on abortion?
A: I think it is less likely that the Court would overrule *Roe v. Wade*, the 1973 decision that legalized abortion, than that it would reduce the scope of that decision to its narrow meaning— that a statute forbidding abortion unless the woman's life was endangered is unconstitutional. That would leave the rest of the matter to the states.

Now, what would happen in the states? Most likely, exactly what was happening before the Supreme Court decision—a wave of liberalization. By 1973, nineteen states had reformed their abortion laws. In almost all the other countries I studied, regulation was left to elected representatives, who made compromises almost everyone could accept.

The great thing about legislation is that you have a chance to undo it. You can get in there and slug it out, and argue and bargain. The system is relatively open, like our society. But once the Supreme Court says something is unconstitutional the whole legislative process, as imperfect as it may be, is brought to a crashing halt.

Q: If there's little chance of rewriting abortion laws, why should we rethink them?

A: Mainly, what I'm concerned about are the kinds of things that go into forming a mentality. I'm worried about forming a mentality that says fetuses are not alive when they are, a mentality that discourages taking responsibility for those who need us.

I see the same thread running through the issue of divorce. We do not require public responsibility for the casualties of divorce by awarding realistic levels of welfare assistance, or private responsibility by collecting realistic levels of child support. Other countries have found ways to assess child support at a high enough level, to deduct it from the absent spouse's paycheck, and to maintain families headed by single women at a decent standard of living. We must ensure that while it may be easy to get rid of your spouse, it isn't easy to get rid of financial obligations to your children.

Q: Why are support awards so low?

A: Studies of support awards show that American judges are by and large protecting the life style of the father at the expense of the children. Europeans use standardized formulas and tables that are based on how much it costs to raise a child. They are adjusted for increases in the cost of living.

Child support is just not a big issue in places like Sweden, the Netherlands, and Germany. When you ask your lawyer, "How much child support am I going to get?" he doesn't give you a half-hour of "It depends on the judge" and this and that. He just pulls a card out from his desk drawer and he gives you a figure, a realistic figure. I'm not saying that all over Western Europe divorced women and children are living a very comfortable life, but they are living decently.

Q: Could Americans be so generous as to say yes, let's help mothers?

A: Generosity is native to America. A great example is the Marshall Plan after World War II, which was awe-inspiring. I hope that somehow we might be able to come up with something like a Marshall Plan for poor children. There are people who would bet against me on that, but you have to keep trying to persuade people that it's in their interest to care. It's a test of our social fabric: Have we become a nation of deracinated individuals, so that a program for the nation's children cannot be brought to light?

FRIENDLY PERSUASION[5]

Daniel: When *Roe v. Wade* was decided in 1973, I basically supported it. I think, ideally, I might have had a law that cut off legal abortion earlier than the present 24 weeks or so. But, nonetheless, it seems to me the present law is tolerable. I make a fairly sharp distinction, however, between the legality of abortion and the morality of it. I think women should ultimately have the choice about whether or not to have an abortion. But I also think that a woman should have an abortion only when there is a very, very serious reason to do so, and she should be prepared to bear a great deal of burden before resorting to abortion.

Sidney: My view is that the conceptus is a member of the human family and is worthy of protection as all powerless human life should be. The only justification I can see for treating this life as a means to an end of a more powerful person—i.e., the mother— is if there is a chance the mother's life is involved. There should be some other way to solve problem pregnancies than by killing. Abortion on demand seems to me a very bad thing for our society, an immoral thing.

So I would like to see the law changed. I would see as the ultimate goal that from the moment of conception, this would be considered a human life. It's certainly not a person, but then neither is a baby a person. I think the boundaries of life have to be treated and protected just like the powerful adult male forms of life.

Daniel: There are two reasons why I hold the view I do. First of all, we are very divided in our society on the issue, particularly on when human life begins or personhood begins. I don't think it appropriate to try to pass legislation on an issue where there is, to me, a great deal of uncertainty and doubt. It is wiser to leave the matter to individual choice, hoping that people will act very conscientiously. Secondly, every country where abortion is illegal has a very high rate of illegal abortions. One way or the other, women

[5]Reprint of an interview by staff writer Joseph Carey. *U.S. News & World Report*. 105:30–1. O 3 '88. Copyright © 1988, U.S. News & World Report.

with seriously troubled pregnancies are, in fact, going to have abortions. So I don't think one can effectively make it illegal. Here, I stand on a traditional principle of law: One should not legislate on those matters where one cannot enforce the law.

Sidney: My response to that would be that in a question of doubt, if a life is at stake, one should take the more protective view. I guess I see the idea of a communal responsibility, of a sense of protection being more important in this case than the autonomy given to the individual woman.

In the Opposing Camps

Daniel: I think there are basically two prochoice movements. One says, look, there are going to be some situations that do present really tragic dilemmas, where there will be great pressure or need or reason for a woman to have an abortion, which has to be taken into account over against the real respect one ought to pay to fetuses. So it's really a hard, difficult, tragic choice. There is, however, another prochoice view which is really saying that the only moral issue is giving women total freedom of choice on the matter, the fetus has no moral standing or moral seriousness and hence, there really isn't a dilemma. For them, the only tragedy is when women aren't given total freedom.

Sidney: That kind of approach is based on a big mistake. It assumes that if I invest my fetus with value—if *I* want it and *I* invest it with value—then it has value. If I don't, then it doesn't. It can be disposed of. And that seems to me a very dangerous precedent.

Daniel: I don't see any clear way of being more restrictive without running into lots of problems. But I would like to see a much more open discussion and debate about the morality of abortion. I'm afraid there are too many women for whom it's a standard method of birth control. We know that there are a number of women who have repeat abortions. That seems to me not a healthy situation.

On the prolife side, what troubles me is the willingness to take a matter of considerable moral uncertainty and simply impose an answer on everyone, which seems to me to go beyond not only the existing political consensus but beyond what I would think would be a justifiable moral consensus on the status of the fetus. It's acting as if we have solved the problem when it seems to me we haven't and it's still an open issue.

Sidney: I guess the people on the opposite side that most upset me are those who exalt control and autonomy. And I hate the people who are violently prolife who seem to be filled with hate, seem to have a totally repressed view of woman. They see a certain view of the family in which women are supposed to stay in their place and stay home. They connect abortion with this whole status quo.

I definitely feel that the prolife program has to go along with a great deal more support for women, for day care and for real alternatives. We have kind of solved the problem of women in this culture by privatization, saying, "It's your problem. Go away; take care of it." I think that has been very bad for women, and a very easy way out for the society.

On Finding Common Ground

Sidney: I think the growth of embryology and fetology and even sonograms [is] making us have more empathy and emotional identification with the unborn. And I think the future of the human race depends on the growth of empathy, the growth of identification with others, especially with the powerless. And I would hope that changes in abortion would be part of a general valuing of life and a part of the peace and ecological movements. The interesting thing about the abortion debate is that we see realignments now of right and left. I think the sense of caring and preserving and loving and supporting is growing within the human species.

Daniel: I'm not that optimistic. I think it's necessary also to point out that Sidney represents one form of opposition to abortion. But as she well knows, there are people in her prolife group that don't represent this transformation at all, but for them abortion is wrong, capital punishment is right, nuclear warfare is right, the right to keep guns is right.

I very much agree with Sidney that there could be a good deal of agreement on changing the conditions that lead women to have abortions. Providing more support, day care and the like. I think it's going to be very hard to find a common ground on the legal issues. Part of the problem on the legal side, unfortunately, is that there aren't many available solutions. You either can do it or you can't do it.

Sidney: I think there are certain compromises. Allowing abortions if you have serious reasons, but not just allowing everybody to do it at all times in all places.

Daniel: One thing that's been occasionally suggested is what if we simply set a 12-week limit? That would represent a significant compromise for prochoice. Would the prolife people be prepared to split the difference, so to speak? My sense is no.

Sidney: I definitely believe that in every step along the way is progress, so I would be willing to look at all steps as a move toward my goal. The reason why the law is so important is behavior shapes feelings and thoughts as well as the other way around. So once you have many, many abortions, it's much harder for people to be sensitive to the seriousness of it or to think a different way. So I think anything that would be a step back toward more seriousness would be positive.

Daniel: I have detected among some prochoice people a kind of unhappiness with the very large number of abortions in our society, particularly the large number of repeat abortions, and a sense that abortion has become too routine. So I think that there is some uneasiness on the prochoice side that might lead some to back down a bit on the present law. Unfortunately, we have not had much opportunity to talk about alternatives and take them seriously.

Sidney: I do see other things happening in society. For instance, the furor over surrogate mothering made some feminists rethink their position that autonomy and control over one's own body is the ultimate principle. I also think the spread of infertility that many women have experienced through repeated abortions or other aspects of the sexual revolution [is] making us rethink the very permissive approach to sexuality that has led to abortion's being necessary.

Daniel: Sidney and I have influenced each other to a considerable extent, and we at least understand how to view the other viewpoint with some sympathy. I wish we had more occasions for people to have some dialogue and discussion which was not acrimonious, in which people were prepared to admit their own hesitations and doubts and worries. An awful lot of people have private doubts and reservations about some of the people on their side of the issues. But we don't live in a society very congenial to bringing those out. I wish we had a situation where everybody could speak a bit more about their honest feelings on the subject and talk and probe together, not merely attack each other.

WE DO ABORTIONS HERE[6]

We do abortions here; that is all we do. There are weary, grim moments when I think I cannot bear another basin of bloody remains, utter another kind phrase of reassurance. So I leave the procedure room in the back and reach for a new chart. Soon I am talking to an eighteen-year-old woman pregnant for the fourth time. I push up her sleeve to check her blood pressure and find row upon row of needle marks, neat and parallel and discolored. She has been so hungry for her drug for so long that she has taken to using the loose skin of her upper arms; her elbows are already a permanent ruin of bruises. She is surprised to find herself nearly four months pregnant. I suspect she is often surprised, in a mild way, by the blows she is dealt. I prepare myself for another basin, another brief and chafing loss.

"How can you stand it?" Even the clients ask. They see the machine, the strange instruments, the blood, the final stroke that wipes away the promise of pregnancy. Sometimes I see that too: I watch a woman's swollen abdomen sink to softness in a few stuttering moments and my own belly flip-flops with sorrow. But all it takes for me to catch my breath is another interview, one more story that sounds so much like the last one. There is a numbing sameness lurking in this job: the same questions, the same answers, even the same trembling tone in the voices. The worst is the sameness of human failure, of inadequacy in the face of each day's dull demands.

In describing this work, I find it difficult to explain how much I enjoy it most of the time. We laugh a lot here, as friends and as professional peers. It's nice to be with women all day. I like the sudden, transient bonds I forge with some clients: moments when I am in my strength, remembering weakness, and a woman in weakness reaches out for my strength. What I offer is not power, but solidness, offered almost eagerly. Certain clients waken in me every tender urge I have—others make me wince and bite my tongue. Both challenge me to find a balance. It is a sweet brutality we practice here, a stark and loving dispassion.

[6]Reprint of a memoir by Sallie Tisdale. *Harper's Magazine*. 275:66–70. O '87. Copyright © 1987 by Sallie Tisdale.

I look at abortion as if I am standing on a cliff with a telescope, gazing at some great vista. I can sweep the horizon with both eyes, survey the scene in all its distance and size. Or I can put my eye to the lens and focus on the small details, suddenly so close. In abortion the absolute must always be tempered by the contextual, because both are real, both valid, both hard. How can we do this? How can we refuse? Each abortion is a measure of our failure to protect, to nourish our own. Each basin I empty is a promise—but a promise broken a long time ago.

I grew up on the great promise of birth control. Like many women my age, I took the pill as soon as I was sexually active. To risk pregnancy when it was so easy to avoid seemed stupid, and my contraceptive success, as it were, was part of the promise of social enlightenment. But birth control fails, far more frequently than laboratory trials predict. Many of our clients take the pill; its failure to protect them is a shocking realization. We have clients who have been sterilized, whose husbands have had vasectomies; each one is a statistical misfit, fine print come to life. The anger and shame of these women I hold in one hand, and the basin in the other. The distance between the two, the length I pace and try to measure, is the size of an abortion.

The procedure is disarmingly simple. Women are surprised, as though the mystery of conception, a dark and hidden genesis, requires an elaborate finale. In the first trimester of pregnancy, it's a mere few minutes of vacuuming, a neat tidying up. I give a woman a small yellow Valium, and when it has begun to relax her, I lead her into the back, into bareness, the stirrups. The doctor reaches in her, opening the narrow tunnel to the uterus with a succession of slim, smooth bars of steel. He inserts a plastic tube and hooks it to a hose on the machine. The woman is framed against white paper that crackles as she moves, the light bright in her eyes. Then the machine rumbles low and loud in the small windowless room; the doctor moves the tube back and forth with an efficient rhythm, and the long tail of it fills with blood that spurts and stumbles along into a jar. He is usually finished in a few minutes. They are long minutes for the woman; her uterus frequently reacts to its abrupt emptying with a powerful, unceasing cramp, which cuts off the blood vessels and enfolds the irritated, bleeding tissue.

I am learning to recognize the shadows that cross the faces of the women I hold. While the doctor works between her spread legs, the paper drape hiding his intent expression, I stand beside the table. I hold the woman's hands in mine, resting them just below her ribs. I watch her eyes, finger her necklace, stroke her hair. I ask about her job, her family; in a haze she answers me; we chatter, faces close, eyes meeting and sliding apart.

I watch the shadows that creep up unnoticed and suddenly darken her face as she screws up her features and pushes a tear out each side to slide down her cheeks. I have learned to anticipate the quiver of chin, the rapid intake of breath and the surprising sobs that rise soon after the machine starts to drum. I know this is when the cramp deepens, and the tears are partly the tears that follow pain—the sharp, childish crying when one bumps one's head on a cabinet door. But a well of woe seems to open beneath many women when they hear that thumping sound. The anticipation of the moment has finally come to fruit; the moment has arrived when the loss is no longer an imagined one. It has come true.

I am struck by the sameness and I am struck every day by the variety here—how this commonplace dilemma can so display the differences of women. A twenty-one-year-old woman, unemployed, uneducated, without family, in the fifth month of her fifth pregnancy. A forty-two-year-old mother of teenagers, shocked by her condition, refusing to tell her husband. A twenty-three-year-old mother of two having her seventh abortion, and many women in their thirties having their first. Some are stoic, some hysterical, a few giggle uncontrollably, many cry.

I talk to a sixteen-year-old uneducated girl who was raped. She has gonorrhea. She describes blinding headaches, attacks of breathlessness, nausea. "Sometimes I feel like two different people," she tells me with a calm smile, "and I talk to myself."

I pull out my plastic models. She listens patiently for a time, and then holds her hands wide in front of her stomach.

"When's the baby going to go up into my stomach?" she asks.

I blink. "What do you mean?"

"Well," she says, still smiling, "when women get so big, isn't the baby in your stomach? Doesn't it hatch out of an egg there?"

My first question in an interview is always the same. As I walk down the hall with the woman, as we get settled in chairs and I glance through her files, I am trying to gauge her, to get a sense of the words, and the tone, I should use. With some I joke, with others I chat, sometimes I fall into a brisk, business-like patter. But I ask every woman, "Are you sure you want to have an abortion?" Most nod with grim knowing smiles. "Oh, yes," they sigh. Some seek forgiveness, offer excuses. Occasionally a woman will flinch and say, "Please don't use that word."

Later I describe the procedure to come, using care with my language. I don't say "pain" any more than I would say "baby." So many are afraid to ask how much it will hurt. "My sister told me—" I hear. "A friend of mine said—" and the dire expectations unravel. I prick the index finger of a woman for a drop of blood to test, and as the tiny lancet approaches the skin she averts her eyes, holding her trembling hand out to me and jumping at my touch.

It is when I am holding a plastic uterus in one hand, a suction tube in the other, moving them together in imitation of the scrubbing to come, that women ask the most secret question. I am speaking in a matter-of-fact voice about "the tissue" and "the contents" when the woman suddenly catches my eye and asks, "How big is the baby now?" These words suggest a quiet need for a definition of the boundaries being drawn. It isn't so odd, after all, that she feels relief when I describe the growing bud's bulbous shape, its miniature nature. Again I gauge, and sometimes lie a little, weaseling around its infantile features until its clinging power slackens.

But when I look in the basin, among the curdlike blood clots, I see an elfin thorax, attenuated, its pencilline ribs all in parallel rows with tiny knobs of spine rounding upwards. A translucent arm and hand swim beside.

A sleepy-eyed girl, just fourteen, watched me with a slight and goofy smile all through her abortion. "Does it have little feet and little fingers and all?" she'd asked earlier. When the suction was over she sat up woozily at the end of the table and murmured, "Can I see it?" I shook my head firmly.

"It's not allowed," I told her sternly, because I knew she didn't really want to see what was left. She accepted this statement of authority, and a shadow of confused relief crossed her plain, pale face.

Privately, even grudgingly, my colleagues might admit the power of abortion to provoke emotion. But they seem to prefer the broad view and disdain the telescope. Abortion is a matter of choice, privacy, control. Its uncertainty lies in specific cases: retarded women and girls too young to give consent for surgery, women who are ill or hostile or psychotic. Such common dilemmas are met with both compassion and impatience: they slow things down. We are too busy to chew over ethics. One person might discuss certain concerns, behind closed doors, or describe a particularly disturbing dream. But generally there is to be no ambivalence.

Every day I take calls from women who are annoyed that we cannot see them, cannot do their abortion today, this morning, now. They argue the price, demand that we stay after hours to accommodate their job or class schedule. Abortion is so routine that one expects it to be like a manicure: Quick, cheap, and painless.

Still, I've cultivated a certain disregard. It isn't negligence, but I don't always pay attention. I couldn't be here if I tried to judge each case on its merits; after all, we do over a hundred abortions a week. At some point each individual in this line of work draws a boundary and adheres to it. For one physician the boundary is a particular week of gestation; for another, it is a certain number of repeated abortions. But these boundaries can be fluid too: one physician overruled his own limit to abort a mature but severely malformed fetus. For me, the limit is allowing my clients to carry their own burden, shoulder the responsibility themselves. I shoulder the burden of trying not to judge them.

This city has several "crisis pregnancy centers" advertised in the Yellow Pages. They are small offices staffed by volunteers, and they offer free pregnancy testing, glossy photos of dead fetuses, and movies. I had a client recently whose mother is active in the anti-abortion movement. The young woman went to the local crisis center and was told that the doctor would make her touch her dismembered baby, that the pain would be the most horrible she could imagine, and that she might, after an abortion, never be able to have children. All lies. They call her at home and at work, over and over and over, but she had been wise enough to give a false name. She came to us a fugitive. We who do abortions are marked, by some, as impure. It's dirty work.

When a deliveryman comes to the sliding glass window by the reception desk and tilts a box toward me, I hesitate. I read the packing slip, assess the shape and weight of the box in light of its supposed contents. We request familiar faces. The doors are carefully locked; I have learned to half glance around at bags and boxes, looking for a telltale sign. I register with security when I arrive, and I am careful not to bang a door. We are all a little on edge here.

Concern about size and shape seem to be natural, and so is the relief that follows. We make the powerful assumption that the fetus is different from us, and even when we admit the similarities, it is too simplistic to be seduced by form alone. But the form is enormously potent—humanoid, powerless, palm-sized, and pure, it evokes an almost fierce tenderness when viewed simply as what it appears to be. But appearance, and even potential, aren't enough. The fetus, in becoming itself, can ruin others; its utter dependence has a sinister side. When I am struck in the moment by the contents in the basin, I am careful to remember the context, to note the tearful teenager and the woman sighing with something more than relief. One kind of question, though, I find considerably trickier.

"Can you tell what it is?" I am asked, and this means gender. This question is asked by couples, not women alone. Always couples would abort a girl and keep a boy. I have been asked about twins, and even if I could tell what race the father was.

An eighteen-year-old woman with three daughters brought her husband to the interview. He glared first at me, then at his wife, as he sank lower and lower in the chair, picking his teeth with a toothpick. He interrupted a conversation with his wife to ask if I could tell whether the baby would be a boy or a girl. I told him I could not.

"Good," he replied in a slow and strangely malevolent voice, "'cause if it was a boy I'd wring her neck."

In a literal sense, abortion exists because we are able to ask such questions, able to assign a value to the fetus which can shift with changing circumstances. If the human bond to a child were as primitive and unflinchingly narrow as that of other animals, there would be no abortion. There would be no abortion because there would be nothing more important than caring for the young and perpetuating the species, no reason for sex but to make babies. I sense this sometimes, this wordless organic duty, when I do ultrasounds.

We do ultrasound, a sound-wave test that paints a faint, gray picture of the fetus, whenever we're uncertain of gestation. Age is measured by the width of the skull and confirmed by the length of the femur or thighbone; we speak of a pregnancy as being a certain "femur length" in weeks. The usual concern is whether a pregnancy is within the legal limit for an abortion. Women this far along have bellies which swell out round and tight like trim muscles. When they lie flat, the mound rises softly above the hips, pressing the umbilicus upward.

It takes practice to read an ultrasound picture, which is grainy and etched as though in strokes of charcoal. But suddenly a rapid rhythmic motion appears—the beating heart. Nearby is a soft oval, scratched with lines—the skull. The leg is harder to find, and then suddenly the fetus moves, bobbing in the surf. The skull turns away, an arm slides across the screen, the torso rolls. I know the weight of a baby's head on my shoulder, the whisper of lips on ears, the delicate curve of a fragile spine in my hand. I know how heavy and correct a newborn cradled feels. The creature I watch in secret requires nothing from me but to be left alone, and that is precisely what won't be done.

These inadvertently made beings are caught in a twisting web of motive and desire. They are at least inconvenient, sometimes quite literally dangerous in the womb, but most often they fall somewhere in between—consequences never quite believed in come to roost. Their virtue rises and falls outside their own nature: they become only what we make them. A fetus created by accident is the most absolute kind of surprise. Whether the blame lies in a failed IUD, a slipped condom, or a false impression of safety, that fetus is a thing whose creation has been actively worked against. Its existence is an error. I think this is why so few women, even late in a pregnancy, will consider giving a baby up for adoption. To do so means making the fetus real—imagining it as something whole and outside oneself. The decision to terminate a pregnancy is sometimes so difficult and confounding that it creates an enormous demand for immediate action. The decision is a rejection; the pregnancy has become something to be rid of, a condition to be ended. It is a burden, a weight, a thing separate.

Women have abortions because they are too old, and too young, too poor, and too rich, too stupid, and too smart. I see women who berate themselves with violent emotions for their first and only abortion, and others who return three times, five times, hauling two or three children, who cannot remember to take a pill or where they put the diaphragm. We talk glibly about choice. But the choice for what? I see all the broken promises in lives lived like a series of impromptu obstacles. There are the sweet, light promises of love and intimacy, the glittering promise of education and progress, the warm promise of safe families, long years of innocence and community. And there is the promise of freedom: freedom from failure, from faithlessness. Freedom from biology. The early feminist defense of abortion asked many questions, but the one I remember is this: Is biology destiny? And the answer is yes, sometimes it is. Women who have the fewest choices of all exercise their right to abortion the most.

Oh, the ignorance. I take a woman to the back room and ask her to undress; a few minutes later I return and find her positioned discreetly behind a drape, still wearing underpants. "Do I have to take these off too?" she asks, a little shocked. Some swear they have not had sex, many do not know what a uterus is, how sperm and egg meet, how sex makes babies. Some late seekers do not believe themselves pregnant; they believe themselves *impregnable*. I was chastised when I began this job for referring to some clients as girls: it is a feminist heresy. They come so young, snapping gum, sockless and sneakered, and their shakily applied eyeliner smears when they cry. I call them girls with maternal benignity. I cannot imagine them as mothers.

The doctor seats himself between the woman's thighs and reaches into the dilated opening of a five-month pregnant uterus. Quickly he grabs and crushes the fetus in several places, and the room is filled with a low clatter and snap of forceps, the click of the tanaculum, and a pulling, sucking sound. The paper crinkles as the drugged and sleepy woman shifts, the nurse's low, honey-brown voice explains each step in delicate words.

I have fetus dreams, we all do here: dreams of abortions one after the other; of buckets of blood splashed on the walls; trees full of crawling fetuses. I dreamed that two men grabbed me and began to drag me away. "Let's do an abortion," they said with a sickening leer, and I began to scream, plunged into a vision of sucking, scraping pain, of being spread and torn by impartial instruments that do only what they are bidden. I woke from this dream barely able to breathe and thought of kitchen tables and coat hangers, knitting needles striped with blood, and women all alone clutching a pillow in their teeth to keep the screams from piercing the apartment-house walls. Abortion is the narrowest edge between kindness and cruelty. Done as well as it can be, it is still violence—merciful violence, like putting a suffering animal to death.

Maggie, one of the nurses, received a call at midnight not long ago. It was a woman in her twentieth week of pregnancy; the necessarily gradual process of cervical dilation begun the day before had stimulated labor, as it sometimes does. Maggie and one of the doctors met the woman at the office in the night. Maggie helped her onto the table, and as she lay down the fetus was delivered into Maggie's hands. When Maggie told me about it the next day, she cupped her hands into a small bowl—"It was just like a little kitten," she said softly, wonderingly. "Everything was still attached."

At the end of the day I clean out the suction jars, pouring blood into the sink, splashing the sides with flecks of tissue. From the sink rises a rich and humid smell, hot, earthy, and moldering; it is the smell of something recently alive beginning to decay. I take care of the plastic tub on the floor, filled with pieces too big to be trusted to the trash. The law defines the contents of the bucket I hold protectively against my chest as "tissue." Some would say my complicity in filling that bucket gives me no right to call it anything else. I slip the tissue gently into a bag and place it in the freezer, to be burned at another time. Abortion requires of me an entirely new set of assumptions. It requires a willingness to live with conflict, fearlessness, and grief. As I close the freezer door, I imagine a world where this won't be necessary, and then return to the world where it is.

BIBLIOGRAPHY

An asterisk (*) preceding a reference indicates that the article or part of it has been reprinted in this book.

BOOKS AND PAMPHLETS

Baird, Robert M. and Rosenbaum, Stuart E., eds. The ethics of abortion: pro-choice vs. pro-life. Prometheus Books. '89.

Barry, Robert L. Medical ethics: essays on abortion and euthanasia. P. Lang Publishers. '89.

Belz, Mark. Suffer the little children: Christians, abortion, and civil disobedience. Good News. '89.

Boston Women's Health Book Collective. The new our bodies, ourselves: a book by and for women. Touchstone/Simon & Schuster. '84.

Burtchaell, James T. Rachel weeping: the case against abortion. Harper & Row. '84.

Callahan, Sidney and Daniel, eds. Abortion: understanding differences. Plenum Press. '84.

Eisenstein, Zillah R. The female body and the law. U of California Press. '88.

Evangelicals for Social Action and Sider, Ronald J. Completely pro-life. Inter-Varsity. '87.

Faux, Marian. Roe vs. Wade: the story of the landmark Supreme Court decision that made abortion legal. Macmillan. '88.

Garfield, Jay L. and Hennessey, Patricia, eds. Abortion: moral and legal perspectives. U. of Massachusetts Press. '85.

Ginsburg, Faye D. Contested lives: the abortion debate in an American community. University of California Press. '89.

Glendon, Mary Ann. Abortion and divorce in Western law. Harvard U Press. '87.

Goldstein, Robert D. Mother-love and abortion: a legal interpretation. University of California Press. '88.

Gordon, Linda. Woman's body, woman's right: a social history of birth control in America. Penguin. '77; rev. ed. '90.

Grenier-Sweet, Gail, ed. Pro-life feminism: different voices. Life Cycle Books. '85.

Harrison, Beverly Wildung. Our right to choose: toward a new ethic of abortion. Beacon Press. '83.

Howe, Louise K. Moments on Maple Avenue: the reality of abortion. Macmillan. '84; Warner Books. '86.

Luker, Kristin. Abortion and the politics of motherhood. University of California Press. '84.

Maguire, Marjorie R. and Daniel C. Abortion: a guide to making ethical choices. Catholics for a Free Choice. '83.

Melton, Gary B., ed. Adolescent abortion: psychological and legal issues. University of Nebraska Press. '86.

Messer, Ellen and May, Kathryn E. Back rooms: voices from the illegal abortion era. St. Martin's Press. '88.

Mihbauer, Barbara and Obventz, Bert N. The law giveth: legal aspects of the abortion controversy. McGraw. '84.

Miller, Hal. The abandoned middle: the ethics and politics of abortion in America. Penumbra Press. '88.

Mohr, James C. Abortion in America: the origins and evolution of national policy, 1800–1900. Oxford U. Press. '78.

Petchesky, Rosalind P. Abortion and woman's choice: the state, sexuality and reproductive freedom. Longman. '84.

Rodman, Hyman and Lewis, Susan H. The sexual rights of adolescence: competence, vulnerability, and parental control. Columbia University Press. '84.

Sass, Lauren R., ed. Abortion: freedom of choice and the right to life. Facts on File. '78.

Sheehan, Patrick J. Women, society, the state and abortion: a structural analysis. Praeger. '87.

Skolnick, Gary E. Abortion: index of modern information with bibliography. ABBE Pubs. '88.

Steiner, Gilbert Y. The abortion dispute and the American system. Brookings. '83.

Sumner, L. W. Abortion and moral theory. Princeton University Press. '81.

Taub, Nadine and Cohen, Sherrill, eds. Reproductive laws for the 1990s. Humana Press. '89.

Terkel, Susan. Abortion: facing the issues. Watts. '88.

Tooley, Michael. Abortion and infanticide. Oxford University Press. '86.

Willke, J. C. Abortion and slavery: history repeats. Hayes. '84.

ADDITIONAL PERIODICAL ARTICLES WITH ABSTRACTS

For those who wish to read more widely on the subject of abortion, this section contains abstracts of additional articles that bear on the topic. Readers who require a comprehensive list of materials are advised to consult the *Readers' Guide to Periodical Literature* and other Wilson indexes.

THE RIGHT TO CHOOSE

Save my law (*Roe v. Wade* plantiff N. McCorvey at Washington, D.C. rally). George Howe Colt *Life* 12:111–12+ My '89

Norma McCorvey, who was known as Jane Roe in the landmark 1973 Supreme Court case *Roe v. Wade*, is speaking out now that the Court's ruling that women have a constitutional right to abortion is in danger of being reversed. McCorvey, who became pregnant in 1969 while she was a resident of Texas, could not afford to keep the baby or go to California for a legal abortion. She decided to give the baby up for adoption, but her adoption lawyer knew about two lawyers who were searching for a plaintiff to contest Texas's abortion laws. The Court's ruling did not come in time for her to benefit from it herself. McCorvey recently marched in a crowd of 300,000 in a prochoice rally in Washington, D.C.

She does abortions: a doctor's story. Elizabeth Kaye *Mademoiselle* 94:150–3+ F '88

In an interview, a doctor who performs abortions discusses how she counsels women who are considering abortion, her emotions about the procedure, and her worry that abortion will be made illegal again.

So much for Prince Charming (excerpt from *Dancing at the edge of the world*). Ursula K. Le Guin *Ms.* 17:101–2+ Ja/F '89

An article excerpted from *Dancing at the Edge of the World*. The threat to abortion rights is greater now than at any time since the monumental *Roe v. Wade* decision. The need for solidarity and action among women is immediate. The Right-to-Life people insist that their goal is the preservation of life, but that phrase appears to be more of a slogan than a goal. What women in the anti-choice movement really want is to share in the male control over women. The writer describes the circumstances of her own abortion and discusses why it was the right thing to do.

Two steps back (consequences of *Webster* decision). Barbara Ehrenreich *Ms.* 18:24–5 O '89

The Supreme Court's *Webster* decision represents the first time in American history that women have experienced a rollback of hard-won rights. The right-to-life rhetoric of the antiabortion movement that was supported by *Webster* is merely a humanistic-sounding front for the agenda of patriarchy. There is reason to believe, however, that today's fundamentalist and antifeminist movements are patriarchy's last gasp. Uncontrolled childbearing is no longer the best way to ensure the survival of the species. Safe, self-help abortions are becoming possible, and the proponents of patriarchy have abandoned their old commitment to protecting women and children in exchange for oppressing them. Most important, feminists are not about to give up a struggle that has been going on for 150 years.

The new abortion wars (political consequences of *Webster* **decision).** Morton Kondracke *The New Republic* 201:17–19 Ag 28 '89

Some observers suggest that the Supreme Court's *Webster* decision, which expands states' power to limit abortion, will benefit the prochoice movement by galvanizing people who take abortion rights for granted. A flood of contributions has more than doubled the National Abortion Rights Action League's budget, and the coalition has gained many new members. Polls show that most Americans have prochoice sentiments, but a large number of people oppose abortion as birth control or for sex selection. This suggests that the fight to regulate abortion in the states will be long and that its outcome is uncertain. In the long run, a consensus may be reached to allow early first-term abortions and to spend more money on preventing unwanted pregnancies, promoting adoption, and improving the life chances of children.

The Right to Live

Winning *Webster v. Reproductive Health Services***: the crisis of the pro-life movement.** James R. Kelly *America* 161:79–83 Ag 12–19 '89

The U.S. Supreme Court's *Webster* decision, which upheld the abortion regulations passed by the Missouri legislature, is a great victory for the prolife movement, but it also represents a crisis. The danger is that this success may tempt the prolife movement to become solely an antiabortion movement, as its critics claim it already is. Prolife activists will not gain the support of the majority of Americans unless the protection of fetal life is linked with general aspirations for a good society. Some prolife groups have clearly demonstrated that they are not merely antiabortionists by providing assistance to women with unwanted pregnancies, and Cardinal Joseph L. Bernardin has persuasively linked opposition to abortion with the fight against war, capital punishment, poverty, racism, and sexism. The movement must adopt a more explicit prolife focus so that it will not be seen as merely trying to turn back the clock on abortion.

The human pesticide (RU-486). David Neff *Christianity Today* 32:16–17 D 9 '88

The development of the abortion pill RU-486 is the latest step in the trend toward treating humans as mere biochemical machines. The pill, developed by the French pharmaceutical company Roussel-Uclaf, induces a miscarriage by blocking progesterone, the hormone that allows the fertilized ovum to implant in the womb. The pill has potentially dangerous side effects. It can cause severe bleeding, and if the abortion is not successful, the child could have severe birth defects. The use of RU-486 is also morally incorrect because the pill makes abortion too easy to choose and undermines the dignity of the human race.

The Catholic legacy & abortion: a debate. Daniel C. Maguire *Commonweal* 114:657–63+ N 20 '87

Catholics are not obliged, due to their history or their moral reasoning, to condemn abortion. The Catholic theological record provides no consistent, enduring, and unanimous condemnation of abortion. In fact, there is no distinctively Christian position on abortion in evidence among early Christians. Some Christians borrowed from the Roman and Stoic view that held that there was no soul until birth, while others subscribed to the Greek view that the fetus was ensouled when sufficiently formed in utero. It was only at the end of the 19th century that the Vatican decided to end debate on the matter and take an absolutist position against it. This prohibition seems to derive more from Vatican politics than from consistent moral views grounded in Catholic theology.

Inside a right-to-life mind. Judith Adler Hennessee *Mademoiselle* 92:173+ Ap '86

Twenty-two-year-old Elsie Lewis is devoting her life to stopping abortion. Until her recent layoff, she worked for the American Life League, a student right-to-life group. She spends much of her free time picketing abortion clinics—an experience she likens to visiting Auschwitz—and has been arrested ten times for her antiabortion activities. She also does sidewalk counseling and sends support money to a woman she counseled out of having an abortion. Elsie believes that there is no difference between a child inside the womb and one outside it and that aborting a fetus is exactly the same as murdering a two-year-old because he is inconvenient. She says she is not ready to spend twenty years in prison for bombing a clinic but doesn't condemn those who take that line of action.

The right to life and the restoration of the American republic. Lew Lehrman *National Review* 38:25–8 Ag 29 '86

The issues of slavery and abortion are in fact the same. Both slavery and abortion challenge the first principles of the U.S. government, which forbid the violation of the God-given rights of any person to life, liberty, and the pursuit of happiness. Just as Lincoln denounced the Dred Scott decision, which held that a black slave was not a person under the Constitution, we now need to denounce *Roe v. Wade*. It is absurd to use the Fourteenth Amendment, which granted personhood to slaves, to deny personhood to the unborn. *Roe v. Wade* has no source of authority in logic, moral law, American history, or constitutional law. The argument that religion shouldn't enter politics may be pragmatic in general, but never when it leads to a denial of first principles.

The H baby incident (fathers' rights and abortion). Michael Fumento *National Review* 40:32-3 Je 24 '88

Prolife advocates hope that *In the Matter of Unborn Child H*, which seems to be on its way to the Supreme Court, will be the first in a series of cases that will erode *Roe v. Wade.* In the Child H case, an Indiana court granted a father's request for an injunction barring his live-in girlfriend from aborting their child. The case is in many ways a perfect test of abortion on demand because the woman's motives for having an abortion were unpersuasive. A ruling for the father would not necessarily entail a complete overturning of *Roe* because the case concerns a person asserting countervailing rights rather than challenging the constitutional right to an abortion. In order to overturn the Child H injunction, however, the court would have to sustain and even extend the rights granted in the *Roe* decision.

Their baby is illegal (Chinese attempt to enforce birth control policy on family of Li Quan Bang, a student in the U.S.). Steven Mosher *Reader's Digest* 133:33-6 Ag '88

Condensed from the April 10 issue of the *Washington Post.* The Chinese and U.S. governments have both ignored the pleas of a Chinese couple who are residing in the United States while one of them attends university and who have had a second child while staying here. Li Quan Bang's wife had an IUD inserted after her first child was born, in accordance with China's one-child policy. When she became pregnant with their second child despite the IUD, Chinese birth-control officials set out to intimidate the couple through the mail into aborting the baby. Li's wife had the baby despite threats that everyone at the factory where she had worked in China would be punished. The couple applied for permission to stay in the United States, but the U.S. Immigration and Naturalization Service has refused their request. The address of the attorney general is provided for comments on the case.

The new politics of abortion (anti-abortion movement). Karen Gustafson *Utne Reader* 19+ Mr/Ap '89

The antiabortion movement has been gathering force and attracting increased attention. The November 6, 1988, issue of *Sojourners* calls Operation Rescue, which stages massive sit-ins at abortion clinics, the biggest and most controversial new development on the abortion front. In Minnesota, antiabortionists have blocked the election of prochoice candidates and influenced legislation, according to an article by Richard Broderick in the December 1988 issue of *Twin Cities.* For many people, respect for women and children is at the heart of the issue. Writing in the October

1988 *Friends Journal*, Nanlouise Wolfe and Stephen Zunes argue that abortion is a symptom of society's negative treatment of women and that the right to abortion alone will not give women complete control over their bodies. Kay Castonguay argues against abortion in the Summer 1986 issue of *Political Woman* on the grounds that it is a way of making women conform to the needs of men.

IF ABORTION WERE ILLEGAL

This is no time for a baby (unplanned pregnancy). Susan Jacoby *McCall's* 115:124-7 Je '88

Accidental pregnancies are experienced not only by unwed teenagers but also by large numbers of married women. Danger zones for unplanned pregnancies in marriage include the period after the birth of a child, the years just before or during menopause, and times of great marital stress. Obstetricians say that, unless they are facing severe marital or economic problems, most married women choose to go ahead with an unplanned pregnancy rather than to end it with an abortion. This decision can result in lingering resentment on the part of parents after an unplanned baby is born. Many women, however, emerge from the stress of an unplanned pregnancy with a heightened sense of their capacity to make productive changes in their lives.

ETHICAL DEBATES

Abortion and moral consensus: beyond Solomon's choice. Madonna Kolbenschlag *The Christian Century* 102:179-83 F 20 '85

The abortion issue gathers all the charged currents of patriarchal politics and feminist ideology into one red-hot focus. But prochoice and prolife views both carry the marks of male mentality; principle and values suppress the weighing of specific contexts to seek the relief of hurt and suffering. Bad faith informs both camps: individualists embrace the control perspective, capitulating to elitism and instrumentality; altruists become fixated on one issue, skewing traditional theology and ignoring embryological research. An impasse may give rise to a dangerous techno-therapeutic morality. Instead an ethic of cocreation would prefer ambiguity over absolutism. Valuing fetal life, for instance, need not preclude observance of higher human values. The Catholic church, a respected moral agent, should consider the circumstances of people and hold personhood above anatomy.

Beyond rights in abortion politics (*Webster v. Reproductive Health Services*). David Heim *The Christian Century* 106:675-6 Jl 19-26 '89

Americans who wish to protect fetal life but not to criminalize abortion need to mobilize in support of compromise legislation. For too long American debate on abortion has been reduced to a moral standoff, pit-

ting a woman's right to choose against a fetus's right to live. The recent
U.S. Supreme Court ruling in *Webster v. Reproductive Health Services*, which
suggested that the Court will increasingly favor state regulation of abortion, has reignited interest groups' simplistic slogans and vociferous
rallies. Many European countries, particularly France, have successfully
balanced different views on abortion. Their measures can serve as models
for new legislation in the United States. A host of family issues, including
child care, parental leave, and child support payments, could be tied to
this legislative initiative.

A tragedy without villains. David R. Carlin, Jr. *Commonweal*
116:517-18 O 6 '89

The political battle over abortion can be seen as a Hegelian tragedy—a
struggle between two goods—rather than a fight between good and evil.
The prochoice contingent prizes freedom of choice, while prolife advocates esteem human life and personhood. Both are important values, yet
one must be denied if the other prevails. Hegel suggested that conflicting
goods can be reconciled in a higher synthesis, a more comprehensive
good in which they both participate. This principle, when applied to the
question of abortion, gives priority to the value of personhood. Universal
freedom is contingent upon the prior assertion that the personhood of
human beings is infinitely valuable. If the value of a person were slighted
to preserve freedom, freedom itself would eventually be undermined.

Family planning and the law. Anne-Marie Dourlen-Rollier
World Health 7-9 Ap '89

Part of an issue on medical ethics, bioethics, and health. Access to family
planning and health services is universally recognized as a social and legal
right, but laws regulating such family planning techniques as modern contraceptives, voluntary sterilization, and abortion vary worldwide. The issue of abortion best illustrates the variety of legal responses to family
planning. Approximately 24 percent of the world's people live in countries where abortion is either prohibited or permitted only to save a
woman's life. Almost 13 percent live in countries that allow abortion on
medical grounds, and 24 percent live in nations where social factors receive consideration. Thirty-nine percent live in countries where abortion
on request during the first trimester of pregnancy is legal.

APPROACHES TO COMPROMISE

**Challenging the legal status of abortion: a matter of moral
obligation?** Vincent J. Genovesi *America* 153:417-22 D 14 '85

The question of whether to challenge the legal status of abortion is more
than a matter of individual conscience. It is indeed the duty of the Church
to proclaim the sanctity of the life of the fetus and to work both directly
and indirectly to protect unborn life. On a direct level, laws that prohibit

abortions in almost all cases should be promoted. An indirect way for the Church to proceed, and one more likely to succeed in the long run, is to attempt to change public opinion on the abortion issue. Abortion must be seen for what it is—a matter of human life and death—rather than as an issue of sexual freedom or women's rights.

A piece of yourself in the world (human embryos frozen for later implantation). James Lieber *The Atlantic* 263:76-80 Je '89

Cryopreservation of unfertilized ova could provide the flexibility of embryo storage with none of the ethical problems. Freezing embryos, which is becoming an increasingly common adjunct to in vitro fertilization, raises serious moral questions. The debate over what should be done with embryos that are not implanted does not fit neatly into either the prochoice or prolife framework. It now seems possible that the frozen embryo issue could erupt into the most wrenching new moral controversy since the abortion debate began. Unlike the abortion issue, however, the frozen embryo issue could be resolved. Although many people value life from the moment of conception, few feel strongly about unfertilized oocytes and sperm cells. If gametes were frozen, the problem of extra embryos would not come up, since embryos could be readied for implantation only when they were needed.

When life begins: embryo research. *Current (Washington, D.C.)* 292:9-10 My '87

A reprint of an unsigned editorial from the November 15, 1986, issue of the *Economist*. A consistent and informed determination of what life is and when it begins could solve the moral quandary surrounding abortions and embryo research. The Warnock committee in Britain has recommended limiting experimentation to the first 14 days of an embryo's existence because during that period an embryo is merely undifferentiated cells. Another point at which the line could be drawn is that at which the brain is developed enough to allow conscious sensation—nine weeks by conservative estimates. If a justifiable limit were imposed, killing a human being on demand—through abortion—would have to stop, and examination of small clusters of cells toward the end of saving lives and fighting disease could continue. Policed sensibly, such research need not be the start of a descent into monstrosity.

The Grand Inquisitor (M. Cuomo's inconsistency in citing ethical positions based on Catholicism). Daniel Seligman *Fortune* 112:197 O 14 '85

Governor Mario Cuomo is quick to reassure New Yorkers that he won't let his religious beliefs on abortion interfere with the state's policy on the matter, but he doesn't hesitate to borrow from Catholic thought to justify his views on the issue of public welfare programs. Citing the fifth-century heresy of Pelagianism, which held that people could earn their salvation without any help from God, Cuomo implies that certain members of society shouldn't be expected to succeed without the state's largesse. By referring to countervailing neoconservative views as heresy, Cuomo exhibits a peculiar tendency to dabble in specious analogizing and selective moralizing.

The great debate (challenge to *Roe v. Wade*)**.** Marilyn Webb *Harper's Bazaar* 122:64–5+ Jl '89

After the Supreme Court makes its ruling in *Webster v. Reproductive Health Services*, the controversy over abortion will move to the state and local levels. The prolife movement holds that abortion is an unacceptable solution to a social problem. Prochoice advocates hold that women will seek abortions regardless of what other options are available and that society must protect them from injury and mutilation. The controversy is also over birth control. Prolifers are determined to prevent RU-486, a French abortifacient, from being introduced in the United States. While prochoicers express contempt for the idea, many prolifers would also like to ban the Pill and the IUD, since both control fertility by sloughing off fertilized eggs. Prolife and prochoice leaders agree that their confrontation will begin in the streets, near the abortion clinics that the prolife Operation Rescue has been trying to close. For those who care about such issues, now is the time to speak out.

Abortion (abortion law declared unconstitutional; cover story; special section; with editorial comment by Kevin Doyle). *Maclean's* 101:2, 8–15+ F 8 '88

A cover story on abortion includes a report on the Canadian Supreme Court's ruling against the federal law prohibiting abortion; an essay on the judgment as a consideration of the reality of women's lives; a profile of Dr. Henry Morgentaler, who has performed an estimated 20,000 abortions at his clinics; a chronology of Morgentaler's court battles; and an examination of the dilemma that Ottawa now faces in contending with the court decision. The Supreme Court of Canada ruled that the federal abortion law was unconstitutional because it violated a woman's right to life, liberty, and security of the person. The decision sparked a new wave of debate between prochoice and antiabortion groups, with the latter vowing to renew its battle. The federal government must now choose between drafting new legislation and leaving the court decision to the provinces to handle as a health concern. The abortion issue seems far from concluded.

Religious belief and public morality (Catholic Church; address, September 13, 1984). Mario Cuomo *The New York Review of Books* 31:32–7 O 25 '84

As a politician and a practicing Catholic, New York governor Mario Cuomo explores the relationship between public policy and religious belief. He argues in response to Catholic bishops that a Catholic politician must weigh the exigencies of religious belief against the political realities of a pluralistic democracy. In the case of abortion, no evidence indicated that Americans favor either a prohibitive constitutional amendment or discontinuation of Medicaid funds for legalized abortion. Far from discouraging abortion, prohibitive laws will most likely polarize the community. Restrictions on the number of abortions cannot be accomplished through legislation. Government can and should, however, develop assistance programs for poor women so that abortion need not be their only option. According to Cuomo, the prolife position is much more than an antiabortion position; it also involves a commitment to improve the quality of life.

A new pill, a fierce battle (RU-486). Steven Greenhouse *The New York Times Magazine* 22–4+ F 12 '89

Dr. Etienne-Emile Baulieu, the creator of the highly controversial abortion-inducing pill known as RU-486, is campaigning to have the pill distributed worldwide. His efforts follow a bitter battle in which Roussel-Uclaf, the French drug company for which Baulieu is a consultant, decided to take the pill off the market due to pressure from Roussel's shareholders and threats and demonstrations from antiabortion protesters. French minister of health Claude Evin subsequently stated that if Roussel did not reverse its decision to withdraw the drug, the government, which owns a 36.25 percent stake in the company, would transfer the patent for the pill to another company. Roussel returned the drug to market and is now working with nonprofit groups to get the pill distributed in Sweden, Britain, and the United States.

In India, they abort females. Jo McGowan *Newsweek* 113:12 Ja 30 '89

The outcry over the use of abortion in India to avoid having female children demonstrates the illogical, inconsistent nature of the feminist position on abortion. Because the custom of marital dowry is still practiced in India, having a girl means great financial hardship for a family. As amniocentesis, which makes it possible to determine the sex of an unborn child, has become more widespread, it has become a tool for sex selection in a nation that prizes sons. Feminists decry the selective abortion of females, yet they view the wider issue of abortion as a question of a woman's right to choose. They cannot have it both ways: if it is wrong to kill a baby just because she is a girl, then it is wrong to kill a baby at all.

The future of abortion (cover story; special section). *Newsweek* 114:14–21+ Jl 17 '89

A cover story examines the battle over abortion. The Supreme Court's recent decision in the case of *Webster v. Reproductive Health Services* affirmed the constitutionality of a Missouri law restricting public funding of abortions and requiring viability testing for fetuses at 20 weeks. The decision did not overturn *Roe v. Wade*, the 1973 decision that established a woman's right to abortion, but it undermined its legal foundation and invited further legislation and litigation. Articles discuss ways in which states may attempt to restrict abortions, the likely impact of the new phase of the struggle on candidates and political parties, the opinions of medical doctors on the issue, the hazards of do-it-yourself abortions, and the conservative activism of the Supreme Court during its current session.

Preventing women from being born (sex selection). Arthur R. Kroeber *The Progressive* 52:14–15 D '88

In India, amniocentesis tests are so often followed by selective abortion of female fetuses that Parliament may soon ban the procedure. India's leading government hospital stopped doing amniocenteses in 1979, when it was discovered that it was being used almost exclusively for sex selection. Since then, however, hundreds of practitioners have begun offering the test. In addition, a sex selection technique developed by American reproductive biologist Ronald Ericsson is now being used in India. Although sex selection does not raise the moral issue that selective abortion does, feminists tend to oppose both procedures.

The pill of choice? (cover story). Joseph Palca *Science* 245:1319–23 S 22 '89

A cover story examines RU-486. RU-486, a drug whose usage is now widespread in France, can be employed in conjunction with prostaglandins to terminate pregnancy within the first nine weeks of gestation. It was developed in the late 1970s in an effort led by Etienne-Emile Baulieu, a leading French scientist. Baulieu argues that it could save thousands of women's lives, a belief that is supported by the World Health Organization (WHO) statistic that nearly 50 percent of the maternal mortality in some countries is due to unsafe abortions. The French pharmaceutical company Roussel-Uclaf delayed distribution of RU-486, apparently in part because of boycott threats from antiabortionists and Catholic hospitals, but the French health minister forced the company to supply the drug. The United States is unlikely to approve the drug soon and has tried to slow its testing by the WHO. Sidebars describe its function and applications, and articles focus on its discovery and uses.

Here come the pregnancy police (legal action against mothers of infants exposed to drugs). Andrea Sachs *Time* 133:104–5 My 22 '89

Prosecutors around the country are seeking legal punishment for women who harm their fetuses by taking drugs. Although there seems to be substantial public support for holding women accountable for their actions during pregnancy, many legal experts, women's rights groups, and doctors strongly oppose legal intervention. They argue that making irresponsible maternal behavior a crime will prompt women who are most in need of prenatal care to avoid it for fear of prosecution. They also maintain that the real goal of intervention is to restrict abortion by establishing that the rights of a fetus, rather than the mother, are primary.